The Prince of Pleasure
and his Regency 1811-20

J. B. Priestley

SPHERE

SPHERE BOOKS LTD.
30/32 Gray's Inn Road, London W.C.1.

First published in Great Britain in 1969 by
William Heinemann Limited
© J. B. Priestley 1969
First Sphere Books edition 1971

Designed and produced by
George Rainbird Limited
Marble Arch House
44 Edgware Road
London W2

Picture Research: Mary Anne Norbury
Design: George Sharp

The text was set in
Monophoto Century 11/13 by
Jolly and Barber Limited,
Rugby, Warwickshire
The text was printed and bound by
Butler & Tanner Limited,
Frome, Somerset
The colour plates and jacket were
originated and printed by
Westerham Press Limited,
Westerham, Kent

PLATE I. (verso of frontispiece)
Snuff-box believed to have been
presented to the 1st Duke of Wellington
by the Prince Regent
gold and enamel
$2\frac{3}{4} \times 3\frac{3}{4} \times \frac{5}{8}$ in. (7 × 9.5 × 1.6 cm.)
Collection the Duke of Wellington

PLATE II. (frontispiece) The Prince
Regent in Garter Robes, 1819, by
Sir Thomas Lawrence
oil on canvas
115 × $80\frac{1}{4}$ in. (292 × 204 cm.)
Pinacoteca Vaticana, Rome

Contents

List of colour plates

Photographic credits and acknowledgments

Fratelli Alinari: p. 160

Courtesy B. T. Batsford for information in connection with Roger Fulford's *The Trial of Queen Caroline*, 1946: p. 265

Brighton Corporation Photograph: p. 30, p. 186, p. 194, PLATE XXXII, p. 249 (below left and right), PLATE XLI, p. 254 (top), p. 256, p. 278, p. 288

The British Travel Association Photo Library: PLATE XL

Carlton Studios, London: p. 193, p. 216 (above left and right)

By kind permission of the Chatsworth Settlement: PLATE V

Copyright the City Art Gallery, Manchester: p. 90 (above), p. 92

Copyright Country Life: p. 42 (below)

Courtesy Terence Davis: p. 292 (map redrawn from *The Architecture of John Nash*, 1960)

Michael R. Dudley, Great Milton, Oxford: p. 120 (below left), p. 291 (above)

By kind permission from the Clerk to the Governors of Dulwich College, London, S.E.21: p. 81

S. Eost and P. Macdonald, London: PLATE X, p. 124, p. 137, p. 192 (below left), p. 156, p. 208, p. 229

F.C.P. Studios and Labs, London: PLATE XV

R. B. Fleming, London: PLATE III

J. R. Freeman, London: all the monochrome illustrations of works in the British Museum, London and p. 13, p. 49, PLATE VII, p. 65 (above right), p. 110 (above), p. 116 (above right), p. 120 (below right), p. 122 (below), PLATE XXI, p. 149, PLATE XXIII, p. 195 (below), p. 240, PLATE XXXVIII, p. 263, p. 264, p. 265, p. 268 (above left), p. 271, p. 284, p. 285

Peter Grugeon, Reading, Berkshire: PLATE I

James Hall, Greenock: p. 104 (above and below)

Geoffrey Harper, Hove, Sussex; p. 268 (above right)

Malcolm L. Keep, London: p. 119, p. 168, p. 169, p. 170

R. Kingsley Tayler, Minehead, Somerset: PLATE XXVIII

The Radio Times Hulton Picture Library, London: p. 17 (below), p. 115 (below), p. 144, p. 158, p. 262

The Royal Collection (Copyright Reserved): p. 19, p. 120 (above), p. 121 (above), p. 123 (above left and below), p. 287

Scala, Florence: PLATE II, PLATE VIII

S.N.A. of Hove, Sussex: PLATE VI

Copyright the Trustees of Sir John Soane's Museum: p. 80

By kind permission·of the Trustees of the Wallace Collection, London: p. 22

By courtesy of the Wellcome Trustees, London: p. 90 (below left), p. 197 (above left)

Derrick Witty, London: p. 46, p. 47, p. 70, PLATE XII, PLATE XIII, PLATE XIV, PLATE XVII, PLATE XVIII, PLATE XIX, PLATE XXII, PLATE XXIV, p. 157, PLATE XXV, PLATE XXVI, p. 183, p. 201, PLATE XXXII, PLATE XXXIV, p. 235, PLATE XXXV, PLATE XXXVI, PLATE XXXIX, PLATE XLI, PLATE XLII

Preface

My interest in this period goes back many years; indeed at one time I hoped to write a long novel with a Regency background. It was in the 1920s that I wrote the article on the literature of the Regency for the 14th Edition of the *Encyclopaedia Britannica*, edited and introduced a selection from Tom Moore's *Diary* for the Cambridge University Press, and contributed the volume on Thomas Love Peacock to the *English Men of Letters* series. But it must be fifty-five years since this particular period, in almost all its aspects, began to fascinate me.

Being closer to a personal impression of an age than to a history of it, this is not a book that calls for footnotes or a full list of sources; but when I have made any use whatever of books published in our own time I have named them in the text or included them in the limited bibliography appearing as an appendix.

As this was a work designed from the first to be amply illustrated I have deliberately omitted from the text descriptions and discussions of certain subjects – such as architecture, furniture, fashions – which are better dealt with in the illustrations and their captions.

Looking for odd facts and revealing quotations, Miss F. M. MacMahon spent months going through Regency memoirs, letters, newspapers. Miss Mary Anne Norbury was equally diligent and tenacious searching for and assembling suitable illustrations. Mr. John Hadfield gave me some sound editorial advice on the final text. So now I thank these three most warmly for their help, while accepting full responsibility myself for the contents of this book.

J.B.P.

Royal Family

On 2 November 1810, His Majesty King George the Third, raving and sometimes violent, was fastened into a straitjacket. He was not released from it for the next eleven days. He was then in his early seventies and had been on the throne for fifty years, succeeding his grandfather, George II, in 1760. He had been more or less out of his mind several times before this. He had suffered a mild attack as early as 1765; there was a worse one in the spring of 1788, and even by the autumn he terrified Fanny Burney by his rapidity of speech, his volubility, his strange vehemence. He ate so quickly that she complained: 'The King is so rapid in his meals that whoever attends him must be rapid also or follow starving.' He was out of his mind again for a few weeks in 1801, and three years later the familiar symptoms returned – endless talking, filled with oaths and obscenities never found in his ordinary speech, bewilderment about persons and events, hours of melancholy, moments of dreadful despair. It was thought even then that he might not be able to continue as King. However, nearly a year later, in January 1805, he was able to read the Address at the Opening of Parliament; though on their return home, according to his daughter-in-law, Caroline, Princess of Wales (a dubious witness, admittedly), he threw her on to a sofa and tried to rape her, and she was able to roll away and escape only because the sofa had no back to it. This story may have been a wild exaggeration but that it should have been told at all is significant, because poor George when in his right mind was unusually chaste and was praised by his humbler subjects for the purity of his domestic life. It was rather as if these earlier fits of madness gave him a holiday from the dull routine of his ordinary existence: he could eat and move around and talk at full speed; he could say anything to anybody; he could dismiss all political responsibilities.

But this time, after those eleven days in a straitjacket in November 1810, there was to be no real recovery. He seemed much better during the earlier months of 1811, though no longer considered fit to rule, but after that he wandered out of this world into one of his own, and there he remained until his death in 1820. With his long white beard the mad old king looked like another Lear. He went blind, was totally deaf during his last years, but did not degenerate into a motionless lump of flesh. He was active enough among his furious fancies. In the white robe he insisted upon wearing, for he was now dominated by the idea of purity, so long as he could still hear anything he played airs from Handel on the flute and harpsichord. His daughter Elizabeth reported: 'He considers himself no longer an inhabitant of this world; and often when he has played one of his favourite tunes, observes that he was very fond of it when he was in the world.' Away from his instruments, he talked and talked and talked – with angels; with Octavius and Alfred, his two sons who died in childhood; with Henry VIII and Cardinal Wolsey and many another long-dead monarch or statesman, setting them right as a conscientious king should do. Although there were hours when he was seventeen again among rosy lads and pretty girls, for the most part he was the ruler of this kingdom of his, with more power now than Parliament had ever ceded to him, and with more and more distinguished subjects seeking advice as they emerged from the mists of Time.

The map of Europe changed, Napoleon fell, death struck his family over and over again, but he was too busy in his dream kingdom to know or to care. His doctors insisted that he was amazingly cheerful, quite happy, perhaps happier than he had ever been before. But we know that on one occasion his attendants watched him sit for a long time, his head down, as if his sightless eyes could pierce the ground; and when finally they touched him, wanting him to go and rest, he said, 'Let me alone. I am looking into Hell.' He could not forget King Lear, and one of the last things he said, dying at eighty-two and remembering that other mad old king, was 'Tom's a cold'.

What was the malady that had driven him insane? All manner of nonsense was talked by his own physicians, of which 'The gout has flown from his feet to his head' is a fair sample. Later he was considered to have been the victim of a manic-depressive psychosis, and much was made, not unreasonably, of the mental instability to be found on both sides of his family. But oddly enough, while I was actually making notes for this chapter a new and – to my lay mind – convincing theory of George's malady was offered to us, first in some articles in the *British Medical Journal* and then in a booklet. These were the work of Dr Ida Macalpine and Dr Richard Hunter, Physician in Psychological Medicine at the National Hospital, London, and a consultant psychiatrist to two other London hospitals; and they were joined in an article about the wider aspects of their theory by Professor C. Rimington, Professor of Chemical Pathology at University College Hospital Medical School, London.

George III, we are told, was in fact suffering from porphyria. The porphyrins are purple-red pigments found in every cell of the human body, and are responsible, through their presence in

Portrait of George III on which the
engraver has indicated by faint lines
in pencil how the hair and beard were
to be trimmed in accordance with
the Prince Regent's instructions
The Royal Collection, Windsor Castle

haemoglobin, for the red colour of our blood. Porphyria is the
result of a dangerous disturbance of porphyrin metabolism. It
occurs when excess porphyrin is formed in the liver or bone
marrow. It can take several forms and has a number of marked
and painful symptoms, which need not be described here as they
make melancholy reading. But two points must be made. A severe
attack of acute porphyria may produce mental manifestations
easily and wrongly diagnosed as hysteria, psychoneurosis, para-
noia or schizophrenia. And our doctors, after examining the reports
of George's physicians, are convinced that all the evidence proves
him to have been suffering from acute intermittent porphyria.
Finally – and this is most important – porphyria is usually hereditary, though it can lie dormant and produce no symptoms in a
person who may in fact be a carrier of the disease.

Charlotte Sophia of Mecklenburg-
Strelitz, wife of George III, 1789,
by Sir Thomas Lawrence
oil on canvas
94¼ × 58 in. (239.5 × 147 cm.)
The National Gallery, London

Now hereditary diseases, often of an unfamiliar sort, have frequently attacked royal families, simply because such families refused to bring in fresh blood but married among themselves. So we need not feel surprised if our new porphyria-hunters now discover symptoms and traces of it in the royal houses of Stuart, Hanover and Prussia. We know about poor George III, but what about his eldest son, the Prince Regent? Well, we are told that the Prince's medical history, from the age of twenty, suggests intermittent if not very acute attacks of porphyria, and that odd character, his wife, Caroline of Brunswick, may have been another victim; she could have inherited porphyria from either or both of her parents. Now the Prince and Caroline were cousins; and their only child, Charlotte, was from the age of sixteen until she died five years later in childbirth often suddenly ill and in pain, the symptoms suggesting porphyria. Finally, three of the Prince's brothers, the Dukes of York, Kent and Sussex, were at various times of life mysteriously laid low and displayed some if not all the family symptoms.

This, I feel, is quite enough about porphyria. However, we ought to bear it in mind. This curious taint in the royal blood, too rich and crimson, may be lurking behind many events in this story.

The idea of this mad old king, no longer to be seen and cheered by his loyal subjects, haunted the Regency like an accusing ghost. The English developed an affection for their 'Farmer George', as they often called him, long before his final breakdown. He had been around for so many years; he was a character, a plain downright character too, though frequently bewildered and crying 'What? What?', like so many elderly London clubmen to this day. He was a faithful and attentive – perhaps over-attentive – husband to his dull and unattractive wife, Charlotte of Mecklenburg-Strelitz. He was an affectionate father, though not a wise one. He was frugal almost to the point of miserliness. And as he grew older and his troubles multiplied and he began at last to stop playing politics, the people either forgave or forgot his dangerous meddling and expensive errors of judgment. He had tried hard to increase the power of the Crown by extending its patronage; he had had a political flair in reverse, almost a genius for distrusting good ministers (the younger Pitt was an exception) and encouraging weak or stupid ministers. He was largely responsible for the loss of the American Colonies; he had personally hired German mercenaries to fight his war over there; he had eagerly assented to the proposed use of Indians by the American Tories; and there is no good old Farmer George in the histories of the United States. But at home – and this king was very much a stay-at-home, never moving outside England – time and his troubles brought him affection and finally a deep compassion. This partly explains the character of the Regency and the personal unpopularity of the Regent himself. There was always a skeleton at the feast – the poor mad old king.

George's Queen Charlotte may have been dull and unprepossessing but she presented him with fifteen children, six daughters and nine sons. As I have already suggested, he was a genuinely affectionate but unwise father. He was so devoted to his daughters that he did not want them to marry at all, and there were bitter complaints from what they called 'the Nunnery'. Three of them did eventually marry, rather late, Charlotte becoming Queen of Würtemberg, Elizabeth the Princess of Hesse-Homburg, and Mary the wife of the second Duke of Gloucester. The youngest, prettiest, and her father's favourite, Amelia, was dying of consumption in the autumn of 1810, and it was generally thought that the king's deep distress brought on his insanity and the straitjacket. Of the nine sons, the last two, Octavius and Alfred, as we have seen, died in childhood. Of the remaining seven, the eldest, George, Prince of Wales and then Regent, is the central figure of this chronicle, and I shall return to him when I have disposed of his six brothers, all of them royal dukes.

These six brothers did much – though their elder, George, Prince of Wales, hardly needed any assistance – to bring contempt and ridicule to the monarchy. The Duke of Wellington was as far from being a republican or a radical as any man in the kingdom, yet he could lump together all the old king's sons and call them 'the damnedst millstones about the neck of any government that can be imagined'. Their characters and styles of life were quite different, but they were mostly alike in being either terrible or laughable nuisances. They were not idiots but too often they behaved like idiots, forgetting they lived in the full glare of royal dukedoms. They were not really as wildly disreputable as they were made out to be, but they were either loud, blundering, and hopelessly without tact or ludicrously eccentric. They were fresh raw meat to the tigerish caricaturists and cartoonists of the time. Though pitied for fathering such a brood, the old king was not entirely blameless. The older sons, with the Prince well out in front, were busy reacting – and too violently – against their father's prim, dull and stingy Court, out of which they burst like children leaving school. This had two important consequences. Instead of marrying dowdy German princesses, they openly kept mistresses, producing no legitimate but plenty of illegitimate children. And instead of trying to live within their not unreasonable allowances, they overspent freely, often on some folly or other, and so were constantly – and at the top of their voices – in debt. They were despised by the wealthier aristocracy for their comparative poverty and desperate shifts, and by the fashionable wits and dandies for their

The Return to Office, 1811, by George Cruikshank – the Duke of York is re-instated
The British Museum, London

Frederick Augustus, Duke of York, 1823, by Sir David Wilkie
oil on panel
23¼ × 20½ in. (59.2 × 52 cm.)
The National Portrait Gallery, London

dull coarse talk and inferior coats and cravats. And they were detested by the ordinary people, skimping to pay for the war against Napoleon, because they seemed so many loud parasites.

Next in age to George, Prince of Wales, about to become Regent and our Prince of Pleasure, was Frederick, Duke of York. He was a dutiful and fairly competent army man, but had to leave the army when it was publicly discovered – and there was a Parliamentary Enquiry – that his mistress, Mary Anne Clarke, was up to her pretty neck in the sale of military commissions and promotions. However, the Regent, who was devoted to him, soon made him commander-in-chief again. *The Dictionary of National Biography* – referred to as *D.N.B.* from now on – tells us he 'had the greatest influence on the history of the British Army', but then it cannot find any fault in him at all. This Duke did marry, in his twenties too, the usual German princess, who was received in London with such enthusiasm in 1791 that a roaring trade was done in imitations of her slipper. But in spite of this fascinating slipper – and the increase in Frederick's allowance to £70,000 a year – the marriage soon failed. The Duchess, the *D.N.B.* tells us, 'retired to Oatlands Park, Weybridge, Surrey, where she amused herself with her pet dogs'. Away from these dogs – a hundred of them at one time – she was in fact a sensible, much-respected woman. A handsome, affable, military-cum-sporting type, the Duke of York was popular enough in his earlier years, but Mrs Clarke's brisk trade and his rigid Tory attitudes, which came to influence the Regent, cost him his popularity. After wasting much money on spectacular building he died of dropsy in 1827.

The next brother, William, Duke of Clarence, afterwards

16

William, Duke of Clarence by Sir
George Hayter
pencil
12¼ × 8 in. (31.1 × 20.3 cm.)
The National Portrait Gallery,
London

Mary Anne Clarke, 1810
stipple engraving

William IV, went into the navy, and though he had to leave the
service, he spent the rest of his life roaring around on an imaginary
quarterdeck, using dreadful language even on solemn occasions.
To people not concerned about the dignity of the monarchy, he
was rather an appealing character, irresponsible, daft, but honest
and open, hiding nothing. He lived in a sailor-home-from-the-sea
fashion with Mrs Jordan, a scandalous but warm-hearted and
generous creature and an excellent actress. She was enthusiastically praised by Hazlitt, Lamb, Byron and Leigh Hunt, and that
ought to be good enough for us. She gave the Duke of Clarence ten
illegitimate children, who all became distinguished FitzClarences
and moved among and married nobility and gentry. She and her
Duke were often so hard up that between pregnancies she had to
return to the stage, not only in London but sometimes on tour.
Once while she was acting, William wrote to her proposing to cut
her allowance of £1,000 a year to £500. She sent as her reply the
bottom half of a playbill that said *No money returned after the
rising of the curtain*. She died in France in 1816. Two years
later, William married Adelaide of Saxe-Meiningen, but both
their children died soon after birth. However, in 1830 he became
William IV and did not do badly as king, in spite of his eccentricities.
Wellington, then Prime Minister, said he could do more business
with him in ten minutes than with George IV in as many days. The
virtuous, who were on the increase, disliked him for the Mrs Jordan
liaison and his coarse manners and speech, but the hearty common
folk were very fond of him. He was the only one of the royal dukes
who ever became really popular.

A very different fellow was the next brother, Edward, Duke of
Kent. He went into the army, where he proved to be such a severe
disciplinarian and so endlessly fussy about trifles that there was
trouble wherever he was in command. Finally, after a mutiny
in Gibraltar, he was recalled and not allowed to return there.
However, this did not prevent his being gazetted field-marshal the
following year. He took his punctilious habits and love of inspect-
ing everything into civilian life, where he was always trying to
make ends meet and never succeeding. He spent some years in
Brussels economising with the help of his French-Canadian
mistress, Madame St Laurent, a less flamboyant lady than the
mistresses of his older brothers. He and the Regent disliked each
other, and he deliberately adopted political opinions as far from
his brother's as possible. By the time the Regent had shown himself
a Tory the Duke of Kent had gone beyond the Whigs and had
landed among the radicals. Indeed, he even corresponded with
Robert Owen, the socialist. In 1818, ridding himself of poor Madame
St Laurent, after twenty-seven years together, he married Victoria
Mary Louisa, widow of the Prince of Leiningen. He did this in the

Edward, Duke of Kent, 1818, by Sir
William Beechey
oil on canvas
29¼ × 24¼ in. (74.4 × 61.6 cm.)
The National Portrait Gallery,
London

Ernest Augustus, Duke of
Cumberland, by George Dawe
oil on canvas
35¼ × 27½ in. (89.4 × 69.2 cm.)
The National Portrait Gallery,
London

(opposite) The Duchess of York,
c. 1810, by Peter Eduard Stroehling
oil on copper
24 × 18¾ in. (61 × 47.5 cm.)
The Royal Collection, London

Augustus Frederick, Duke of Sussex,
1789, by Guy Head oil on canvas
37¼ × 31¾ in. (94.5 × 80.7 cm.)
The National Portrait Gallery,
London

hope of fathering an heir to the throne; and he of all the royal
dukes drew a winner, for his daughter Victoria was crowned
queen seventeen years after his death. Not from egotism but from
a desire to prove that we are all in history, I must add that for some
years I was myself a subject of Queen Victoria, daughter of this
same Edward, Duke of Kent.

Now we have Ernest, Duke of Cumberland and eventually King
of Hanover, where he lived on and on into a different epoch
altogether, not dying until 1851, the year of the Great Exhibition.
He spent his youth and earlier years with the Hanoverian army
and saw much hard service with it – he was ferociously courageous
– up to 1796, when he returned to England and became a lieutenant-
general in the British Army. He had lost an eye in battle and had
an ugly menacing aspect, and his reputation was so sinister that
it was popularly (but wrongly) believed that he had fathered a
child on his sister Sophia and had murdered his valet. He was a
violent reactionary, and his force of character, uncommon among
these brothers, made it easy for him to influence the Regent.
To the radical press he was not an expensive clown, as the other
dukes seemed to be, but a villain and a horror. One reason for the
great popularity of Victoria as a young girl was that at least she
would be keeping Uncle Ernest, Duke of Cumberland, off the throne.
It was unfortunate for England that the most forceful and in many
respects the ablest of the royal brothers should have hated and
loudly condemned any sign of reform.

In sharpest contrast to the sinister Cumberland was the next
brother, Augustus, Duke of Sussex. He was a mild man, but firm
in his liberal opinions, a collector of books, a modest patron of the
arts and sciences. There is one innocently approving sentence in
the *D.N.B.* that seems to tell us a great deal about him: 'In his later
years he was in great request as chairman at anniversary dinners.'

The seventh son of George III was Adolphus, Duke of Cambridge.
He was a military man, and might be said to be a watercolour version of his brother Cumberland. He had no debts, no fancy mistresses, and had a son and two daughters by his marriage to Princess Augusta of Hesse-Cassel. He acted as viceroy in Hanover for
many years, returning to England when brother Cumberland in
1837 became King of Hanover. He was more or less active in the
conservative interest until his death in 1850, when he was described
as 'emphatically the connecting link between the throne and the
people'. But as this was the opinion of the *United Service Gazette*, it
may not have been everybody's. His admirers said he was prudent;
some other people thought him mean. What is certain is that he
is the last figure in our procession of royal dukes.

We must now go to the head of the procession, to the showiest
figure of all, the old king's eldest son and therefore Prince of Wales,

Adolphus, Duke of Cambridge,
anonymous British artist
oil on canvas
35¼ × 27½ in. (89.5 × 69.9 cm.)
The City Museum and Art Gallery,
Birmingham

soon to be Prince Regent and eventually to reign as George IV. He was born in August 1762 and before the end of December 1765 he had been created a Knight of the Garter. He was brought up plainly and strictly – perhaps too plainly and strictly – at the Bower Lodge at Kew. He was well educated, learnt quickly, acquired various accomplishments of a more social kind; he grew up to be tall, rather bulky, fairly handsome in a florid fashion, and had easy and engaging manners, though he did not always display them to his tutors or even to his father.

While still in his 'teens and not his own master, the Prince gradually became involved, after many secret romantic assignations, with Mary Robinson – *Florizel* to her *Perdita*, the part in which he first saw her – an actress and writer without much talent but an unusually beautiful woman, as everybody, including the numerous artists who painted her, enthusiastically agreed. This was his first great affair and it set a sexual pattern that he was to follow, with some absurd enlargements, for the rest of his life. For Mary Robinson was already married and a few years older than he was; she had a fine but full figure; and after she had been his mistress for two years, during which he had set her up in what was called then a 'splendid establishment' and had poured jewels into it, he broke off the affair, suddenly and coolly, indeed treating her very badly. She was probably a vain and rather silly beauty – but then he could hardly be considered modest and wise, at that or any other age. The reason he dismissed her so heartlessly was that he was bored and wanted a change. The romance of *Florizel* and *Perdita* vanished; the pleasure principle now took over and went to work on him, never stopping for the next forty-odd years. It is the secret of his charm, his folly, his inner emptiness.

As soon as the Prince was out of his father's control and could act independently, with an establishment of his own in Carlton House, he began to follow another pattern, this time not new and personal to him but old and traditional. Over and over again in English history the heir to the throne, on reaching independence, has immediately sided with the group, cabal, class, political party, opposing his father the king. The son must widen the distance between himself and his father. The Prince of Wales must not be a blurred copy of the King but somebody quite different, with his own set, his own policy and outlook, his own style of life. So, because King George's sympathisers, chosen instruments, ministers, were Tories, the Prince immediately surrounded himself with Whigs.

This was inevitable, almost a mechanical move. It is doubtful if at any time – and later events will support this, as we shall see – the Prince had any genuinely personal political convictions. He was entirely at the mercy of situations and immediate influences. His mind was not strengthened by the development of any political

(opposite) Mrs Robinson ('Perdita'),
1781, by Thomas Gainsborough
oil on canvas
90 × 60¼ in. (229 × 153 cm.)
The Wallace Collection, London

philosophy because there was nothing in his mind to nourish its growth. An oak tree cannot rise out of macaroons and madeira on the green baize of a card table. Some of the English statesmen of this period, the 1780's, were notorious lovers of pleasure, but even so they were not completely dominated and enslaved by the pleasure principle; they were able to think and work and make strenuous efforts well beyond its grasp. But the Prince never enjoyed this freedom; he was always busy trying to enjoy everything else.

However, he quickly embraced the Whigs, entertained their leaders and so was soon in the constant company of three remark-

(above left) Charles James Fox, before 1798, by K. Anton Hickel
oil on canvas
52 × 44½ in. (132 × 113 cm.)
The National Portrait Gallery, London

(above right) Whig Statesmen and their friends gathered around the bust of Charles James Fox (detail), c. 1810, by William Lane
(top row left to right) 5th Duke of Devonshire, 2nd Earl Fitzwilliam, 1st Baron Crewe, 3rd Earl Bessborough, Dudley Long North, 1st Marquess of Cholmondeley, Lord Robert Spencer; (sitting left to right) 3rd Lord Holland, 2nd Earl Upper Ossory, Richard FitzPatrick, 2nd Marquess Townshend, 13th Baron St John
chalk
21 × 27½ in. (53.4 × 72.4 cm.)
The National Portrait Gallery, London

(opposite) George, Prince of Wales, drawn from life, 1794, by John Russell
black and red chalk
19 × 13½ in. (48.5 × 34.5 cm.)
The Courtauld Institute Galleries, London

able men: the great Charles James Fox, the redoubtable and splendid Edmund Burke, the brilliant, witty and versatile Sheridan. Sheridan was the only one who survived into the Regency proper, and I shall consider his character, career and talents when we arrive at the year of his death, 1816. But Burke must be separated from the other two Whig leaders. His interest in the Prince was entirely political; he was never a boon companion, never a member of the raffish Carlton House set. Any influence he might have had on the young Prince would have been all to the good. This cannot be said of Fox and Sheridan. Outside their public life, which they took seriously, they were the boon companions any young prince on the loose would welcome.

When not feeling called upon to make a sudden strenuous effort, Sheridan was lazy, extravagant and dissolute. And Fox – the larger personality – was even more astonishingly and outrageously divided. Dark, heavily-built, sensual and dissipated, he yet had a strange sweetness in his essential character, enormous charm. He was a great man, perhaps the finest debater the House of Commons has ever known, and no mere party manager-leader (he was faulty there) but a genuine statesman. He had the wisdom and the courage to welcome and then defend the French Revolution;

and if his policy had succeeded, there might have been no Napoleon, no years of war, and the whole course of European history might have been changed for the better. But in his private life he was reckless and defied all respectable opinion. Sitting night after night and sometimes whole days at the gaming tables, he threw away all his own money and any he could borrow, sinking more and more deeply into debt. He lived openly with his mistress, Mrs Armistead (or Armstead as she was sometimes called), who was said to have been originally a 'waiting woman' or superior maid-servant. However, she is described as having some education and excellent manners, and Fox, who refused to repair his fortunes by marrying any of the rich heiresses his friends found for him, was as much devoted to her as she was to him, and finally in his last years made her his wife. But there was the long liaison, the public scandal.

With a pair of wild spendthrifts like Fox and Sheridan keeping him company night after night, the young Prince was not likely to imitate his father's frugal habits. He was soon in debt and he never really got out of it. Yet for this his father, the careful George III, is at least as much to blame as his own self-indulgence and the bad example set him by Fox and Sheridan. The King had been unwise in first keeping his son, a full-blooded, high-spirited youth, so close to a dull and cheese-paring Court. He had been even more unwise when he had allowed the Prince of Wales his independence and his own establishment at Carlton House. Previously, the heirs to the throne had been granted £100,000 a year, but now the King had obstinately and foolishly insisted that *his* eldest son must accept only £50,000 – and this at a time when money was worth less than it had been when the royal heirs received £100,000. By drastically cutting down his son's official allowance in this fashion, the King hoped he would soon learn the value of money. And this was folly, as a better student of human nature would have known, because it had precisely the opposite effect. It is possible that the Prince, thoughtless and naturally self-indulgent and extravagant, might have behaved in exactly the same fashion whatever income he had been given. But as it was, he was not unreasonably resentful and felt that this allowance was ridiculous. He soon came to believe that money itself was ridiculous, a kind of fairy gold that a pleasure-loving prince had not to take seriously.

The inevitable result was that from the first the gay and lavish Prince of Wales began to spend money recklessly. He was soon in debt and had to resort to moneylenders. (Often he sent his chef to negotiate the more delicate transactions.) This of course proved to be a vicious circle: he had to incur further debts to pay existing ones, and he had to pay more and more for less and less money actually received. (His I.O.U.'s were snapped up at a discount.)

(opposite) Mrs Fitzherbert, engraving
after Richard Cosway
The British Museum, London

So he went forward, though not noticeably bowed, under an increasing load of debt, both as Prince and then as Regent, and had to make frequent appeals, often through his Whig friends, both to the King and to Parliament for some special grant that would temporarily release him. These demands for public money – especially when the country was at war – when contrasted with his extravagant mode of life, and with the King's frugality, soon began to undermine his initial popularity as England's smiling florid young Prince. With the increasing load of debt – and at one point it must have amounted to several millions in our money – came an increasing disapproval and sharp opposition to him, from the King and the Tory Ministers, from the fiery radicals, and from the growing and largely puritanical middle class.

However, we must return to the 1780s and the youth of the Prince, Here I quote from Robert Huish's *Memoirs of George IV* published not long after the King's death. Behind Huish's florid verbiage and pious head-shakings there is always a glitter of malice. He writes:

> Previously to the attachment of the Prince to Mrs Fitzherbert, the passions, it was well known, treated him with as little reserve as the meanest of their votaries; and, under their influence, he was continually seen in those pavilions of Pleasure, where honour is not known, and female virtue for ever vanished. It was, therefore, very fortunate for himself, and of course beneficial to the nation, if he could become stationary somewhere, and in particular with a person whose situation in life entitled her to every attention which the laws of his country would allow him to bestow . . .

But before introducing Mrs Fitzherbert, I feel something must be said about the various stories told by Huish and others. They suggest that the Prince at this time was not only exhibiting himself in 'those pavilions of Pleasure' but was also busy playing Don Juan or a Lovelace to somebody's Clarissa. In other words, he was engaged in elaborate plots to seduce virtuous young women, to trap and then deflower trembling virgins, aided by various titled ladies ready to act as procuresses – or indeed as anything imaginable. These stories seem dubious because they appear to me to be out of character. The cool long-range seducer is in love with the game not the girl. A Don Juan, as distinct from a Casanova, is really indulging a deep-seated hatred of Woman herself. The Prince might have agreed to take part in some elaborate plot against an innocent girl's virtue, chiefly because he was easily persuaded, but this was not his type of rôle nor part of his sexual pattern.

Mrs Fitzherbert fitted the pattern exactly. She was older and more experienced in the traffic between the sexes than he was, having been married then widowed twice before she met him. She

PLATE III. Tankard and cover, 1817, by Edward Farrell
A fine example of Regency silver-gilt
11¾ in. (29.8 cm.) high
By kind permission of Christies, London

was also a full-bodied woman whose charms matched the Prince's opulent taste. Again, she was no bedazzled actress or singer; she had a good Roman Catholic family and marriage background and a reasonable position in society; and she was no inflammable romantic but a careful lady. After they first met, in 1785, she resisted his pressing attentions and then slipped away to France where she knew he could not follow her. (It was said that once there she gave herself generously to a handsome marquis.) The Prince now offered to marry her, and with some show of reluctance she agreed, returned to England, and in secret went through a marriage ceremony with him late in December, 1785. After this they lived together as man and wife for many years, and she was accepted by the best society, not excluding the other members of the royal family. But not as the Princess of Wales, still as Mrs Fitzherbert. So – was she the Prince's wife or only his mistress? Were they or weren't they truly married? We arrive at one of those *Through the Looking-Glass* situations so often created by the hazy convolutions of the English official mind.

Now to disentangle this. So far as marriage is determined by a religious ceremony, they were married. So far as marriage is a legal binding tie, they were not married and never would be. Two huge solemn Acts stood in the way. The Marriage Act, only thirteen years old, declared that any marriage contracted by a member of the royal family under the age of twenty-five, without the King's consent, was invalid. The Act of Settlement laid down that if the heir apparent married a Roman Catholic he forfeited all right to the crown. Legally the Prince was not married, and he must have known that the ceremony would not be valid in law when he asked Mrs Fitzherbert to become his wife.

But the idea that he behaved like a villain in a melodrama, deliberately deceiving a trusting loving woman, must be rejected. It is false to his character, devoted to instant pleasure and not to foresight and planning, and equally false to hers. She was no infatuated girl but a shrewd woman of the world. Indeed, he was far more warmly attached to her than she was to him. She admitted in confidence that she was attracted by the rank and not the person of the Prince. Constancy she could not expect from such a pleasure-loving, emotional flibberty-gibbet – the jealous angry scenes she often made later probably came from wounded vanity – but so far as he was capable of love or even a fairly steady devotion, it was given to her and she was certainly the most important woman in his life. Their association lasted on and off until 1803 – and it is perhaps significant that she finally broke with him because he demoted her down the table at a big official dinner party at Carlton House. She retired with a pension of £6,000 a year (worth, say, about £50,000 now), and with only herself to keep, for there

PLATE IV. Caroline Amelia Elizabeth of Brunswick, 1804, by Sir Thomas Lawrence
oil on canvas
55¼ × 44 in. (140 × 111.8 cm.)
The National Portrait Gallery, London

Her Royal Highness Caroline,
Princess of Wales and Princess
Charlotte, *c*. 1798, engraving by
Francesco Bartolozzi after Richard
Cosway
The Royal Pavilion, Brighton

were no children, she was not too badly treated. As for him, he cherished sentimental memories of her, fondled keepsakes, and had her portrait round his neck when he died, about twenty-seven years after they had parted.

There was certainly one brief period, back in 1795, when the Prince and Mrs Fitzherbert were not living together. And for a very good reason. In April of that year he really *did* get married, and this time legally and in anything but secrecy. George III wanted an heir in the direct line, through his eldest son. And this son, our Prince, was now at his wits' end for money: he owed £630,000, a stupendous sum for those days. He agreed to marry if his debts were paid and his income more than doubled. There were also a few minor items like £27,000 to prepare for the marriage, £26,000 to complete Carlton House, £28,000 for jewels and plate – making a total of about £700,000 in our money. For once the Prince drove a hard bargain; but he was to regret it. The bride chosen for him was his cousin Caroline, daughter of George III's sister Augusta and the Duke of Brunswick. It was a bad choice; it brought together two unstable families; it also brought together two unstable persons who had never before set eyes on each other; and that wedding day, 5 April 1795, was to prove disastrous for everybody intimately concerned in its ceremony.

Now we seem to move into a comedy, not smiling like one of Shakespeare's but harsh like one of Ben Jonson's. To begin with, the naval squadron sent to escort Caroline from her German shore to Greenwich was compelled by bad weather to turn back, so that she was kept waiting for weeks. Next, the lady chosen to bring the bride from Greenwich to St James's was none other than the handsome and malicious Lady Jersey, with whom the Prince had been philandering for some time. And if this was a bad beginning, worse was to follow. Bride and groom took an instant strong dislike to each other. Her verdict was that he was too fat. The Prince saw her for the first time with James Harris, Lord Malmesbury, who had escorted her from Brunswick, at his side, and he whispered, 'Harris, I am not well; pray get me a glass of brandy.' His immediate revulsion is not easy to understand because at that time, aged twenty-seven, Caroline, a blonde with fine eyes, was said to be quite pretty. On the other hand, she was ungraceful, moved badly, was gauche and loud in her manner, and was privately thought by her family to be a little unhinged. However, in spite of this dislike at first sight, the royal pair somehow contrived, with astonishing speed, to produce a child, the unlucky Princess Charlotte being born in January 1796.

Some months before the birth the Prince and Caroline had agreed to lead separate lives, though at first within the establishment of his household. The exact reason for this separation has never been discovered, though there are hints that the Prince soon shrank from any intimate contacts with his wife, finding her peculiarly repellent. What we do know for certain is that it was not long before he returned to the more wholesome and opulent charms of Mrs Fitzherbert, to whom he was more deeply devoted than ever. He even made a will expressing a wish that they should be buried together. Mrs Fitzherbert's conscience did not trouble her because her spiritual advisers, who had received special instructions from Rome, assured her that she might return to the Prince. Indeed, to show that all was well, she entertained the fashionable world to a splendid public breakfast, a good last act to the comedy of the Royal Marriage.

All this took place many years before the Prince was officially appointed Regent, early in 1811. But, even more than his extravagance and debts and dissolute mode of life, it was the immediate breakdown of his marriage and his separation from his wife and daughter that made him unpopular with a large section of his father's subjects. Though London might be packed with prostitutes, many of them in their early teens, its citizens liked to think that their kings and princes were leading firmly established and unsullied domestic lives. Because this Prince of Wales had obviously broken the rule, it was tempting to believe that he was much worse, more debauched and defiant of all regal decorum, than he actually was.

During these years before the Regency he spent more and more of his time in Brighton, where he indulged his expensive passion for building and elaborate decoration until in the end he achieved his fantastic Pavilion. Both before and after he broke with Mrs Fitzherbert, his life there – rising late, riding in the afternoon, giving a dinner or supper party every few days – was fairly regular and not noticeably wild. The popular notion that it was all one huge orgy, with drunken feasts every night and with gay girls or bewildered virgins hurried in along secret passages, was so much nonsense. This man, soon to be Regent of the United Kingdom and afterwards its King George the Fourth, was far from being a kind of decadent Roman Emperor in top-boots, waisted coats and cravats. The truth about him is less spectacular, wild and scandalous, but more complex and really more fascinating.

His weaknesses are quickly discovered. He was absurdly extravagant; he was clearly self-indulgent, in all things and not only at the dinner table; and he was maddeningly thoughtless and incapable of any consistency and steady purpose. The Duke of Wellington said he was the most extraordinary compound of talent with buffoonery and good feeling, a medley of the most opposite qualities with a great preponderance of good, that he ever saw in any character in his life. Another shrewd contemporary, Thomas Philips, brings us closer to him:

> The Prince is influenced by caprice and has no steadiness. I have seen something of him. He has the power of giving a proper answer to whoever addresses him upon any subject, but nothing fixes him. The person who last spoke to him makes an apparent impression, but it is gone when another person or subject comes before him, and his tailor or bootmaker will occupy his mind to the doing away of any other consideration to which his attention might before have been drawn . . .

This might be the portrait of a giant child. Again, the Prince's growing love, after spells of quiet living, of being the centre of attraction, the host magnificently arrayed on great glittering occasions, suggests an adolescent making his dreams come true. Moreover, though he was notorious for his affairs, he was in fact quite the opposite of a character like Louis XV with an insatiable appetite for sex. His so-called mistresses were increasingly older than himself, and he devoted himself to them not for nights of passion and erotic adventures but chiefly out of a growing fondness for cosy (and possibly platonic) companionship and a rather sentimental domesticity, a style of life that later became fashionable under his niece, Victoria. Instead of being a cold-hearted libertine, which he was so often reputed to be, he was really a rather soft-hearted overgrown boy. So far as he was a man, he was not a bad man but a foolish one.

A story told of him, to his credit, before he became Regent gives us a clue to his essential nature. At a time when he was desperate for money he heard of an army officer who had just returned from abroad with a wife and family and was in great distress. He contrived to borrow a few hundred pounds and insisted upon taking the money himself to the officer. This unusual insistence is significant. He wanted the immediate pleasure of relieving the officer's anxieties himself. By the next day he might easily have forgotten the wretched man and thrown away the money on some frippery. His heart was warm but his head was never steadily in its service.

He was an easy and affable prince and indeed often had great charm, as Scott and Byron (at first) and many another have testified. Though his personal taste was uncertain, he was a generous patron of the arts, and we English, as will be seen, owe him much for this patronage. Most of us, men or women, would rather have spent an evening with him as host than with any English monarch between Charles II and Edward VII, two others largely dominated by the pleasure principle. But, even more than they do, he justifies the title I have given him – Prince of Pleasure. If he was too self-indulgent and idle-minded, he was also unfortunate in his time. He would have made a splendid show-figure for a nation richly prosperous, with contented subjects everywhere; but as it happened his extravagant love of pleasure gleamed and flared against a dark background of frustration, poverty and despair. So a man who was anything but coldly ill-natured, who was over-anxious for admiration and affection, was already, before he took over the country from his mad old father, the target of derision, contempt, detestation.

But I have kept the Prince, no doubt corseted in some magnificent uniform, too long waiting in the wings to make his grand entrance as Regent. Now the curtain must rise both on him and on his Regency.

1811

The Regency

In January 1811, after much argument, Parliament passed the Regency Bill. It was largely modelled on the one put together as far back as 1788, when the King had had his first very serious attack. The Bill formally appointed the Prince as Regent but it did not give him all the power his father had enjoyed, and there were various restrictions that would not be removed until the following year. But the Regent could form a government; it would have to be announced before he was sworn in by the Privy Council on 6 February. Unable to make up his mind, he was genuinely ill with worry. There was a complicated political situation here but I do not propose to explain it in detail. The political scene was now smaller and duller because the two great leaders, William Pitt for the Tories, Charles James Fox for the Whigs, had quitted the stage, both dying in 1806. Had Fox been still alive, there is no doubt that the Regent would have asked him to form a government. But without him the Whigs were not firmly united, and their new and more moderate leaders (in favour of continuing the war against Napoleon) had never been members of the Whig Old Guard (wanting peace with France) that had been so close to the Prince. So after much dithering he asked the Tories, under Perceval, to continue in power. This brought him enemies and no real new friends. The Tories still mistrusted him. The Whigs, who had been out in the political wilderness with him for years and had thought that he would return them triumphantly to power, were disappointed and angry, feeling he had betrayed them.

They had a case, but so, under the pressure of his new responsibilities, had he. Lacking a powerful leader, the Whigs of 1811 were disunited and could not be called a party. Many of them would have wanted to sue for peace now when the war was at last taking a turn for the better. But the Regent, not the man to reject an heroic rôle that required no personal heroism and sacrifice, began to see himself as Napoleon's great antagonist. Moreover, as he frankly declared much later, now that he was Regent, taking care of his father's dominions, he felt it was right to abandon many of his old Whig friends because he thought 'their liberal and anti-monarchical sentiments unfavourable to good government'. So the Tories were back, as they would keep coming back, confident in

A French exile's impression of Pall Mall, showing Carlton House on the left
engraving by Dubois after Courvoisier
The London Museum, London

their belief that when they were not in power some great law of nature had been temporarily and absurdly suspended.

Meanwhile, three weeks after being sworn in, the Regent held his first levée at Carlton House, now in his element as a regal impresario. His guests have left us varied accounts of the occasion and its setting. 'Great crowds, splendid liveries, and hussars of all colours,' we are told. 'Carlton House finer than anything in England and not inferior to Versailles or Saint Cloud,' another English guest declared. The Hanoverian Minister admitted that the palace at St Petersburg beat everything in vastness 'but was not equal to this in elegance and richness'. Others thought Carlton House overdone – 'not a spot without some finery upon it, gold upon gold – a bad taste' – and it was even said that the apartments had so much superfluous finery that 'supposing the owner not to be known, they would give an unfavourable idea of the kind of mind he must have'.

The Regent himself, though willing to entertain and be entertained, was said to be passing through a rather silent and serious phase at this time, and was 'supposed to be engaged with religion, and read daily a chapter or two of the Bible with Lady Hertford'. She was now his favourite companion but no mistress, for though she was described as 'an extraordinary fine woman, a *Juno*', she was also frigidly virtuous, very dignified, intelligent and with fairly wide interests. The Hertfords, immensely wealthy, were connoisseurs, and the Regent often consulted them when making his lavish purchases of furniture, bronzes, porcelain, gold and silver plate. But they were also rigid Tories. There was no chance of the Regent following the Whig tradition of reform while under their influence.

Was reform urgently necessary? To answer that we must now

36

take a look at the country and the nation that our Prince of Pleasure asked to support him. The population of England was still under ten million; the whole of Great Britain about thirteen million. London was passing the million mark, but the provincial industrial cities, though growing fast, were all under a hundred thousand. The nation had been at war with France on and off for many years, and was still at war with Napoleon's Empire, which had denied most of Western Europe any British imports, even though there was much smuggling. However, the British Navy controlled the seaways; the industries were flourishing; and a new manufacturing class prospered. But no cheap food was entering the country, as it would do much later, and this was chiefly due to the operation of the Corn Laws. These were endlessly debated before, during and after the Regency, and I do not propose to allow them to detain us here. It is sufficient to say that the Corn Laws protected the home market for wheat, no matter how high the price rose, by proportionately increasing the tariff against imported wheat. This benefited the landowners and larger farmers at the expense of everybody else. The lot of the smallholder, with no great fields of wheat, was miserable; and that of the farm labourer was worse still. Vast numbers of them in the North and the Midlands went to work, often together with their wives and children, in the mines and foundries and new factories, in spite of the pitiful wages, long hours, and appalling conditions. In the South, where there were few industries, where a labouring man could not afford to travel and might easily be arrested as a vagabond if he were found some miles from home, there were thousands half-starved on poor relief. Moreover, there were several bad harvests during the Regency, sending the price of home wheat soaring.

Though protesting often enough, these people could not demand reform in Parliament because for the most part they were not represented there. Some sympathetic Whigs and angry radicals might speak or write on their behalf, but under Tory governments the persons who were solidly represented were the big landowners and the wealthier farmers, with the price of wheat in their pockets. The Reform Bill, spreading the franchise, was still years away; the new industrial districts were hardly represented at all; and England still had its 'rotten boroughs', which meant that all too often influential landowners could give away seats in Parliament as if they were snuffboxes. The laws protecting property were still very harsh indeed. It has been suggested that in no other European country were there so many offences on the statute book that demanded the death penalty. In theory, if not always in practice by this time, you could be hanged for 'privately stealing in a shop, warehouse, coach-house or stable to the amount of five shillings', or 'stealing to the amount of forty shillings in a dwellinghouse'.

(above) Sports of a Country Fair,
1810, coloured engraving published
by Thomas Tegg
The British Museum, London

If you escaped the hangman, you might be transported to New South Wales and go through hell in the convict ships. The lash, applied with dreadful severity, was common; the pillory had yet to be abolished. The prisons were filthy shambles. The police were inadequate, badly organised, and often dishonest. Reform in many different directions was now long overdue.

A poor man with a growing family might be tempted to risk hanging by stealing a sheep because such families both in town and country were rarely able to enjoy meat. Their diet chiefly consisted of bread and butter and potatoes, frequently half-rotten, washed down with strong tea. True, a farm labourer with a good employer might have a cottage with a garden, and grow some vegetables and even keep a pig. But without his own vegetables and at least a share of a pig to give the children an occasional bit of bacon, a labourer receiving day wages of a shilling or so and an allowance of bread for his family would be existing on a diet dangerously lacking in proteins and fats. Moreover, even the bread was often darkish unappetising stuff because it had been made out of adulterated flour. This probably explains the traditional dislike, lasting into the present century, of the English working class for brown bread.

Such a man might be entirely cut off from London and its doings, and even if he could read there would be no newspaper for him. But rumours would spread, stories filter out, probably by way of the innumerable domestic servants. So it is hardly likely that these poor people would give a cheer for the Regent when they heard about his grand midsummer fête.

(opposite) The Gothic Conservatory
at Carlton House from W. H. Pine's
History of the Royal Residences, 1819
The Royal Institute of British
Architects, London (Drawings
Collection)

About two thousand guests – the men wearing court dress or uniforms – were invited to Carlton House for 9 p.m. on 19 June, 1811. The Regent made his entrance at 9.15 wearing the uniform of

a field-marshal, which he was entitled to wear because he had recently appointed himself a field-marshal. And a particularly splendid one too, for even the seams of his coat were heavily embroidered, and there was a perhaps apocryphal story that it had cost as much as it weighed – two hundred pounds. He was joined by the exiled French royal family, the Bourbons, who were received in a room specially hung with blue silk and stitched gold fleur-de-lys. The main supper table filled the two-hundred-foot length of the Gothic conservatory. In front of the Regent's seat was a large circular basin which fed a stream that meandered, between banks of flowers, down to the end of the table, and offered flashing glimpses of gold and silver fish, all alive. The less important guests, streamless and fishless, had supper served to them at tables in the garden. Even out here, we are told, tureens, dishes, plates, were all silver. There were hot soups and roasts as well as an ample supply of excellent cold food; in addition to other wines there was iced champagne for everybody; peaches, grapes, pine-apples, and other fruits in or out of season were piled up everywhere; and, it was said, 'there was no crowding, hurry or bustle in waiting; everything was done as in a private house.' Some of us would like to visit that private house.

Tom Moore the poet, a kind of pet minstrel to the Whig aristocracy, was one of the guests and was enchanted half out of his mind. 'Nothing was ever half so magnificent,' he gasps. 'It was *in reality* all that they try to imitate in the gorgeous scenery of the theatre ... assemblage of beauty, splendour, and profuse and magnificence ... women out-blazing each other in the richness of their dress.' Then he adds, 'The Prince spoke to me, as he always does, with the cordial familiarity of an old acquaintance.' (This big show with 'cordial familiarity' in the middle of it was typical of the Regent and explains his limited short-range popularity.) But not all were enchanted – 'a paltry thing of bad taste' was one verdict. And another and better poet than Moore, Shelley, who was not there, wrote, 'It is said that this entertainment will cost £150,000. Nor will it be the last bauble which the nation must buy to amuse this overgrown bantling of Regency.' However, the Regent had whetted the appetite of that section of the London which longed – and indeed still longs – to live vicariously through royalty and its possessions. For three days after the fête these people were admitted by ticket to inspect the grand apartments. On the last day about thirty thousand stormed Carlton House, with the result that ladies 'were to be seen all round the gardens, most of them without shoes or gowns; and many almost completely undressed, and their hair hanging about their shoulders' – there had been such pushing and shoving and tugging and tearing in the day's long stampede. This was the end of the expensive show (though Shelley's £150,000 proved to be a wild

Tom Moore (detail), about 1830, by
Sir Thomas Lawrence
oil on panel
24 × 30 in. (61 × 76.2 cm.)
Collection Mr John Murray, London

exaggeration) that may have brought the Regent some new admirers but did nothing for his credit with the country. It merely sharpened the wits of the politicians and writers who already disliked him.

Moore's 'assemblage of beauty, splendour, and profuse magnificence' consisted largely of members of the aristocracy. It is they who have given the Regency its raffish air and rather gamey flavour. This was a ruling class nearing the end of one stage of its development. It blazed, crackled, fizzed in a torrid Indian Summer. It over-acted in a series of farewell performances. These were not like the aristocrats of the earlier eighteenth century, gravely magnificent but secure and serene, able to shape and colour the appearance of a whole age. Since then there had been the French Revolution, the *emigrés* haunting London, the huge menace of Napoleon, the new rich men and the sullen masses of industry, and everything was changing and the future uncertain. The Edwardian upper class found itself in a similar position and behaved accordingly, offering us pale reflections of the more full-blooded and reckless Regency types.

Like most aristocracies either decadent or about to transform themselves, this of the Regency was not really very aristocratic. Many of its haughty peers, perhaps the haughtiest, had not come out of ancient landed families but out of dubious eighteenth-century fortunes. And if an indifference to money was ever an aristocratic virtue (and I have my doubts), most of the Regency lords and ladies had forgotten it was. Indeed, apart from physical courage and a certain devil-may-care individualism – not to be despised in any age of careful conformity – the old aristocratic virtues and characteristics were fast disappearing. Too many of the landowning politicians of the Regency, the men who hooted in the Commons or Lords any modest attempt at reform, were hard and narrow, either without imagination and generosity or secretly frightened. Too many of the others, men or women, simply tried hard, often desperately, to amuse themselves, to defy boredom, like the Regent himself. There was about them a suggestion of keeping going while the going was good. Though still making much of their exclusive closed ranks, in fact they opened them to almost anybody who had either plenty of money or the wit and impudence to be entertaining. The old standards of conduct had almost vanished: *Noblesse Oblige* had been guillotined.

When in London these people lived and spent most of their time in a comparatively small area between Grosvenor Square and St James's. Dinner parties were frequent and rarely on a small scale, and on many occasions they must have looked magnificent. But the food and drink – though a great deal better than the bread and butter and strong tea of the more unfortunate common people –

were not always remarkable. Gronow, whose *Recollections* offer a fairly dependable guide to fashionable life in the Regency, first introduces us to a grand dinner of the period:

> Mulligatawny and turtle soups were the first dishes placed before you; a little lower, the eye met with the familiar salmon at one end of the table, and the turbot, surrounded by smelts, at the other. The first course was sure to be followed by a saddle of mutton or a piece of roast beef; and then you could take your oath that fowls, tongue and ham, would assuredly succeed as darkness after day . . .

This is lavish fare, but some further remarks he makes on Regency dining will not reduce most of us to envy:

> The universally-adored and ever-popular boiled potato, produced at the earliest period of the dinner, was eaten with everything, up to the moment when sweets appeared. Our vegetables, the best in the world, were never honoured by an accompanying sauce, and generally came to the table cold. A prime difficulty to overcome was the placing on your fork, and finally in your mouth, some half-dozen different eatables which occupied your plate at the same time. For example, your plate would contain, say, a slice of turkey, a piece of stuffing, a sausage, pickles, a slice of tongue, cauliflower, and potatoes. According to habit and custom, a judicious and careful selection from this little bazaar of good things was to be made, with an endeavour to place a portion of each in your mouth at the same moment. In fact, it appeared to me that we used to do all our compound cookery between our jaws . . .

Quite so; but it will appear to most of us that they were doing it the hard way.

The wines, Gronow tells us, were chiefly sherry, hock and port, for claret and even burgundy were then considered 'poor, thin, washy stuff'. Most men and many women drank heavily 'as soon as they had tasted their soup; as from that moment everybody was taking wine with everybody else till the close of the dinner.' This 'taking wine' meant that two people, having agreed to do this, raised their glasses to each other and then drank together. 'A glass of wine with you, Sir' often occurs in Dickens; and to my astonishment, when I lived in London just after the First World War, I found a few elderly gentlemen still following this custom. After the ladies had left the table and the room, the Regency men did as their fathers and grandfathers had done and settled down to some hours of drinking port, some of them emptying several bottles and ending up almost speechless. This meant that (Gronow again) 'female society amongst the upper classes was most notoriously neglected; except by romantic foreigners, who were the heroes of many a fashionable adventure that fed the clubs with ever-acceptable scandal.' However, aristocratic women were not altogether

Rees Howell Gronow (detail), engraving by J. C. Armytage, from a miniature
The British Museum, London

Detail of the façade of White's Club, St James's, London

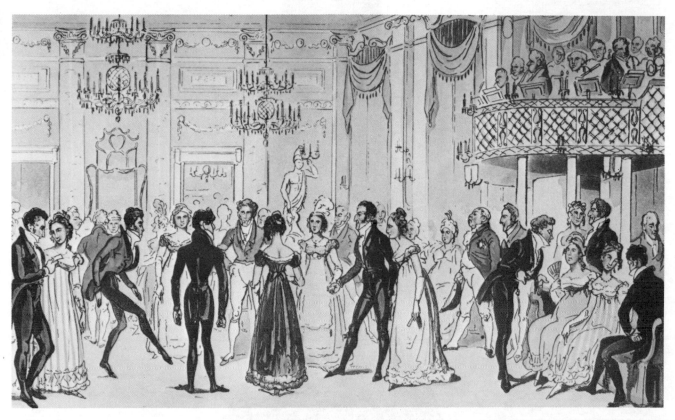

Highest Life in London – Tom and Jerry 'Sporting a Toe among the Corinthians at Almacks in the West', from Pierce Egan's *Life in London,* 1821 – drawn and etched by I. R. & G. Cruikshank
The British Museum, London

neglected; some of them, notably Lady Bessborough and Lady Melbourne, had several illegitimate children, whose fathers were rarely those 'romantic foreigners'. The children of the Countess of Oxford (of the Harley family) were known as the *Harleian Miscellany* because their fathers were supposed to be such a mixed lot.

Of the clubs that were being fed with scandal the two most important were White's and Watier's. White's can still be found in St James's Street though dandies no longer lounge in its bow window eyeing the women and passing rude remarks about the men. It was probably the most popular social club among Regency upper-class men, who made an election to membership fairly difficult. Watier's, Byron's Dandy Club, which had Brummell as its president for some years, was notorious throughout this period for its wild night-long gambling, which claimed the value of many an old estate. This passion for gambling and betting – not only on horses; there were Regency characters who would bet on anything, two flies on a wall – is significant. Taken together with the solemn devotion to fashion, with all the whimsicalities and eccentricities we shall shortly come to, with so much almost automatic sex, it suggests a whole class of men, like the Russian aristocrats later, cut off from the main stream of life, existing for pleasure and sooner or later finding themselves in a desert. I am not trying to

43

Sydney Smith, 1840, by Henry
Perronet Briggs
oil on canvas
49½ × 39½ in. (124 × 100 cm.)
The National Portrait Gallery,
London

Henry Luttrell, 1845, engraving after
Count d'Orsay
The British Museum, London

(opposite) Going to White's –
caricature of 2nd Baron Alvanley,
1823, engraving published by S. W.
Fores
The British Museum, London

Princess de Lieven, 1812–20, by Sir
Thomas Lawrence
oil on canvas
18⅛ × 15⅛ in. (46.1 × 38.4 cm.)
The Tate Gallery, London

moralise, but too much has been made, to please popular fancy, of the roistering and rip-roaring life of the Regency dandies and rakes. A longer look shows the fog of boredom creeping over them, and not infrequently a moonless night of despair.

The ladies might be barred from the men's clubs, but they had their own place, given up to suppers, gossip and dancing. This was Almack's, severely exclusive and most despotically controlled by a group of patronesses, such as the Ladies Castlereagh, Jersey, and Cowper (the best-liked of them), the Princess Esterhazy, and the Countess Lieven. 'Many diplomatic arts,' we are told, 'much finesse, and a host of intrigues were set in motion to get an invitation to Almack's.' Persons engaged in commerce had no hope of going. And not only had the male guests to have some skill in dancing but they also had to wear knee-breeches and white cravats. One night even the great Duke of Wellington, who happened to be wearing trousers, was firmly refused admittance. A ball and a supper were given there once a week during the Season; voucher-invitations were issued by the despotic patronesses; and girls new to the fashionable world suffered and wept if they were not on the List, for reasons suggested by the following verse, 'Advice to Julia':

> All on that magic LIST depends;
> Fame, fortune, fashion, lovers, friends:
> 'Tis that which gratifies or vexes
> All ranks, all ages, and both sexes.
> If once to Almack's you belong,
> Like monarchs, you can do no wrong;
> But banished thence on Wednesday night,
> By Jove, you can do nothing right.

This verse was written by Henry Luttrell. who was fond of scribbling such things to amuse his friends, and he had a great many friends and was in fact one of the most welcome diners-out and wits of Regency society. His social success offers us a good example of that society's inconsistencies. He was the illegitimate son of a gardener's daughter and an Irish peer, who gave him a sound education and then just enough to live on, by fashionable London standards, for the rest of his life. By dining out almost every night or staying for weeks in great country houses, he managed nicely. He had no claim to wealth, position and influence, nor, strictly speaking, birth; but he was charming and very amusing, so he was warmly invited everywhere. He could be called one of the entertainers of the wealthy Whig society (dominated by Lady Holland), like Tom Moore, who sang his Irish ditties after dinner, or the sturdier and far wittier Sydney Smith.

If I have to choose one man to represent the fashionable world

45

of the Regency, both in its reckless behaviour and its whims, quirks, eccentricities, then my choice would fall on William, Second Baron Alvanley, son of a successful though unpopular lawyer and politician who became a peer only in 1801. (No ancient titled family here, we observe, for all this talk of exclusiveness.) Unlike his father, this second Lord Alvanley was immensely popular in society, one of its central figures. He was famous for his humour and wit (but it does not wear well so I shall not quote it), his smiling good nature, dinners that were considered the best in London, and cheerfully reckless behaviour. He inherited an income worth between £60,000 and £70,000 in our money, began squandering it in all directions, and was soon – but hopefully rather than hopelessly – in debt. He was one of the Regency characters who would not only keep losing his money at the gaming tables but would also bet on anything anywhere. So the club betting book would read: *January 11th, 1811 – Lord Alvanley bets Sir Joseph Copley twenty guineas that a certain person outlives another certain person.*

It was Alvanley who once enjoyed a cold apricot tart so much that he ordered his chef to have a cold apricot tart on the sideboard every day throughout the year. He often stayed in country houses, and one of his reckless eccentricities was so well known that servants were ordered to sit up outside his bedroom, for after reading late he would extinguish his candle either by throwing it on the floor and aiming a pillow at it or by pushing it, still alight, under the bolster.

Lord Alvanley could be equally eccentric on other men's behalf. Once, knowing that his friend Lord Allen was miserable in the country because it was so quiet, Alvanley, a fellow guest at some country house, hired a hackney coach to drive to and fro outside Allen's window all night, with the coachman's assistant, the 'boots', calling out, 'Half-past two and a stormy night!'

Some of these titled eccentrics did not hire coachmen but carefully imitated them, in dress, speech, manner, occupation, even going to the length of delivering imaginary parcels. One of them, Akers, had his front teeth filed and paid fifty guineas to 'Hell Fire Dick', driver of the Cambridge Telegraph coach, to teach him to spit in the familiar coachman's style. The most notorious of these amateur coachmen was Sir John Lade, whose wife Letty had been the mistress of 'Sixteen-string Jack', a highwayman who was hanged in the 1770s. She was even more notorious than her husband, chiefly for her foul language. The Lades drove their own coach, and they behaved like professional coachmen who were going out of their minds. In 'The Devil's Drive', Byron wrote sardonically about all these coach-mad lunatics:

A fashionable Full Dress for November 1806, engraved and coloured for *Le Beau Monde* Collection Mrs Doris Langley Moore, London

A fashionable Morning Walking Dress for November 1806, engraved and coloured for *Le Beau Monde* Collection Mrs Doris Langley Moore, London

The Devil first saw, as he thought, the mail,
Its coachman and his coat;
So instead of a pistol, he cocked his tail,
And seized him by the throat.
'Aha!' quoth he, 'what have we here?
'Tis a new barouche and an ancient peer!'

So he sat him on his box again,
And bade him have no fear,
But be true to his club, and staunch to his rein,
His brothel and his beer;
'Next to seeing a lord at the council board,
I would rather see him here.'

Incidentally, Conan Doyle gives us a lively and fairly accurate account of these dandies and eccentrics in his tale, *Rodney Stone*. It is chiefly concerned with pugilism, but then bare-fist fighting, which drew immense crowds and large bets from the sporting gentry, was one of the passions of the age. And cricket too was beginning its long reign over the English.

I have already mentioned the dandies, and now we ought to take a closer look at them. The wildly eccentric fops were not true dandies. One of them was Sir Lumley Skeffington, known as 'Skiffy', who wrote indifferent plays, painted his face, perfumed himself liberally, and wore coloured satin suits. Another was Henry Cope of Brighton, called its 'Green Man', for everything he wore was green, so were all his rooms and possessions, and it was said he ate nothing but green fruits and vegetables. He was one of the sights of the town, was probably more than half dotty, and ended his life by throwing himself off the cliff at Brighton. Somewhere between the eccentrics and the true dandies was a man like Lord Petersham, who was said to have had a different snuffbox for every day of the year, taking care to choose one that suited the weather, not risking a cold by using a light snuffbox in an East wind.

The true dandy dressed soberly but at a cost of money, time and trouble quite out of proportion to any sensible demands. All this was a deliberate affectation, not without a glint of humour in it. To discuss for hours the shape of a cravat, to shrink with horror from a badly-cut coat, to spend half the day choosing clothes and putting them on, these were moves in a game being played with a mock solemnity. In its indifference to serious matters and its intense concentration upon trivia, Regency dandyism (as some French writers realised, much later) was a half-defiant, half-humorous way of life. There was in it a good deal of poker-faced impudence, and to be temporarily successful it needed a considerable audience of non-dandies, ordinary people who were either amused or shocked. Three generations later Oscar Wilde in his talk and writing would reproduce something of the style, tone, atmosphere, of Regency dandyism, even though there was none of Wilde's homosexuality among its chief figures.

The most important of them, the high priest of dandyism, was of course George (Beau) Brummell. I made the point earlier that this Regency aristocracy in its desire to be amused would forget noble birth or great wealth and open its ranks to welcome a discreet entertainer. Brummell's grandfather was probably a personal servant; his father was a government clerk who became private secretary to Lord North when he was in office. It is possible that Lord North tossed him a few small sinecures; and we know that he married a woman who had money. But the total capital inherited by our Brummell, the Beau, would hardly equal the income of many of his friends and admirers. So he could not boast of either birth or wealth. However, he was educated at Eton, where he made many useful friends. He had an unusually pleasing appearance and manner, a certain dry wit, and any amount of cool impudence. He probably met and charmed the Prince quite early, long before the Regency, and he was given a commission in the Prince's own regiment, the Tenth Light Dragoons. However, he soon left the army to become a man of fashion, and after a few years the leader of it, the dictator in the world of the beaux.

It was he who decided what the well-dressed man should wear, who remodelled the dress coat, decreed that cravats should be starched, and brought pantaloons into fashion. He was the first man to wear evening dress of black. He denounced showy materials, fantastic suits, frills and perfume for men; he was fastidiously clean when too many men of position were downright dirty (the fat old Duke of Norfolk could only be washed and cleaned up when he was too drunk to know what was happening); and his constant aim was towards a sober but exquisite perfection. When he was told about a man who was so well-dressed that everybody turned round to stare at him, Brummell replied, 'Then he is not well-dressed.'

That sharp and original character, Lady Hester Stanhope, declared that Brummell was no fool, and reported how he once said to her, 'If the world is so silly as to admire my absurdities, you and I may know better, but what does it signify?' He had genuine good taste in everything – his house, furniture, library and all his possessions were much admired – but in his agreeable cool style he built up the absurdities and slyly encouraged myths about himself – that only in one distant place could his washing be done properly, that his boots had to be cleaned in champagne, that it took three people to make his gloves, and so forth, deliberate exaggerations that annoyed and alarmed his creditors. For in this year, 1811, he was already deep in debt; he was no longer on good terms with the Regent; and his reign over the beaux was not to last much longer. But we shall meet him again – and on a famous occasion.

Harriette Wilson, 1825, engraving published by Robert Jones
The British Museum, London

Amy Wilson, engraving reproduced from *The Fortunes of Harriette,* by Angela Thirkell, 1936

One of the few spiteful references to Brummell, calling him cold and heartless and satirical, can be found in the *Memoirs* of Harriette Wilson. She and her sisters Amy and Fanny were successful courtesans, and in that capacity, and also simply as hostesses, were well acquainted with almost all the Regency men of rank and fashion, from Dukes (including Wellington) downwards. Their father kept a small shop in Mayfair, and he was either extremely cynical or absent-minded because his daughters were off on their own, being kept as mistresses by members of the aristocracy, while still in their very early teens. (Later, Harriette so identifies herself with rank and fashion – at least with the male half – that she can denounce the impudence of persons in trade trying to force their way into good society.) The *Memoirs* were first published in 1825, when Harriette had already gone to live in France; they appeared then in paper parts and the demand for them was so great that the publisher-bookseller, Stockdale, had to erect a barrier outside his shop. They must have disappointed many readers then and since; they are not at all salacious and keep well away from any sexual frankness; indeed, their general tone tends to be mincingly genteel and there is an irritating falseness throughout. Yet they keep us moving in a long gallery of Regency aristocrats, bucks and beaux. Walter Scott, a sound judge, said of them, 'There is some good retailing of conversations, in which the style of the speaker, so far as known to me, is exactly imitated.' He met Harriette once, years before the *Memoirs* appeared, and declared: 'She was far from beautiful . . . but a smart saucy girl with good eyes and dark hair, and the manners of a wild schoolboy.'

Even after awarding points for sauciness, good eyes and uninhibited manners, I must confess I find it hard to understand why Harriette and her sisters were able to keep so many Regency men of rank and fashion buzzing and swarming round them night after night. It is easy to understand the attraction of the notorious mid-Victorian cocottes. This was not based entirely on their sexual availability and (no doubt) expertise; in their free-and-easy company a man, bored at home, could smoke and drink and exchange ribald remarks and stories, behave in fact as any quite devoted young couple might do today, when wives are no longer reproachful angels. But in the high society of the Regency few women were already adopting this angelic rôle (though Byron found one, as we shall see); beautiful women of rank and wealth and easy sexual morals were not difficult to find, as the innumerable liaisons of the period amply testify; so why should their men leave them to look into Harriette's box at the opera or take supper with her and her sisters afterwards?

The best answer that comes to my mind is that these girls chanced to become fashionable, and that the various dukes and the

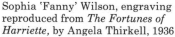
Sophia 'Fanny' Wilson, engraving reproduced from *The Fortunes of Harriette,* by Angela Thirkell, 1936

(above left) Match Bill at Lord's, 1816 – Lord's Cricket Ground was opened in 1814
The Marylebone Cricket Club, London

(above right) The Ladies of Surrey and Hampshire, 1811, by Thomas Rowlandson
watercolour
9 × 13½ in. (22.9 × 34.3 cm.)
The Marylebone Cricket Club, London

Alvanleys and Brummells were all dominated by fashion. Just as it was fashionable to go fox-hunting, to attend and bet on bare-fist fights sometimes lasting for hours, and even by now to patronise cricket (with elegant variations too, for in this year '11 females of Surrey were backed against 11 of Hampshire by 2 noblemen for 500 guineas a side'), so too it was fashionable to go to bed or stay out of bed, talking scandal, with Harriette Wilson.

A little sidelight on the manners and morals of the time can be provided by one of its well-known characters, Colonel 'Dan' Mackinnon. 'A great swell both in Lisbon and London,' his fellow-officer Gronow tells us. 'His calm smile, black eyes and splendid figure when he strutted in uniform down St James's Street, struck everyone with admiration.' He was notorious for elaborate practical jokes. Once, landing in Spain, he impersonated the Duke of York and he kept it up, with the connivance of his regimental friends, for several hours until at last, when a huge bowl of punch was served at a mayoral banquet, he horrified his hosts by suddenly diving his head into the bowl and throwing his heels into the air.

When Wellington arranged to visit a convent near Lisbon, Mackinnon went in before him (it was rumoured he had paid several secret visits to that convent), disguised himself completely as a nun, and was even singled out as one of the best-looking of them. As his antics with the punchbowl suggest, he was equally notorious for his acrobatic feats; bets were made on his agility – going round a room entirely on the furniture or scrambling over a difficult rooftop – and one night at Covent Garden he went right round the auditorium by running along the ledges of the boxes. High-spirited, athletic, handsome, he was – as they liked to say then – a great favourite with the fair sex. After a passionate liaison with a lady

William Wyndham, 1st Baron
Grenville (detail), *c.* 1800, by
John Hoppner
oil on canvas
29 × 23½ in. (73.7 × 59 cm.)
The National Portrait Gallery,
London

'of high birth and aristocratic connexions', he stayed away from her, so she wrote him a letter full of reproaches, threatening suicide, and demanded the return of a lock of hair she had given him. The cheerfully whimsical but brutal Mackinnon did not reply but sent his orderly to her with a large packet of locks of hair, blonde to red, black to grey, and a message asking her to pick out her own property. Such characters were best employed fighting the Peninsular War, and it is only fair to add that they did – and won it.

Before we leave high society, we can at least enjoy a glimpse of three of its great ladies, widely different in character. The first is the Duchess of York, the former Prussian Princess already mentioned in the first chapter. Her passionate interest in dogs was ridiculous – at one time she had a hundred and at all times she had several large, embarrassing and rather dirty dogs sharing her apartment – but most of her visitors tried to ignore this absurdity because she was a pleasant hostess who liked to invite wits and men of letters to her house, Oatlands. A tiny woman with china-blue eyes, she had plenty of character and a will of her own. She disliked the royal family, refused to recognise Mrs Fitzherbert, and showed affection for Princess Caroline. There was a real friendship between her and Brummell, and they continued to exchange letters when, as we shall see, he had to leave England and was living in poverty in France. Many men hard to please, like Charles Greville, admired her dignity, good manners, hospitality, her generosity to her poorer neighbours; and her death in 1820, when she was only in her early fifties, brought grief to a wide section of society.

Incidentally, it was this Duchess of York – and not, as we are often told, the Prince Consort, years later – who first introduced and popularised the German custom of giving Christmas presents. She turned her dining room into a kind of Christmas fair, to which all her servants and many local children were invited, to see the decorations and all the presents piled up and then receive their share of the gifts. No doubt there are times when we wish these customs had never been imported from Germany, but there must be few of us who have not enjoyed in childhood and youth such Christmas treats. And we owe them largely to this Regency Duchess of York.

Lady Holland was the great Whig hostess of the time. She was originally Lady Webster (married at sixteen), ran off with Henry Richard Fox, third Baron Holland, and when her divorce came through, in 1797, she married him – a good move because he was rich, sensible and very patient. She was an imperious woman, not a fool but slightly absurd, and at her crowded dinner table she sat somewhat raised above her guests and treated the table talk as if it were a symphony she was trying to conduct. Many guests resented her sharp bossy manner, but the wits – and to give her

William Lamb, 2nd Viscount
Melbourne (detail), 1836, by Sir Edwin
Henry Landseer
oil on panel
23½ × 17¼ in. (59.8 × 43.8 cm.)
The National Portrait Gallery,
London

PLATE V. Lady Caroline Lamb, 1813,
by Thomas Phillips
oil on canvas
36 × 27½ in. (91.5 × 69.8 cm.)
The Devonshire Collection,
Chatsworth, Derbyshire

credit where it is due, she kept on inviting them – were generally
a match for her. Once when the dinner table was already over-
crowded, she abruptly told Luttrell to make room for another
guest, and he replied, without stirring, 'It certainly must be made,
because it doesn't exist.' Again, asking for trouble, she sharply
ordered the redoubtable Sydney Smith to ring the bell. 'Oh yes,'
he replied, 'and shall I sweep the floor?'

She was very much a political hostess. Creevey wrote in 1812:
'Lady Holland said to me on Sunday in the drawing room after
dinner – "Come here and sit by me, you *mischievous toad*, and
promise you won't begin upon the new Government with your
jokes. When you do, begin with those Grenvilles" . . .' Brougham,
at the radical end of the Whigs, wrote to Creevey: 'Nothing, for
instance, can be more unpropitious than the plan of carrying on the
party by a coterie at Lady Holland's elbow . . .' Tom Moore in his
Diary often takes us to Lady Holland's dinner parties, and over and
above the amusing stories and the remarks of the wits what is so
impressive about them is the wide range and the high level of the
talk there. If there is equally good talk at dinner parties nowadays,
then I have been unlucky for some time in my invitations. Regency
society was not all gaming, debts, booze and affairs: it could offer
some superbly good table talk.

Lady Melbourne was also a great Whig hostess but had little
else in common with Lady Holland. Born as early as 1752 she was
really an eighteenth-century figure, with many of the characteristics of that age, but she lived on into the Regency long enough to
become the close and adored friend of Byron. She was then fat and
elderly, so it was simply a friendship, enlivened by mutual flirta-
tiousness. 'Had she been a few years younger,' he declared, 'what
havoc might she not have wrought in my affections!' And he wrote
of her, 'The best friend I ever had in my life, and the cleverest of
women.' Married at sixteen to a dullish, weak, rich man – who spent
forty years in Parliament and spoke only once – she took a number
of lovers, among them Lord Coleraine, the Duke of Bedford, and,
probably the most important, Lord Egremont; and she had six
children, possibly all illegitimate. Her second son, William, the
Lord Melbourne who was Victoria's first prime minister, was
generally supposed to be one of her children by Lord Egremont.

Her reputation was far from spotless, yet she took care never to
flaunt her affairs in public. 'Anyone,' she said, 'who braves the
opinion of the world sooner or later feels the consequences of it.'
(Her son William's wife, Caroline Lamb, and Byron, should have
remembered this.) It is the dictum of a worldly woman, and this is
what she was, her only world, outside her garden, being the tiny
world of London society and politics. But, within these limitations,
Lady Melbourne was a remarkable woman, as so many of her

MOLINEUX. CRIBB.

contemporaries acknowledged. She was rather tall but shapely, had an attractive mouth, challenging dark eyes, a full-blooded femininity; but she was entirely free from tiresome tricks and caprices, never cadging for sympathy, and actually disliked talking about herself. It was she who said, 'No man is safe with another's secrets, no woman with her own.' She was very much a woman, enduringly devoted to the few people she cared about, yet she had the mind and ambitious outlook of a shrewd politician. From 1816 to 1818, when she died, she was miserable, gross, doped with laudanum. Yet on her deathbed she told her son William to aspire to great things, and commanded her daughter Emily to be true not to her husband, Lord Cowper, but to her first and most distinguished admirer, Lord Palmerston. Twenty-one years later, Emily, now a widow, married Lord Palmerston, and shared, 'with tact and grace', the years of his greatest fame. So, while Lady Melbourne cannot be held up as an example to high-spirited young ladies, she was indeed a remarkable woman, taking much that was best in the eighteenth century into the dubious Regency.

It was dubious in more senses than one. In this London of raffish high society, of gaming clubs and prizefights, of theatres and the opera and the circus and Vauxhall Gardens, there were more and more people, not entirely belonging to the middle and lower classes, who strongly condemned all such things. There was an inevitable swing of the pendulum. Those who lived for amusement, with our Prince of Pleasure at their head, were increasingly denounced by people who believed that all amusement, even a hand at cards or a dance or two, was so much hell-bait. Some of these puritanical prejudices came from the various nonconformist sects, old hands at disapproval, but now the most active and influential disdainers and denouncers of pleasure belonged to the Evangelical Low Church.

Probably the two best-known converts to Evangelicalism were William Wilberforce, justly celebrated for his long campaign against slavery, and the writer Hannah More. A rich young man of immense personal charm, an M.P. and a close friend of William Pitt, a welcome guest because he was an excellent singer and an amusing mimic, Wilberforce was converted while still in his twenties. Later he became the most prominent member of the 'Clapham Sect', a group of public-spirited Evangelicals who did much good service for reform. He was never as narrow-minded and bigoted as most Evangelicals, including Hannah More. She had had an early career as a writer of tragedies, when she was a close friend of Garrick and his wife. Her conversion was slow, but thorough in the end. Though already an elderly woman at the time of the Regency, she was indefatigable in all the various activities of the Evangelical movement and was its most popular author.

Hannah More, 1827, by Augustin Edouart
silhouette
8¾ × 11 in. (22.2 × 28 cm.)
The National Portrait Gallery, London

PLATE VI. Tom Cribb ('Black Diamond') the Boxer in combat with Tom Molyneux of Virginia, about 1810
Newcastle yellow-glazed ware
5⅝ in. (14.3 cm.) high
The Art Gallery and Museum, Brighton

William Wilberforce, 1828, by Sir
Thomas Lawrence
oil on canvas
38 × 43 in. (96.6 × 109.3 cm.)
The National Portrait Gallery,
London

Her *Practical Piety* and *Christian Morals* sold out before publication and then went into many editions. She had, of course, turned
her back on the theatre long before, denouncing it in all sincerity
but also discovering there was a far larger public for her piety than
there had ever been for her plays.

A great many Evangelical societies, some charitable but most
of them concerned with propagating the Bible, came into existence
in the years just before the Regency. The most notorious of these
was the Society for the Suppression of Vice. Its object was to
suppress Sabbath-breaking (first of all), then blasphemous and
licentious books, prints, drawings, etc., together with private
theatricals, fairs, brothels, dram-shops, gaming houses, lotteries,
and fortune-tellers. On the whole it was not successful though it
worked hard, often through informers, at warning, threatening,
and bringing actions against the wicked. So it was able to put an
end to 'the shameful practice of Rowing Matches and Boat Races
on Sundays' on the Thames above Westminster Bridge. It was also
a constant menace to liberal authors and publishers. Men who
disliked it, like Sydney Smith, accused it of trying to curtail or
banish the amusements and pastimes of the lower orders while
remaining oblivious to similar pastimes of the rich and lordly.
This Sabbatarian bigotry was very hard on working folk who had
only this one day in the week to get out and about and amuse
themselves. But Hannah More had declared: 'The amusements of
a Christian must have nothing in them to excite the passions which
it is his duty to subdue; they must not obstruct spiritual-mindedness,
nor inflame the lust of the flesh, lust of the eye and pride of life.'

For my part I find little 'spiritual-mindedness' in this Evangelical movement, which was to throw a shadow over much of English life, and encourage cant and humbug, for the next hundred years. Dickens's Chadband and Pecksniff came out of it. It was puritanism again but with a difference, having none of the strength and depth of the old puritans, ready to defy and march against authority. These tea-and-meeting and rather slimy new puritans did not challenge the Establishment – the *Thing* as Cobbett called it – and made it clear to the Poor, whom they were always solemnly addressing, that they had no *right* to the benevolence of the rich, that the bounty of the affluent would be given only to those Poor who were Evangelically religious and proper in conduct. The Good Poor, being well instructed, received what had been done for them as a matter of *favour*, not of *right*. (The temptation to join the Bad Poor must have been very strong, and I suspect that my own great-great-grandparents never resisted it.) Even the terrible scarcity of those years – and now I quote from one of their addresses to the Poor – 'has also enabled you to see more clearly the advantages you derive from the government and constitution of this country – to observe the benefits flowing from the distinction of rank and fortune, which has enabled the *high* so liberally to assist the *low* . . .' It was complacent cant of this kind that encouraged the upper and middle classes to keep the shockingly ungrateful working people in their place. And it partly explains why electoral reforms and any improvement in hours, wages, working conditions, were so slow to arrive.

Moreover, this Evangelicalism, based more on fear than on love, and theologically and intellectually contemptible, was responsible

The Spirit moving the Quakers upon Worldly Vanities, 1819, by George Cruikshank – the Quakers are mounted on hobby horses
The British Museum, London

for some profound psychological effects, which long outlasted the Regency. If the Regent himself was the victim of the pleasure principle, these people were the slaves of an anti-pleasure principle. And, unlike the Regent, they shaped and coloured the next world by their prejudices. By concentrating on some passages of the Bible and ignoring others, they worshipped a deity presumably ready to condemn people to everlasting torture for being unrepentant about playing whist, singing in taverns, or attending a performance of *Twelfth Night*. Children were taught to believe that their lightest actions and preferences might make the difference between everlasting bliss or appalling damnation. The stories written for them and very widely read – Mrs Sherwood's *The Fairchild Family* is a notable example – were life-denying, fear-inspiring, and sometimes downright sadistic. They began to twist minds that would live on, often acquiring much influence, well into the Victorian Age.

With this Evangelicalism so widespread and active and its new puritanism so hard at work, clearly the Regency was an age and a society of wild extremes. It is during these unusual ages of extravagance and astonishing extremes – of power and helplessness, wealth and poverty, licentiousness and austere priggishness, the permissive and the puritanical – that literature, as if energised by a current passing between opposite poles, becomes richly creative. Whatever the reason might be, it is certain that this decade of the Regency astounds us by its literary genius and talent. There were alive together in these years – Blake, Wordsworth, Coleridge, Byron, Shelley, Keats, among the poets; Scott and Jane Austen among novelists; Coleridge again, Hazlitt, Lamb, Leigh Hunt, among critics and essayists. In this place they are merely names on the programme, but later, I trust, we shall see them making entrances and exits, illuminated and sharply defined on the great stage.

Before ringing down the curtain on 1811, we must allow the Regent himself a brief appearance. Towards the year's end, he slipped and hurt his ankle while showing his daughter how to do the Highland Fling. A gallant effort, for he was a heavy man and his ankles were known to be weak. He was in bed for two weeks. There were wild rumours, much alarm. Scott reported that in Edinburgh they were not only alarmed but stunned. After learning that the Regent, in such pain and with so much irritation of his nerves, was nearing delirium, Lady Bessborough cried, 'What will become of us if, as well as our King, our Regent goes mad?' His brother, the sinister Duke of Cumberland, was less sympathetic; and the stricken Regent quarrelled with him – 'from hearing of his saying that his Brother's illness was *higher* than the foot, and that a blister on the head might be more efficacious than a poultice on the Ankle.' And not a bad line, I think, for the Curtain.

1812

The Romantics

There are some years that seem to have a curious character of their own, as if they were bent on exaggerating some particular human quality by shaping events to illustrate it. 1812 is one of those years. It will show us its personages chiefly being romantic in a pejorative sense, defying calm judgment, ignoring a reasonable view of things.

The first and most famous of these self-deceivers was Napoleon himself, who had almost all of Western Europe safely in his grasp. Supreme power and a restless insatiable ambition were clouding his judgment, and he was already more sluggish in mind and body than he had been in his greatest days. One of his oldest friends, Marmont, said of him: 'Napoleon was at this period living in a non-existent world, created by his own imagination. He built structures in the air, he took his desires for realities, and gave his orders as if he was ignorant of the true state of affairs and as if the actual facts had been hidden from him on purpose.' Had he been attending to the realities of his situation, before attempting anything else he would have gone down into Spain himself, collected 200,000 of his veterans, and swept Wellington and his British Expeditionary Force into the sea. As it was, now half in dreamland, he pulled out some of his best troops from Spain to join the army of 600,000 that would invade Russia. These men came from all parts of the Empire, but by far the greater number – alas for them – from the southern half of it where Russian winters were unimaginable. They marched towards Moscow and most of them were never seen again.

Wellington was no romantic, and if he had not Napoleon's genius for battle, he was at least cool, long-sighted and able to profit by his opponents' mistakes. He faced some disadvantages: he had too few British troops, divisional commanders who tended to be ineffectual, and allies he could not always trust – the Spaniards made daring and ferocious guerillas but lacked discipline and steadiness as regular soldiers. But Wellington enjoyed some supremely important advantages. Instead of being compelled to live off the land (and a savagely hostile land too) as the French armies had to do, his expeditionary force had the sea at its back, with the triumphant British Navy keeping open his line of supply. He also had the best-trained infantry in Europe, its musketry fire,

A monument erected to commemorate the raising of the Siege of Cadiz in consequence of the glorious Victory gained by the Duke of Wellington over the French, near Salamanca, on the 22 July 1812, drawn and etched by Robert Shipster, Woolwich
The British Museum, London

as Marmont acknowledged, the most murderous, which explains why his casualties were almost always far fewer than those of the French. Again, though he was far outnumbered, he never had to face a properly unified command. The French Marshals were suspicious of one another, quarrelsome and unco-operative until it was too late. By 1812 Wellington had already outfought the ablest of all Napoleon's Marshals, Masséna, who was then replaced by Marmont, a superb administrator and organiser but no genius in actual battle. In January Wellington took Ciudad Rodrigo, in April Badajos, and then crushingly defeated Marmont at Salamanca and marched into Madrid. He had to retire again because Soult moved from Andalusia, but soon he was once more on the move and by the following summer he was driving Soult out of the Pyrenees and about to enter France. Napoleon's own spectacular defeats were elsewhere, but this Peninsular War, which he had never really understood and had always treated too lightly, might be said to be the creeping cancer of his Empire.

It was also during this fantastic year that the United States, suffering from the Royal Navy's blockade and annoyed by its high-handed behaviour on the seas, declared war on Great Britain. The result was one of the most scattered wars in all history, ranging rather than raging from Canada down to Louisiana, from the Great Lakes to the mid-Atlantic, with flotillas engaged anywhere except on land, and hastily assembled small forces advancing and retreating, winning and losing, all over the place. The American privateers were finally so numerous, active and bold that they doubled the London insurance rates for British shipping. Two events stand out in this strange war, though neither happened as early as 1812. A British squadron, moving by river, landed four thousand regular soldiers within reach of Washington, where they burned the Capitol. This infuriated the Americans without inspiring the British, who afterwards never included it among their triumphs of arms, whereas at times, arguing with my American friends, I have caught a gleam in their eyes that might suggest they were remembering that once we burned the Capitol. The other event was the successful defence of New Orleans by Andrew Jackson and his men, the British invaders being finally defeated with the loss of two thousand men and a couple of generals. In these days we see battles on television while they are still being fought, but in those days communications were very slow, so that nobody on either side, banging away in Louisiana, knew that the peace treaty between their two countries had already been signed. However, this post-treaty victory did much for American morale and the increasing depth of national feeling. Peace arrived at the end of 1814 but the war it ended began in 1812, perhaps not surprisingly – an odd war beginning in an odd year.

(opposite) The Duke of Wellington, *c.* 1812, by Juan Bauzit
watercolour
13 × 9¾ in. (33.1 × 24.8 cm.)
The National Portrait Gallery, London

The Regent, though wearing many splendid uniforms, was of course far from all this cannonading. But he claimed to have been in action, later even at Waterloo; and we do not know to this day whether he was solemnly fooling his listeners or really believed – after all those uniforms and guns firing salutes – that he had been in a battle or two.

Early in 1812 the government kept its promise of a year before, and the Prince's wider powers as Regent were confirmed. He could now form a government but dallied and dithered over the idea of a possible coalition, which would take some of his old Whig friends into the cabinet. He even asked Perceval, leader of the Tories and now Prime Minister, to draft a letter from him suggesting coalition to the chief Whigs. As this whole idea was distasteful to Perceval, who was not ready to welcome any Whigs as colleagues, the letter he drafted was very far from being a masterpiece of persuasion; and the Regent remarked, 'It is a great misfortune to Mr Perceval to write in a style that would disgrace a washerwoman.' One complication, out of many, was that the moderate and more responsible Whig leaders not only mistrusted the Regent but were also strongly in favour of Catholic Emancipation (long overdue), a policy the Regent detested and would hardly discuss. In all this, what the Regent really wanted – and the wish came from his heart, not his head – were places in the government for a few members of his Whig Old Guard, like Sheridan. But then something happened that was totally unexpected, strange and startling, and somehow typical of this peculiar year.

On 11 May, Spencer Perceval, who had been Prime Minister since 1809, was murdered in the lobby of the House of Commons. The man who shot him, Bellingham, was suffering from a persecution mania, though his original grievance may not have been altogether unreasonable. He had been sent to prison in Russia, and the British representative there, Leveson Gower, to whom he had appealed, had done nothing for him. He came back, a bankrupt, with a fierce grudge against the British Government. He said he would have preferred to kill Leveson Gower, but Leveson Gower was not available and the Prime Minister was, so he would do. Perceval was no statesman, just a hard-working administrator and Tory party manager; but his death threw everything into confusion again.

The Regent tried for a coalition once more, but the Whigs objected, among other things, to the important places in the Regent's household occupied by Lord and Lady Hertford and their son, Lord Yarmouth, all strongly Tory. This Lord Yarmouth is the Hertford, immensely rich, who was afterwards turned into 'Lord Steyn' in Thackeray's *Vanity Fair*, and into 'Lord Monmouth' in Disraeli's *Coningsby*. The Regent now sent for all manner of

PLATE VII. The Battle of Waterloo (detail), 1815, drawn and etched by William Heath and aquatinted by R. Reeve
The Royal Collection, Windsor Castle

(above left) Robert Banks Jenkinson,
2nd Earl of Liverpool, *c.* 1827, by
Sir Thomas Lawrence
oil on canvas
92 × 56 in. (254 × 143 cm.)
The National Portrait Gallery,
London

(above right) The Assassination of the
Right Honourable Spencer Perceval
in the lobby of the House of Commons
11 May 1812
coloured engraving
The Royal Collection, Windsor Castle

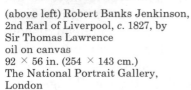

PLATE VIII. Percy Bysshe Shelley
(detail), 1845, by Joseph Severn
paper on canvas
40⅛ × 48⅞ in. (102 × 124 cm.)
The Keats Shelley Memorial House,
Rome

politicans, rather like a man trying to work a card trick he does not quite know, with sticky cards too. Creevey told in his diary: 'I begin to think that his reign will end in a day or two in downright insanity. He first sends for one person and then another.' Then, later: 'It really begins to be almost too farcical to write about this madman and his delay.' Finally, on 8 June: 'Well, this is beyond anything. Castlereagh has just told us that . . . His Royal Highness has appointed Lord Liverpool Prime Minister. Was there ever anything equal to this?'

Lord Liverpool, a dutiful and pious High Tory, immediately put together a Tory government that was to be dominated for years by Lord Castlereagh, who was both Foreign Secretary and Leader of the House. Castlereagh was cold, narrow, obstinate and hard-working, a man who devoted himself intensely to the wrong side in almost every great issue. No politician of the Regency exerted a stronger, wider or worse influence, and no man was more strongly and widely detested by everybody outside the Tory Establishment. 'I met Murder in the way,' wrote Shelley, 'He had a mask like Castlercagh.' And ten years after 1812, when Castlereagh, worn out, no longer in his right mind, cut his throat, Byron wrote:

> Oh Castlereagh! Thou art a patriot now;
> Cato died for his country, so didst thou:
> He perished rather than see Rome enslaved,
> Thou cutt'st thy throat that Britain may be saved.

Castlereagh fought hard against Napoleon, but for the wrong

A Procession from Wales to Manchester Square, N.B. by way of Yarmouth, 1812, by George Cruikshank – A procession is approaching the residence of the Marchioness of Hertford in Manchester Square where the lady is seen dressed in regal attire on the balcony waiting to receive the *cortège*. First comes a sledge drawn by a sorry hack and inscribed 'Yarmouth Troll' on which stands Yarmouth; then follows the Prince Regent riding on a goat, with a leek in lieu of a whip, and exclaming 'All hail, Sweet Queen!' followed by his suite also on goats
The British Museum, London

reasons, wanting to preserve or restore systems that were not worth preserving or restoring and in the end would have to go. Though foreign and not home affairs were always his immediate concern, he must be held largely responsible for the deep discontents, the rioting, the savage legislation and the brutal suppression, that we shall discover in the later years of the Regency.

As soon as Liverpool became Prime Minister the Whigs, who had imagined that the Regent would reward them after the long years they had spent in the political wilderness with him, loudly denounced his ingratitude and perfidy. And they did not overlook Lady Hertford – 'that unseen and separate influence which lurked behind the throne – an influence of odious character, leading to consequences the most pestilent and disgusting.' The most ambitious, energetic and eloquent of the extreme Whigs, Brougham, declared henceforth he would attack the Regent 'in terms which would not have been too strong to have described the latter days of Tiberius'. He was an able advocate and now offered his services to the Regent's neglected wife, Princess Caroline, a move that would have important consequences in a few years' time. If there had been public opinion polls in those days, the Regent's popularity would have been plainly seen taking a dive. Unfortunately for him – and it has been a familiar situation in England – while the Tories had the power, the extreme Whigs and the radicals had the talent, which they used without stint to denounce or ridicule him.

One story began to leak out during this summer of 1812 that in the end did the Regent's reputation more harm than all his extravagances and debts. It involved him as a husband and a father. We shall have to take a long look later, when they reach the centre of the stage, at his wife Caroline and his daughter Charlotte. Here it is sufficient to say that at this time, by the Regent's express orders, not only did they live separated from him but also completely separated from each other. And Charlotte was not a child; she was well into her teens. Once a week, mother and daughter dined at the same table but always surrounded by a carefully selected company. The Regent would not allow them to meet in private. Naturally both of them protested, Caroline with particular vigour. It was not long before people learnt how the Regent was playing the callous tyrant in his family life, as if he were not a foolish man but a downright cruel one. Actually there was no intentional cruelty in his behaviour at this time but there was certainly a monumental stupidity, in terms of his public reputation almost determinedly self-destructive. He was now busy encouraging all the talent ranged against him.

But one man of very great talent, Byron, either pretended to be or was indeed temporarily charmed by the Regent. In June of this year he attended a ball in the gracious presence of His Royal Highness, who summoned Byron to his side and – as Murray the publisher told Scott – 'displayed an intimacy and critical taste which at once surprised and delighted Lord Byron'. The poet himself referred to 'a tone and taste which gave me a very high idea of his abilities and accomplishments . . .' It may be that Byron was genuinely bowled over, but there is some ambiguity here – as there often is with Byron – because certain verses he wrote during this year are obviously hostile to the Regent. But it is possible that at this time Byron, still only in his middle twenties, did not quite know where he was, his head reeling from the intoxication of sudden and enormous success. He was now, to use the old phrase, the literary lion of the season.

In 1809 his satirical *English Bards and Scotch Reviewers* had brought him some favourable attention in London literary circles,

An excursion to R(agley) Hall, 1812, by George Cruikshank – The devil driving a carriage assisted by Cupid, blindfolded, as a postboy in which are the Regent and the Marchioness of Hertford, pass a 'Female Asylum' where the Prince's earlier favourites are seen looking from the windows and upbrading him with his faithlessness; the Earl of Yarmouth on a jackass is leading the way as an outrider. Ragley Hall was the home of the Marquis of Hertford · The British Museum, London

but he was still unknown to the general reading public when he set out, that year, with his friend Hobhouse for a lengthy tour of Spain, Portugal, Greece and Turkey. Out of this tour, together with a great deal of ultra-romantic posing, came the first two cantos of *Childe Harold's Pilgrimage*, published in the March of this highly suitable year, 1812. As we all know, for his words have been quoted to death, he awoke to find himself famous. It is not surprising. Society was eager to praise this kind of semi-narrative and semi-lyrical verse that described exotic regions and had as hero-narrator a wonderfully romantic type, both a sated voluptuary, clearly of high rank, and a sin-haunted remorseful wanderer. Here he is in the last two verses of the second canto:

Sir John Hobhouse, Bart., engraving by Charles Turner after James Lonsdale
The British Museum, London

> Then must I plunge again into the crowd,
> And follow all that Peace disdains to seek?
> Where Revel calls, and Laughter, vainly loud,
> False to the heart, distorts the hollow cheek,
> To leave the flagging spirit doubly weak;
> Still o'er the features, which perforce they cheer,
> To feign the pleasure or conceal the pique;
> Smiles form the channel of a future tear,
> Or raise the writhing lip with ill-dissembled sneer.
>
> What is the worst of woes that wait on age?
> What stamps the wrinkle deeper on the brow?
> To view each loved one blotted from life's page,
> And be alone on earth, as I am now.
> Before the Chastener humbly let me bow,
> O'er hearts divided and o'er hopes destroy'd:
> Roll on, vain days! Full reckless may ye flow,
> Since Time hath reft whate'er my soul enjoy'd,
> And with the ills of Eld mine earlier years alloy'd.

Byron was to write much better than this – especially in satire and a few superb lyrics – but here is the beginning of his legend, soon to capture all Europe, the first glimpse of the archetypal figure of romanticism.

The truth about Byron is far from being simple. In his secret life he was a true romantic but in most of his work he appears as a bogus romantic. This will be easier to understand if we take him on three different levels. As Childe Harold and as the poetic young nobleman at parties – with the chestnut curls, the strangely pale face, the scornful mouth, the whole attitude of weary disdain – he was putting on a performance, both in life and literature. On the next level, where we find him among his close friends and in his journals and letters, he seems an eighteenth-century type brought up to date by certain elements of Regency dandyism. He is more outside romantic literature than inside it; he can hardly be de-

George Gordon Byron, 6th Baron
Byron, 1813, by Richard Westall
oil on canvas
29½ × 24½ in. (74.9 × 62.3 cm.)
The National Portrait Gallery,
London

Lady Elizabeth Foster, 1805 by Sir
Thomas Lawrence
oil on canvas
92½ × 56⅛ in. (235 × 145 cm.)
The National Gallery of Ireland,
Dublin

scribed as an artist; he is a man in society merely writing stuff
about Corsairs and the like late at night over brandies and sodas;
and the women he really prefers are not creatures of romance but
tend to be coarse, hearty and rather cynical dames. But on the
third level, down in the dark, probably because of his unhappy and
calvinistic childhood, he really is a bewildered, haunted, half-
frightened and half-fatalistic being, never shaping his own destiny
but drifting towards disaster in this world and doom in the next.
There is nothing bogus down here, where he really is a tragic
figure, and one – in spite of all his faults of taste and temper –
deserving our compassion.

When, in the spring of 1812, there stepped out from this cloaked
melancholy figure of Childe Harold an astonishingly handsome
young Lord Byron, the double appeal to women was irresistible.
The girls in their innocence thought how Childe Harold might
still be saved by the love of a pure woman. And the style of their
letters to him testifies to the influence of popular sentimental
fiction in the Regency. Older society women, no longer concerned
with purity or rescuing anybody, looked at that disdainful fine
profile and wondered about all that bold voluptuousness mentioned
in his verse. Now invited everywhere, Byron was enjoying high
society for the first time; it had ignored his existence before he
went for his long tour abroad; and, in spite of his liberalism, never
deep-seated, here was the glittering company he wanted. Now he
was to startle and then entertain it by staging a romantic comedy
with its most eccentric young woman, a far more reckless exhibitionist than he was – Caroline Lamb.

Her family background – even though Caroline herself was
brought up strictly enough – was not one to encourage propriety
and chastity. Her mother, Lady Bessborough, had had a long and
notorious affair with Granville Leveson Gower and had had
two children by him. Her aunt, the Duchess of Devonshire, was
well known for various scrapes and scandals, had had an illegitimate daughter by Charles Grey, and finally lived in a *ménage à trois*
with her husband and his mistress (also her own best friend), Lady
Elizabeth Foster. Caroline as a young girl was slight and agile
with odd but attractive looks, at once wild and delicate; she was
also impulsive, eccentric (and really neurotic), but held to be
delightful in her own family circle. Anything might happen, it was
thought, when she was around. One scandalous rumour described
an evening at Devonshire House when Caroline was carried into
the dining room, hidden under a silver dish cover, to emerge on the
table completely naked. (I have never been able to understand these
familiar girl-in-pie stories, because this would be no treat for
women guests, and most men, myself included, would rather have
a genuine pie on the dinner table than a naked girl upsetting the

sauce boats.) This story was probably quite untrue, but its very existence as a rumour suggests the kind of reputation, the particular legend, growing up around her.

In 1805, when she was twenty, William Lamb – much later to be Prime Minister as Lord Melbourne – proposed to her. He had loved her deeply and dearly, he said, for several years; and she 'adored him'. But as a love match it did not last very long. An amiable cynic, devoted to books and a quiet life, William Lamb could be tolerant of but could not sympathise with her neurotic romanticism, lack of restraint, demand for constant excitement. Without any public separation, they went their own way, and her way, restless and discontented as she was, inevitably led to one affair and possibly to several others. Always wanting to attract attention, she played the wild tomboy, and even in 1811, and now twenty-six, she could vex her elderly relatives by her antics in public, for example, when 'she had jumped over a couch at some assembly', lowering her character, they said, 'by such improprieties'. But there were other times when she would escape attention by disguising herself as a pageboy, her slight figure and short curly hair, easily hidden, helping the masquerade. This then was Caroline Lamb, so much loose gunpowder only waiting for Byron, so handsome, so romantic, and the talk of the town, to toss a lighted match into it.

Curiously enough, although theirs was so famous an affair, endlessly discussed and then described in print over and over again, we have no clear single account of how they first met. One version, which we owe to Byron's relative, Dallas, tells us that Caroline read an early copy of *Childe Harold* and then dashed off an enthusiastic, though anonymous, letter to him. Two days later, she wrote again, this time giving him the address of a shop in Old Bond Street where he could leave a reply. Byron told Dallas he would not reply to the letters but then changed his mind – 'on finding his correspondent to be a fine young woman, and distinguished for eccentric notions, he became so enraptured, so intoxicated, that his time and thoughts were almost entirely devoted to reading her letters and answering them.' Dallas adds that Byron 'professedly despised the society of women, yet female adulation became the most captivating charm to his heart.' Moreover, Lady Caroline Lamb, a few years older than he was, had belonged all her life to the high society in which he was moving now for the first time. And Byron, even after he left England in disgust, was always sharply conscious of birth and rank. In Italy he was very much the milord.

The second and far more popular version of their first meeting does not mention any previous correspondence. It was when fashionable hostesses were trying hard to exhibit him to their guests, when, to quote the Duchess of Devonshire, 'the subject

Morning Dress – engraved for
La Belle Assemblée, 1 December 1812
Collection Mrs Doris Langley Moore,
London

of conversation, of curiosity, of enthusiasm almost, one might say, of the moment, is not Spain or Portugal, Warriors or Patriots, but Lord Byron.' In this heady atmosphere, Byron and Caroline attended the same ball. But when he was taken towards her to be introduced, Caroline, instead of being eager and fluttery, stared hard at him for a moment and then, without speaking, turned away. This was not good manners but obviously it was an effective trick to make a man, already being spoilt by women, feel piqued and challenged. That night Caroline made the famous entry in her diary: 'Bad, mad, and dangerous to know.' But of course she ignored this moment of insight. The introduction trick had immediately concentrated Byron's attention on her. An ultra-romantic affair, taking place as much in public as in private, was inevitable. They were Paola and Francesca in Regency costume.

They exchanged passionate letters and verses. They were seen everywhere together, and after late parties she would always leave in his carriage. Caroline was wildly indiscreet: if he had been invited somewhere and she had not, she would hang about outside the house; and more than once, when he had company in his rooms, she would suddenly turn up in her favourite masquerade as a pageboy. Even the patient and amiable William Lamb had to warn his wife that she was going much too far. Her mother's house-keeper told her bluntly, 'You have exposed yourself to all London, you are the talk of every Groom and Footman about the Town.' But neither of the romantic lovers objected to being talked about; they adored it. Caroline, no longer restless and discontented, had found a superbly romantic rôle, the mistress, half-crazy with love, of the country's handsomest poet, and she played it for all it was worth – indeed, for more than it was worth. She was more in love with the rôle than with the man. And Byron was not really in love at all. His vanity was tickled; certain feelings of social insecurity and personal inferiority (he was very conscious of his lameness) were quietened; and if she could be histrionic, then so could he.

There is an ironic comedy here. While people imagined that these reckless lovers were wearing themselves out in each other's arms, it is more than likely that they never actually made love at all. There are several good reasons for believing this. First, men and women who sleep together and are passionate in private are apt to avoid public demonstrations of their devotion. Secondly, Samuel Rogers, the banker-poet, who knew both Caroline and Byron quite well and was himself a cynical man of the world, no sentimentalist except in his verses, declared their relationship to be platonic. Thirdly, their behaviour does not really suggest two people with a tremendous sexual attraction for each other, anxious to get away and be by themselves. Fourthly, strange as it may seem, their tastes and temperaments make a platonic relationship more than likely. Caroline could be happy with a romantic rôle played in public; she was a type who wanted to indulge her imagination, not her senses. This is not true of Byron, of course, but what *is* true is that Caroline was not really his kind of woman; she was too slight and angular, physically altogether too skinny, and far more restless, excitable, unpredictable, than the kind of women who really did attract him. It was vanity and not sex that kept this affair going. He wrote later: 'I was soon congratulated by my friends on the conquest I had made, and did my utmost to show that I was not insensible to the partiality I could not but perceive. I made every effort to be in love, expressed as much ardour as I could muster, and kept feeding the flame with a constant supply of *billets doux* and amatory verses . . .'

The tone of these remarks, hardly in the best gentlemanly tradition, might suggest a man hiding a wound to his vanity after being dropped by a woman. But this was not the case. Caroline still pursued him, creating emotional scenes he disliked, when he was rapidly tiring of her. His vanity now declared against her because she was beginning to make him look a fool. Furthermore, he was soon deep in another affair, anything but platonic, with Lady Oxford, mother of the 'Harleian Miscellany'. She was really his type, though almost old enough to be his mother, and it was a satisfying affair for both of them, enabling Byron to enjoy a quiet country life with a sensible well-read woman and her delightful children. However, the oddest but most important outcome of this whole performance with Caroline was the close friendship he formed with her mother-in-law, Lady Melbourne. Being essentially an eighteenth-century *grande dame*, Lady Melbourne had no patience with all this showing-off romantic nonsense, and she and Byron agreed that he ought to marry a sensible girl with money, if only to keep Caroline, now wilder than ever, at a distance. Lady Melbourne suggested her niece, Annabella Milbanke, only twenty, a provincial heiress now living in London – calm, quiet, well-behaved, all that poor Caroline was not. Half-heartedly, Byron proposed to Annabella and was turned down, much to his relief. Afterwards, good judgment deserted them both, and the marriage they made in 1815 was a disaster.

We shall meet Byron and Annabella again, but poor wild Caroline cannot be allowed to escape into later chapters. The patient William Lamb took her to Ireland, and Byron continued to write to her there, though he told Lady Melbourne he was now weary of the affair and only wrote to Caroline to end it gradually. Lady Melbourne took care that Caroline should learn this; there was a furious quarrel, which Byron welcomed, needing an excuse to break off the affair once and for all. 'As to yourself, Lady Caroline,'

PLATE IX. The Prince Regent in Profile, *c*. 1814, by Sir Thomas Lawrence
oil on canvas
27 × 20½ in. (68.6 × 52 cm.)
The National Portrait Gallery, London

he wrote to her, 'correct your vanity which has become ridiculous – exert your caprices on others, enjoy the excellent flow of spirits which make you so delightful in the eyes of others, and leave me in peace.' It was a brutal dismissal and sent Caroline to bed for a couple of weeks.

Later, when she was staying in the country alone, almost out of her wits, she devised an anti-Byron ceremony. While she burnt him in effigy, village girls dressed in white had to dance round the pyre. Dressed as one of her own pages, Caroline threw into the flames Byron's book, his ring and chain, and copies (not the originals) of his letters to her. One of her pages had to recite verses she had composed for this ceremony:

> See here are locks and braids of coloured hair
> Worn oft by me, to make the people stare;
> Rouge, feathers, flowers, and all those tawdry things,
> Besides those Pictures, letters, chains and rings –
> Burn, fire, burn, while wondering Boys exclaim,
> And gold and trinkets glitter in the flame . . .

It was not such verses and antics that finally alienated her from society; it was chiefly the publication of a novel, *Glenarvon*, in 1816 – a wildly romantic tale (though it included some of Byron's actual letters to her) that offered its readers some recognisable caricatures of persons in her circle and prominent in high society. This could not be forgiven, and Caroline Lamb was *out*. Her husband and family did what they could for her, trying to make her live a quiet life in the country, discouraging her from dashing up to London to embarrass them. She wrote other novels and a good deal of verse, but never succeeded in establishing a literary reputation, though she herself, easily recognised under various names, figured in several novels, notably by Bulwer Lytton and Disraeli. By an evil chance, in July 1824, she met Byron's funeral procession on its way to Newstead, a shock from which she never really recovered. She died in 1828. She could be – and we have plenty of evidence that she often was – a fascinating creature, even if always too excitable and vain. She suffered from Byron's vanity but suffered even more from her own. She was ruined not by him but by her own highly neurotic temperament and deeply divided personality. If she had been born into our time, she would have had a very different medical history; but in the Regency her case was hopeless.

The last important event in the London of 1812 was the trial in December of the two Hunts, namely John and the critic, essayist and poet, Leigh Hunt. They had to face a charge of having the intention 'to traduce and vilify His Royal Highness the Prince of Wales, Regent of the United Kingdom'. If it was the Regent himself who originally demanded their prosecution, he took a step that largely helped to ruin his reputation, for all liberal writers for many years proceeded to attack it – as far ahead as 1855, when Thackeray lectured on *The Four Georges* and delivered the most damaging assault of all. It has been one of the persistent weaknesses of the English Establishment that it has always tended to underrate the influence and importance of writers, so many mere scribblers in its eyes. Oddly enough, the Regent in some respects contradicts this opinion; he took care to charm the few authors he did meet and he gave his official patronage to Literature itself. Perhaps he himself never demanded that writers should be prosecuted, but he was partly responsible for a savagely reactionary government.

The Hunt story goes back to 1808 when the two brothers, then very young men, together produced *The Examiner*, a weekly paper attached to no political party but decidedly liberal and reformist in its opinions. It had a tiny circulation – there were no huge circulations then – but it was popular and widely read, at least in London. The government kept a keen eye on *The Examiner* and the Hunt brothers. Early in 1811 they were prosecuted for an article protesting against brutal flogging in the army, but Brougham, brilliantly defending, got an acquittal. (Shelley, then at Oxford, wrote to Leigh Hunt congratulating him, and so began a friendship of great value to both men.) And now we arrive at 1812 and a touch of fantasy. At a political dinner of the progressives, the customary toast to the Regent was deliberately left out. So on 12 March the

James Henry Leigh Hunt, 1815, by Thomas Wageman
pencil
8¼ × 6½ in. (21 × 16.5 cm.)
The National Portrait Gallery, London

Morning Post, bursting with indignation and loyalty, printed an extravagant panegyric to the slighted Regent, crying, 'You are the *glory of the People* – You are the *Maecenas of the Age* – Wherever you appear you *conquer all hearts*, wipe away tears, excite *desire and love* and win *beauty* towards you – You breathe *eloquence*, you inspire the Graces – you are an *Adonis* in loveliness . . .'

This sycophantic bosh was too much for Leigh Hunt, and ten days later in *The Examiner* he gave his own account both of the *Morning Post* and of its adored Prince, pointing out – 'That this Adonis in Loveliness *was a corpulent gentleman of fifty*! In short, that this delightful, blissful, wise, pleasurable, honourable, virtuous, true and immortal PRINCE was a *violator of his work, a libertine over head and ears in debt and disgrace, a despiser of domestic ties, the companion of gamblers and demireps, a man who has just closed half a century without one single claim on the gratitude of his country or the respect of posterity.'* This was really a double attack – on the Regent himself, of course, but also on a hypocritical press and the society represented by its readers. *The Examiner* had fired these guns before, but this was its strongest blast. So the Hunt brothers were prosecuted, though their actual trial did not take place until December, 1812. This time Brougham was not successful, and the Hunts were sentenced to two years in prison – and in separate gaols – and a fine of several hundred pounds. After the sentence they were told privately that if they gave a solemn pledge not to attack the Regent in future, both the imprisonment and the fine would be considerably reduced. This offer they rejected at once, and John Hunt was sent to Clerkenwell while Leigh Hunt (in bad health too) was condemned to pass two years in the Surrey gaol.

It is at this point that the scene unexpectedly changes, the grim vista suddenly vanishing, the harsh sentence dissolving into thin air. This was an age that was inconsistent, odd, running to extremes, so that while it had not yet abolished public executions or terrible flogging for minor offences, yet it could send Leigh Hunt to prison and make him quite comfortable, better off than he would be today. He had forfeited his liberty, but in every other respect he might almost have been at home. He had a room, no damp cell, and he had its walls, we are told, 'papered with a trellis of roses, the ceiling painted with sky and clouds, the windows furnished with Venetian blinds, and an unfailing supply of flowers.' He was allowed his books and a piano. Charles Lamb said there was no other such room, out of a fairy tale. Leigh Hunt could work – and did, even continuing to edit *The Examiner*. He was constantly visited by his wife and his friends; Tom Moore brought Byron. And when Jeremy Bentham visited the gaol, the prisoner was playing battledore.

Jeremy Bentham (detail), 1829, by
Henry William Pickersgill
oil on canvas
80½ × 54½ in. (205 × 138 cm.)
The National Portrait Gallery,
London

The Prince of Pleasure

(above) The Nightmare, *c.* 1782,
by Henry Fuseli
oil on canvas
29⅝ × 25¼ in. (75.5 × 64 cm.)
Goethehaus Goethemuseum,
Frankfurt-am-Main

(below) William Blake, 1807,
by Thomas Phillips
oil on canvas
35¼ × 27¼ in. (89.5 × 71.8 cm.)
The National Portrait Gallery, London

Bentham was an authority on prisons, having designed a completely rational one of his own, called 'The Panopticon'. He was now an elderly man, having been born in 1742, and was no Regency figure, though in fact he outlived it by twelve years. He might be described as an English end-product of the French Enlightenment, much of his work having been done years before the Revolution. But he cannot be ignored here because it was during these years that he found some important disciples, such as Brougham and the Scots historian and journalist, James Mill (father of John Stuart Mill). 'Benthamism', generally known later as Utilitarianism, began to have some influence and to be widely discussed.

Curiously enough, the phrase we associate with Bentham and his followers – 'the greatest happiness of the greatest number' – was not originally his; he discovered it in a pamphlet by Joseph Priestley; but he saw in it at once the light that would illuminate and guide the rest of his extremely industrious life. (He enjoyed an ample private income, so he could do what he pleased.) He was one of those characters – and most of us have met them – who while being severely rational and critical somehow preserve in their private life an innocent and cheerful simplicity that is almost naive. It is as hard to dislike Jeremy Bentham as it is to agree with him. He is not really a philosopher but a kind of systematic engineer of rational reform, especially of the Law. What other men regarded with solemn awe he examined, took to pieces, and then proceeded to scrap, as being irrational and not conducive to anybody's happiness. His over-simplifications were rarely acceptable to educated minds, but he furnished much good ammunition to men battling for reform, some of it still needed in England to this day. However, his belief in *laissez faire* government, his refusal to understand the irrational elements in our nature, his indifference to a whole world of values, have weighed heavily against him, except as a splendid character, which indeed he was. If his 'greatest happiness of the greatest number' principle were ruling London today, then the National Gallery, the Royal Festival Hall and the Old Vic Theatre would now be running Bingo every night.

However, I cannot conclude a chapter called 'The Romantics' with Jeremy Bentham. What about the painters? It can be said at once that the average run of Regency artists, the hard-working and fairly successful painters who sent their work, year after year, to the Royal Academy exhibitions, were not romantics. But the exceptional men, to whom we turn now, arrived at romanticism far earlier than the poets did. For example, Fuseli, a Swiss whose real name was Füssli, and Blake had been painting and drawing for years before Coleridge contributed a line to *Lyrical Ballads*. And Thomas Lawrence, the most successful portrait painter of the age, might be said to have added a rather theatrical Byronic quality to his eighteenth-century masters long before Byron himself captured London. Much of our own rather romantic attitude towards the Regency probably owes something to the impression Lawrence's portraits have left with us. But this, of course, is not true of the greatest of them all, the one towering genius of nineteenth-century English painting, Joseph Mallord William Turner, who was in fact born a few years after Wordsworth, Coleridge and Scott.

Turner's greatest work, in which he would paint the elements themselves – especially his late watercolour sketches – came long after the Regency; but already, in this year 1812, he had exhibited at the Royal Academy his *Snowstorm: Hannibal and his Army crossing the Alps*, in which Hannibal is a mere excuse for offering us a huge and violent sky. It was also in 1812 that he went down to Devonshire and took his little sketchbooks out in the fishing boats, often in the foulest weather, to record immediately his impressions. (There can never have been another artist who endured and braved

Snowstorm: Hannibal and his Army crossing the Alps, exhibited 1812, by Joseph Mallord William Turner
oil on canvas
57 × 93 in. (145 × 267 cm.)
The Tate Gallery, London

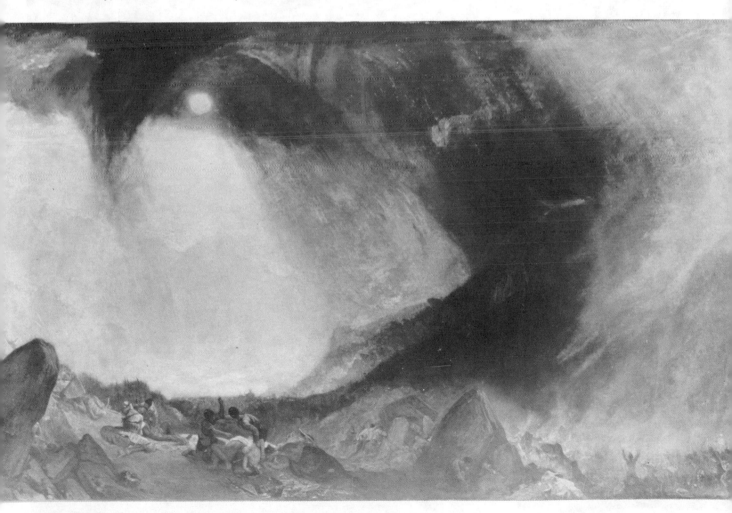

so much for his art. He was as indomitable as he was perceptive and industrious. What a man!) Again, it was in 1812 that he bought, and greatly altered, the house in Queen Anne Street that was to be his official London address – he had others, for other purposes – for the next thirty-nine years. In this house was the gallery where he exhibited his pictures. Like many of our greatest creators, Turner, though entirely unconventional and careless of appearances, was no fool about money and was a hard bargainer when he wanted to be. Though the Royal Academy was at his disposal he needed a gallery of his own, even though it soon looked shockingly neglected and was bitterly cold, because these were the days of the private patron, before the picture-dealers arrived in any large numbers to control the art market.

These private patrons, with the Regent high on the list, were often able to buy masterpieces from great collections in France, Italy, Spain, broken up after the French Revolution and during the Napoleonic wars. Notable and public-spirited connoisseurs like Sir George Beaumont would allow artists to examine and then if necessary carefully study famous foreign work in their collections, even going to the length at times of actually lending them. In 1812 there were still no public galleries. It was two years later when the first of them, the Dulwich Gallery, was made accessible to the public, and it was not until 1824 that the National Gallery was opened. Throughout the Regency, and indeed for long afterwards, the importance of the Royal Academy, in which the Regent himself took a genuine interest, can hardly be exaggerated. There, to its

(opposite) Sir John Soane's Museum, 1812–13, by Sir John Soane

(below) Dulwich College Art Gallery, by Sir John Soane – opened to the public in 1814

A shilling well laid out – Tom and Jerry at the Exhibition at the Royal Academy, from Pierce Egan's *Life in London*, 1821 – drawn and etched by I. R. & G. Cruikshank The British Museum, London

PLATE XI. The First Steamboat on the Clyde – Henry Bell's *Comet* built 1811 (detail), 1812–20, by John Knox oil on canvas
44 × 62$\frac{3}{8}$ in. (111.8 × 158.5 cm.) The Art Gallery and Museum, Glasgow

annual Exhibitions, went the patrons and the increasing number of art critics, allowed more space for their notices than most critics can find nowadays, It was difficult in these years for an artist to succeed without the support of the Royal Academy, and he was not likely to continue being successful without becoming one of its members. Turner was fortunate; he was elected a full Royal Academician in 1802, when he was only twenty-seven, so by 1812 he was an established if puzzling and controversial figure, a supremely romantic painter not yet understood in this year to which I have given the title: 'The Romantics'.

One last brief entry for 1812. A few weeks before Byron became famous and when Caroline Lamb was still wondering what to do with herself and while young Leigh Hunt was braving prosecution in *The Examiner*, a convivial and rather unreliable Navy clerk, John Dickens, had a son and called him Charles. Forty years later, in *Bleak House*, there appeared an affected aesthete and sponger, Harold Skimpole, who was a caricature (rather cruel, in my opinion) of poor old Leigh Hunt's known weaknesses. But do I mention this simply to drag Dickens into the Regency? Not at all. The Regency had been left behind only fifteen years when Dickens brought out his first book. And in all his earlier novels we can discover types, characters, situations, attitudes, that might be called grotesque fragments of Regency life and manners persisting into another chapter of history.

1813

Pride and Prejudice

The title I have given this chapter applies to a great deal more than Jane Austen's novel. But her *Pride and Prejudice* did actually make its first appearance in 1813. It was a revised version of a novel she had written as long ago as 1796. And I for one agree with those critics who consider it her best all-round performance, inferior in this particular or that to one or other of her later novels but more representative than they are of all her wonderful qualities. These are often not fully appreciated just because too many English-speaking people have had to read *Pride and Prejudice* at school, before they were ready for it.

Fashionable persons in 1813 were not telling one another that Miss Austen's Elizabeth Bennet was the best heroine the English had been offered since Shakespeare. (And surely she is.) They had much else to discuss. First, the famous Madame de Staël, who arrived in London in the summer of 1813, accompanied by her son and daughter and a handsome young husband, whose hand she had accepted but not his name. She was getting on, thickening and coarsening, no treat for the spectator, and she talked everywhere at great length; but this was expected of so formidable a blue-stocking. Lady Holland told Mrs Creevey, 'The great wonder of the time is Madame de Staël. She is surrounded by all the curious, and every sentence she utters is caught and repeated with various commentaries.' The Regent wanted to meet her, and she was presented to him at the end of June. They sat and talked for three-quarters of an hour, after which she declared he could not have been kinder. Disrespectful and mischievous fellows like Sheridan, Brummell and Alvanley amused themselves mystifying her, making her believe all manner of nonsense. As she had been exiled by Napoleon, Byron expected to find her a rebel like himself, but she disappointed him by being, as he said, 'all for the Lord of Israel and the Lord of Liverpool'. However, when she settled down and entertained in her own house, he saw her fairly frequently, but irritated her by looking bored and making cynical remarks about love, a subject that always inspired Madame de Staël to eloquence. At one dinner, talking to Caroline Lamb (Byron was not there), Madame announced emphatically that Byron was totally insensible to real passion, that he was a kind of demon who had no right to make love.

PLATE XII. George 'Beau' Brummell, 1805, by Richard Dighton
watercolour
20 × 16 in. (50.8 × 40.7 cm.)
Collection Sir Owen Morshead

The Cyprian's Ball at the Argyle Rooms, Regent's Street, from Robert Cruikshank's *The English Spy,* 1826 The British Museum, London

Anne Louise Germaine Necker, Baronne de Staël Holstein, 1818, engraving by Jean Nicolas Laugier after Marguerite Gérard The British Museum, London

This was reported to Byron, who replied pointedly, not having any designs himself on Madame de Staël, 'True enough, but rather premature.'

Another and more exciting topic held the fashionable world enthralled from July onwards. At the centre of it was one of the most famous remarks that have come down to us from the Regency. Brummell and Alvanley and their two friends, Sir Henry Mildmay and Henry Pierrepoint, had together won a great deal of money gambling at Watier's. They decided to celebrate their good fortune by giving a ball at Argyle Rooms. The Regent was no longer on speaking terms with Brummell and was rather hostile to Mildmay, but the four dandies decided they ought to invite him. When he arrived, with the four hosts standing to receive their guests, the Regent shook hands with Alvanley and Pierrepoint but then went forward, deliberately ignoring the other two. Then came the famous remark. 'Alvanley,' cried Brummell in a clear high tone, 'Who's your fat friend?'

Nothing could have been better calculated to infuriate the Regent, whose vanity was easily wounded and who was especially sensitive about his bulk. There was now no hope of any reconciliation. Our Prince of Pleasure and the greatest of his dandies were never to exchange another word. And it is not too fanciful to suggest that Brummell's famous question represents a high peak of self-confident impudent dandyism, from which it rapidly descended and was never the same again.

Later, Brummell and the Regent came face to face on only two occasions. The first was in a crush, waiting for carriages, after the opera. Brummell was accidentally driven back until he was quite close to the Regent. We can now take up an eye-witness account:

> In order to stop Brummell, therefore, and prevent actual collision, one of the Prince's suite tapped him on the back, when he immediately turned sharply round, and saw there was not more than a foot between his nose and the Prince of Wales's. I watched with intense curiosity, and observed that his countenance did not change in the slightest degree, nor did his head move; they looked straight into each other's eyes, the Prince evidently amazed and annoyed. Brummell, however, did not quail or show the least embarrassment. He receded quite quietly, and backed slowly step by step till the crowd closed between them, never once taking his eyes off those of the Prince . . .

A report of the later occasion comes from Jesse:

> His Royal Highness was going to the Picture Gallery in Pall Mall, and Brummell, who was walking with some other men about ten yards in front of me, was exactly opposite the door of the Exhibition as the low, dark red carriage stopped. Brummell evidently saw it and saw who was in it, although he pretended not to do so, and when the two sentinels presented arms, he, with an air of pretended surprise and mock dignity which was most amusing, gravely raised his hat as if the salute had been for him; as he did this he passed, turning his head very graciously towards the sentries and his back to the carriage window, which was quite close to. I saw, as I paused, the angry look of the Regent, but he said nothing . . .

There had been a time when the Prince frequently called at Brummell's house just to watch him dress, and once – so Moore tells us – the Prince 'began to blubber when told that Brummell did not like the cut of his coat'.

I have had no particular admiration for dandies since the age of seventeen, when I briefly aspired to be one; but to me there is something appealing about Beau Brummell at the height of his fame and cool impudence. In his clashes with the Regent it is the Beau who has the princely style. But his luck ran out. (He blamed it on the loss of a lucky sixpence with a hole in it.) Gambling losses piled up his debts. In 1816 he had to leave England, to escape arrest, and he never returned, living for many years at Calais, where his English friends visited him and helped him with money, and then later at Caen. His last years were horrible, revealing an appallingly malicious irony in events. In 1837, according to the *D.N.B.*, 'he began to show signs of imbecility; he held phantom receptions of the beauties and magnates of the old days. Soon all care of his person went, and from carelessness and disease his habits became so loathsome that an attendant could hardly be found for him.' And he had been the most fastidious dandy in London, indeed in all Europe. He died in a Caen asylum in 1840.

But not forgotten, in England or France, where he appeared in many memoirs and essays and, under fictitious names, in various novels. In the days of his absurd glory, try as we may to avoid acknowledging it, there is something mysteriously impressive about Beau Brummell.

It is hard to believe that Brummell ever set foot in one of England's industrial regions. Yet his avoidance of all colour, his insistence upon a perfection of black and white, at a time when he created the fashions for well-to-do men, may have contributed something to the sombre nineteenth-century style, generally attributed to the influence of industry, men who owned engines and factories wanting to look rather like them. Though they did not move in Brummell's circle, there were growing numbers of wealthy men during the Regency who owned more and more factories and

(below left) Sir Richard Arkwright, *c.* 1790, by Joseph Wright of Derby
oil on canvas
29½ × 24½ in. (74.9 × 62.3 cm.)
The National Portrait Gallery, London

(below right) The Embankment, Taeth Mawr, Tre-Madoc (detail), 1810, by Matthew Duborg after Horace W. Billington
38 × 54 in. (96.6 × 137 cm.)
Collection Sir Arthur Elton, Bart.

installed more and more steam engines in them. They were hugely self-confident among the cotton mills in Lancashire, where Arkwright, the successful inventor, declared that he had only to live long enough and he would be able to pay off the National Debt.

The Regency was a time of industrial expansion rather than invention. The real breakthrough had occurred in the last quarter of the eighteenth century. English gentlemen were still wearing satin breeches and powdered wigs when, unknown to most of them, the Industrial Revolution changed the history of the country – and indeed of the world. (For good or evil? It is still an open question.) Some more conservative trades – wool, for example, as against cotton – resisted change and the new inventions; and Cartwright's wool-combing machine, invented in 1790, was not brought into general use until the Regency. Again – keeping to the wool trade, in which I was humbly engaged from 1912 to 1914 – the long Napoleonic war created difficulties both in raw supplies and export markets; English sheep had become progressively better

Henry Cort, anonymous
The British Museum, London

James Watt (detail), 1792, by Carl
Fredrik von Breda
oil on canvas
49½ × 39½ in. (126 × 100.2 cm.)
The National Portrait Gallery,
London

for meat than for wool; the finer wools had been imported for centuries from Spain, occupied by the French in 1808; and it was not until after the war that the first wool cargo from New South Wales was carried to Britain.

Most of us in our childhood learnt something about Watt and Stephenson and their engines, but nobody told us anything about Henry Cort (1740–1800), who perhaps made the greatest single contribution to British industry. 'He seems a good simple man but not very knowing,' Watt said on first meeting him. Knowing or not, he revolutionised the process of converting pig iron into bar iron, by-passing the increasingly expensive use of charcoal and speeding up the whole manufacture. His process involved re-heating the pig iron with coke, stirring it with rods until much of the carbon and impurities had burnt away, then passing it through rollers that pressed out any dross that remained. And as the iron-masters had become too dependent on Sweden and Russia for their charcoal, some foundrymen's greeting in song to Cort was sharply topical:

That the wood of old England would fail to appear,
And tough iron was scarce because charcoal was dear.
By puddling and stamping he prevented that evil,
So the Swedes and the Russians may go to the devil.

More and more tough iron was needed, together with a new precision in the production of engine parts. Indeed, faced with the problem of manufacturing the steam engine, the Society of Engineers was once told that 'Neither the tools nor the workmen existed that could manufacture so complex a machine with sufficient precision.' But as in so many projects, then and now, the demand soon created the supply, and in the Midlands, Lancashire and Yorkshire more and more steam engines huffed and puffed like angry giants.

The steam engines devoured more and more coal, coming generally from mines in the neighbourhood of the factories. So the Black Country, with Birmingham its capital, East Lancashire and the West Riding of Yorkshire, all had their convenient coalfields. They also had communities of miners as far removed from the ordinary life of the region as members of an alien race. A journalist of this period could describe the miners of the Black Country arriving in the streets of Birmingham like 'aborigines straying into the urban purlieus of a civilised country', staring about them and being stared at – 'with their black faces and strange speech'. (This sense of being quite separate, not discouraged by the miners themselves, lasted into my lifetime. As a well-grown teenager, I played football occasionally against teams in mining towns and always felt I was in a strange – and very rough – world.)

Earlier coal mining had been largely opencast, that is, shallow and not demanding deep shafts and galleries far underground; but as the demand increased, the surface coal could not satisfy it, and even pits three hundred feet deep, as they often were in Yorkshire, were soon inadequate. This was particularly true in Northumberland and Durham, which led coal production, and to a lesser degree in Cumberland, where the mines soon went under the sea; and in all these districts the shafts went deeper and deeper, and more and more galleries, to reach the coal face, ran out from them. This rapidly heightened the danger of what was – and still is – a dangerous trade.

The lower the working, the greater the risk of encountering fire damp, the deadly explosive gas. When candles were still being used, some rich seams had to be abandoned because they were altogether too dangerous. The miners could not work in the dark, and naked lights were appallingly hazardous. There were frequent explosions, and in May 1812, at a pit near Gateshead, ninety-two men and boys were either burnt to death or suffocated. So in 1813 a Dr Clanny of Sunderland produced the first safety lamp. It was used in some pits, but it was generally considered to be too unwieldy: air had to be fed to the lamp through a water container by means of hand bellows. Something better had to be found. So, still in 1813, a society of coal owners was formed, to consider the problem, its President being Ralph Milbanke, the father of Annabella, the future Lady Byron. But what the society did and how the problem was solved belong to chapter VI.

Meanwhile, it was the mines that brought railways nearer and nearer. To get the coal away from the pitheads, the mine owners were committed to the regular transport of heavy loads; more and more horses were needed; and the war had sent up the cost of fodder. Tramways and iron rails, for horse traffic from the mines, had been laid down for some time. What was needed now was an effective steam locomotive. There were many experiments between 1801 and this year, 1813, and I have here on my desk some detailed

John Evans who was buried without food or light, during the space of 12 days and nights in a coalpit, near Wrexham 120 yards below the surface of the earth, 27 September 1819, engraving by R. C. Roffe after A. R. Burt
The Department of Industry, The National Museum of Wales, Cardiff

(below left) Dr Clanny's Safety Lamp from the *Transactions of the Society Instituted at London for the Encouragement of Arts, Manufactures and Commerce*, 1817
The Wellcome Institute of the History of Medicine, London

(below right) View of the Railway from Hetton Colliery to the depot on the banks of the river Wear, near Sutherland in the county of Durham, with the locomotive and other engines used on the same, about 1810 – coloured engraving
The Science Museum, London

TREVITHICKS,
PORTABLE STEAM ENGINE.

Catch me who can.

Mechanical Power Subduing
Animal Speed.

(above left) Trevithick's London
locomotive, 1808 – 'catch-me-who-can'
The Science Museum, London

(above right) A Victorian photograph
of William Hedley's 'Puffing Billy'
which dates from 1813
The Science Museum, London

accounts of them which I propose to ignore, believing that most readers would find them tedious while the technologically-minded would want even more details. With so many inventors and engineers at work, there was much dispute then and afterwards as to which of them was taking the lead. The credit probably goes to Richard Trevithick, an ingenious Cornishman largely handicapped by his lack of perseverance: he could invent a promising engine but did not trouble to improve it. This gave a chance to the stubborn Northerners. Two of them, Blenkinson and Murray, built a two-cylinder locomotive in 1812. (Trevithick's patent had covered the use of two cylinders, but he never seems to have actually introduced them into his engine. He was paid £30 for this part of his patent.)

By August 1812 two Blenkinsop/Murray locomotives, the *Prince Regent* and the *Salamanca*, went into use at the Middleton colliery in the West Riding. And the first public trial of the *Prince Regent*, a contemporary notes, 'was witnessed by thousands of spectators', cheering to see it flash past at ten miles an hour. In 1813 two more of these locomotives, which were still clumsy, were built, and one of these was sent for a short trial up to Tyneside, where George Stephenson, ambitious and determined, was living and working only a few miles away. It would be another twelve years before the Stockton and Darlington Railway would attract the attention of the general public; but it would not be long after that to the time when railways began to cover most of England. Incidentally, back in 1813 one William Hedley constructed a locomotive that worked, though it and its successors were clumsy and really too heavy for the cast iron plateway. But the point here is – that Hedley's first locomotive was called *Puffing Billy*, and it is a fact that as a child,

Sir Richard Arkwright's Cotton Mill
at Cromford, near Matlock (detail),
about 1783, after Joseph Wright of
Derby
oil on canvas
36 × 44⅞ in. (91.4 × 114.2 cm.)
Collection Mr James M. Oakes

PLATE XIII. A collier at Charles
Brandling's Middleton Colliery, near
Leeds, showing one of John
Blenkinsop's locomotives in the
background (detail), 1814 – Blenkinsop
was a 'viewer' or superintendent at
the colliery
lithograph by Ernst Kaufmann of
Lahr, near Baden – illustrated after
George Walker in *The Costume of
Yorkshire . . . being fac-similes of
original drawings,* 1885, Plate III
7⅞ × 11⅞ in. (20 × 30 cm.)
The Science Museum, London

in that same part of the world, I often heard any railway engine
called a *Puffing Billy.*

One feature of this industrial development may surprise many
readers just as it did me. William Blake pointed a finger at 'the dark
satanic mills', but during the Regency, while they may have been
still 'satanic', most of the larger mills were far from being 'dark'.
Here I can quote a German visitor to Manchester writing to a
friend at home:

> The modern miracles, my friend, are to me, the machines here and the
> buildings that house them called *factories.* Such a block is eight or nine
> storeys high, sometimes has forty windows along its frontage and is
> often four windows deep. Each floor is twelve feet high, and vaulted
> along its whole length with arches each having a span of nine feet. The
> pillars are of iron, as is the girder which they support and the enclosing
> walls are as thin as cards, attaining on the second floor a thickness of
> less than two feet six inches. It is said that a storm wrecked one such
> building in that neighbourhood before it had been completed; that may
> be true, but a hundred of them are now standing unshaken and exactly
> as they were erected thirty or forty years ago. A number of such blocks
> stand in very elevated positions which dominate the neighbourhood;
> and in addition a forest of even taller boiler-house chimneys like needles,
> so that it is hard to imagine how they stand upright; the whole presents
> from a distance a wonderful spectacle especially at night, when
> thousands of windows are brilliantly illuminated by gas-light . . .

And of course it is this brilliant illumination by gas-light that
surprises us. We associate these years with candles and lamps, and
not gas-light.

It was another German who was chiefly responsible for the wide

(above left) Introduction of Gas; or
Throwing a New Light on the Subject,
by George Cruikshank – Friedrich
Winzer addressing bystanders
The British Museum, London

(above right) The Blessed Effects of
Gass, 1813, engraving published by
S. W. Fores
Collection Sir Arthur Elton, Bart.

PLATE XIV. Full and half dress for
April, *c.* 1809
Collection Mrs Doris Langley Moore,
London

use of gas to light streets and factories. There had been experiments
with gas – not always coal-gas – during most of the eighteenth
century. As early as 1730 a Cumberland mine owner had led fire
damp through a pipe from the workings in one of his pits to the
surface, where it burned continuously. And one of his neighbours
at Whitehaven offered to light the town by gas from his pits,
conducting the gas through pipes laid under the street, and though
his offer was refused, it was said he supplied light to his own office
in this fashion. Out of the many later experimenters, two are really
important, one English, the other French. William Murdock
worked, first in Cornwall and then in Birmingham, for the famous
engineering firm of Boulton and Watt. In 1792 he generated gas
from coal and used it to light a room in Redruth, Cornwall. In 1798
he moved to Birmingham and could work on a larger scale. He
seems to have succeeded in lighting the main building there by gas,
but, for various reasons, in 1801 the firm told him to discontinue his
experiments. The French pioneer of gas was Philippe Lebon, who
had more ideas than Murdock, gave demonstrations that attracted
much attention (James Watt's brother, Gregory, visited him), but
was not able to find any financial backing; and in November 1804
he was robbed and stabbed to death in the Champs Elysées. His
early death – he was only thirty-seven – left the Continent without
any interest in gas lighting for many years.

On the other hand, industrial England was deeply interested.
The Napoleonic and American wars had cut down the supply of
whale oil and Russian tallow, and the cost of lamp oil and candles
was rising steeply. Moreover, the cotton mills especially were bad
fire risks; insurance premiums were a heavy charge; the mill

95

owners were ready to welcome any source of light that was economical and reasonably safe. Murdock set to work again, together with many others, notably Samuel Clegg, a chemical engineer, probably the first person to purify gas by passing it through water to which lime had been added. Before the Regency began, a number of factories – and some public buildings on holiday occasions – had gas blazing away. But we have kept the other German, mentioned earlier, waiting too long. His name was Friedrich Albrecht Winzer (1763–1830), and he had seen Lebon's demonstrations. He had little or no scientific knowledge and no mechanical skill, but his tremendous enthusiasm for gas lighting, which defied all obstacles, finally

(below left) Detail from one of the plates in F. C. Accum's *A Practical Treatise on Gas-Light,* 1815, published by R. Ackermann
The Science Museum, London

(below right) A Gas Holder, Dover, possibly *c.* 1820, anonymous British artist
grey monochrome wash
9¾ × 16 in. (24.6 × 40.4 cm.)
Collection Sir Arthur Elton, Bart.

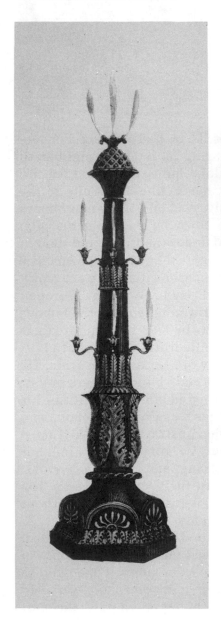

brought him to England, where he changed his name to Frederick Albert Winsor. What he saw, in a kind of gas-lighted vision, was that it was absurd to keep on supplying individual buildings with their own gas plants; there would have to be general supplies through mains radiating from central gas-generating stations. He hammered away at this until some important persons began to realise he was not just another monomaniac. He talked these persons – peers, bankers, businessmen – into forming a committee that would apply to Parliament for a charter. Finally, in 1812, The Gas, Light and Coke Company received its charter; and shortly afterwards the oil lamps in the parish of St Margaret's, Westminster, were replaced by gas, and crowds of curious people followed the lamp-lighters on their rounds. The insurance companies promptly accepted smaller premiums for any mills or public buildings lit by gas.

By the end of 1815 there were twenty-six miles of gas mains in London alone, and, as we have learnt already, the mills around Manchester presented 'a wonderful spectacle especially at night', with their thousands of windows so 'brilliantly illuminated by gas-light'. But there were some people who lived not far from these mills who did not appreciate their brilliant appearance at night, and indeed resented this whole rapid development of industry. They were known, both among themselves and to outsiders, as 'Luddites'. It was in this year, 1813, that there occurred at York the last and most ferocious mass trial of these Luddites, over a dozen being afterwards hanged and many others sentenced to transportation. It was no fun working with the factory engines in 1813 – long hours, bad conditions, pitiful wages – but it was even worse to make an active protest against them.

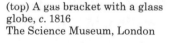

(top) A gas bracket with a glass globe, *c.* 1816
The Science Museum, London

(above left) Detail from one of the plates in F. C. Accum's *A Practical Treatise on Gas-Light*, 1815, published by R. Ackermann
The Science Museum, London

(above right) Rolling Mills, Merthyr Tydfil, *c.* 1810, by Thomas Horner pen and ink and grey wash
11¾ × 18⅞ in. (29.9 × 47.9 cm.)
The National Museum of Wales, Cardiff

The Luddites belonged to a working-class movement more complicated than it is generally imagined to be, and with much hazier outlines. It did not simply amount to some groups of workers in the North resenting and then smashing machines. Indeed, the movement began in Nottingham and was supposed to be directed by a mysterious (probably legendary) King Lud or Ludd living in Sherwood Forest. And the fundamental grievance here was that people were having to produce shoddy material, chiefly because the employers, for quicker and easier profits, were compelling them to use wide frames instead of the narrower stocking frames they had always used. These workers began to hold secret meetings, to plot and to riot, because there was nothing else they could do. The Combination Acts penalised any attempt by working men to combine against their employers. It is true that the Acts did not allow employers to combine, but this was farcical, the prohibition never being enforced. But workmen who attempted any common action were often tried and sent to prison; defendants were compelled to give evidence against one another; and though appeals were

Henry Addington, 1st Viscount
Sidmouth (detail), 1833,
by George Richmond
oil on canvas
23¼ × 15¼ in. (59.7 × 38.7 cm.)
The National Portrait Gallery,
London

PLATE XV. Regency interior lit by
gaslight – Ackermann's Art Library
(detail), *c.* 1812–15, by J. Bluck after
Augustus Charles Pugin
aquatint
9¼ × 11⅛ in. (23.5 × 28.2 cm.)
Collection Sir Arthur Elton, Bart.

PLATE XVI (overleaf). Pit-head of a
coalmine with steam winding gear,
c. 1820, anonymous British artist –
although rarely done and clumsy
some Newcomen engines were made
rotative at the end of the eighteenth
century and adapted to winding from
shallow pits
oil on canvas
37⅜ × 60¼ in. (95 × 153 cm.)
The Walker Art Gallery, Liverpool

possible – and sometimes succeeded because their legal superiors suspected local magistrates of not knowing much law – very few working men could afford to make an appeal. If there had been no Combination Acts in force, it is doubtful if there would have been any Luddites in Nottingham, holding secret meetings and arranging passwords and various hand-and-face signals of brother-hood.

It was the Luddite movement further north, in the textile industries of the West Riding and Lancashire, that began as a protest against the introduction of machinery, chiefly the new power-looms. Here the smashing of machines by heavy hammers led to factories being guarded by armed watchmen, to the firing of mills, to men being killed on both sides, to whole companies of regular soldiers being hurried north. The situation was not a simple one, for two quite different reasons. Most of the Luddites only wanted to be rid of the machines. But they were joined by some men who had been wanting a violent revolution for years – such as the Old Jacks (Jacobins) and the Paineites, with Tom Paine as their hero. And the conspiratorial atmosphere, the secret meetings, the supposed orders from King Lud, the passwords and signals, encouraged this revolutionary feeling. These people in Yorkshire and Lancashire were really remote then from London, and hardly knew what was happening there, even though Cobbett might be sending them his papers and pamphlets, and 'Orator' Hunt, a famous demagogue, might come down to deliver one of his impassioned speeches. The whole King Lud idea suggests rather simple uneducated men.

The second reason why the situation was more complicated brings us to the attitude of the authorities. Very few of the Luddites may have been in favour of a general insurrection, but they were going to be accused of plotting it. There was great and growing discontent, political, economic, industrial, and one way to suppress it, over and above all the Acts of Suppression already in force, was not to minimize but to exaggerate its threat to law and order and the Establishment. A general insurrection, a French Revolution at home, might be imminent: the country and its constitution were in danger. From Lord Sidmouth at the Home Office to lords lieutenant and commanding officers, to land-owning magistrates and wealthy employers, these were the cries repeated over and over again. Even the sceptics on this side knew they had here a wonderful catch-all to discourage protesters and reformers of every sort. And if the general insurrection line was weak, it had to be strengthened. So the loose ranks of the Luddites not only contained government spies and paid informers but also a fair number of *agents provocateurs*, to keep things hotted up. Our storytellers of today who are so fascinated by espionage and counter-espionage, agents and

A commemorative medallion, 1810, by
Thomas Wyon, senior, after
Peter Rouw, junior
The reverse side shows Joseph
Hanson of Strangeways Hall who
was sentenced to imprisonment and
fined 12 May, 1809. 396,000 penny
subscribers contributed to a
testimonial for his sufferings in the
cause of the weavers
white metal
diameter 1⅝ in. (4.2 cm.)
The City Art Gallery, Manchester

double agents, might try giving East and West Berlin a rest,
putting Manchester and Leeds in their place and going back to the
days of the Luddites.

Byron was in the House of Lords when a Bill passed by the
Commons was being debated by the peers. It was a Bill asking for
the death penalty for Luddites caught smashing frames and looms.
Byron's own estate, Newstead, was close to Nottingham, so that he
knew something of the Luddites there. He attacked the Bill in a
memorable speech, which ended:

> Suppose it passed. Suppose one of these men, as I have seen them –
> meagre with famine, sullen with despair, careless of a life which your
> lordships are perhaps about to value at something less than the price
> of a stocking-frame – suppose this man (and there are a thousand such
> from whom you may select your victims) dragged into court to be tried
> for this new offence by this new law, still there are two things wanting
> to convict and condemn him; and these are, in my opinion, twelve
> butchers for a jury and a Jeffreys for a judge . . .

But in spite of the poet's generous eloquence, the Bill was passed
and became law.

The reformers and radicals protested against the savage punish-
ment of the Luddites, but they had no sympathy with this machine-
smashing. The power looms in the Lancashire and Yorkshire
textile trades meant vastly increased and easier production; they
represented progress. Even Cobbett, who might have been expected
to understand and sympathise with the Luddites, surprisingly
denounced them. And indeed those handloom weavers who took
their big hammers to the machines have come down in history as
specimens of a prejudiced, short-sighted, stupid working class.
But perhaps because I grew up in their region I cannot dismiss
them so easily. The weavers who worked at home were paid
abominably low rates, and often to survive at all they had to be at
their looms from dawn until after dusk. But if they wanted an
afternoon off, they could take it. Though necessity might drive
them hard, they were to some extent their own masters. They
worked to their own needs, their own rhythms, their own moods.
They were not dominated by and geared to machines.

Something of their protest has lingered to this day in English
industry. Even now many strikes occur in those very industries
where the hours are reasonable and the wages comparatively
high; but they are also the industries, like the manufacture of
motor cars, in which men have to adapt themselves most completely
to the rhythm and unceasing demands of machines. Men who are
able to work at their own gait and in their own fashion may not
earn half as much as men employed in high-pressure plants, but
it is not they who keep coming out on strike. What lingers on among

PLATE XVII. Regency Ornament
composed of a two-handled vase
containing a variety of flowers formed
of shells of various colours
height of shade 26 in. (66.1 cm.)
The Victoria and Albert Museum,
London

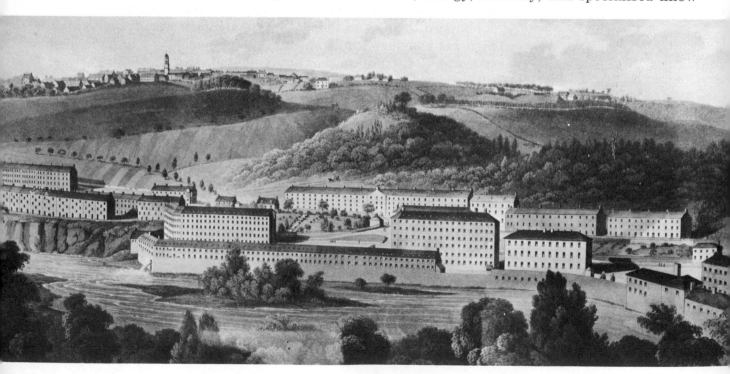

Robert Owen, engraving by B. Danck
The Gourock Ropework Co. Limited,
Port Glasgow

(below) The Town of Lanark (detail),
1825, engraving by and after I. Clark
The Gourock Ropework Co. Limited,
Port Glasgow

the English, who still do not relish time-and-motion studies and computer managerial policies, was probably at the heart of the old Luddite protest.

It was in this year that Robert Owen went to London and met Francis Place, who, it is said, helped him to revise his pamphlet, *A New View of Society*. The two men were very different in temperament and experience, but were alike in their deep sympathy with the working class, and in the further and very important fact that they were themselves reasonably successful employers and business men. The usual gibe against reformers and radicals – that they would not know what to do in positions of responsibility – did not apply to Owen and Place. And both men were more or less self-educated.

Place was a Londoner who was apprenticed to a breeches-maker, was later thrown out of work (and almost starved) because he led a strike, but finally ran a prosperous tailor's shop at Charing Cross. He was prodigiously industrious, not only in his business but also as what we should now call a 'social and political researcher'. He mastered all the details of the various Acts and repressive laws to which he objected, and his chief function – he disliked public speaking – was to supply material to other reformers, especially those in Parliament or prominent journalists, to organise committees, draft petitions of protest, and act as the general strategist of reform.

He was a dull writer, though he wrote tirelessly, but by sheer single-minded devotion, energy, industry, and specialised knowledge, he became one of the most valuable and influential figures in the workers' movement and the whole struggle for reform.

Except in his broad sympathies, Robert Owen was a very different character. He was an intuitive Welshman who worked hard enough and easily mastered business but throughout his adult life (he was born in 1771 and lived until 1858) he was dominated by one great idea, to which he gave all his energy and enthusiasm. This was the idea of co-operation, applied first to industry and then more widely in other fields.

He was a cotton spinner, and after some valuable experience in Lancashire he was able to take over some mills at New Lanark in Scotland. There he did something that is common enough now, when we should regard Owen as the originator of 'paternalism' in industry, but which was wildly original at the opening of the nineteenth century. He took care of his work-people (he called them industry's 'living machinery') both inside and outside the mills, giving them better wages and conditions, seeing that they were properly housed, and making sure their children were decently educated. He claimed to be the first founder of infant schools. Five per cent interest was paid on capital investment, but all profits above that would be spent on education and improved living conditions for the work-people. And though he had been called a mere 'reasoning machine', his experiment was successful from every point of view and soon attracted much attention both at home and abroad.

Francis Place (detail), 1833, by Samuel Drummond
oil on canvas
$35\frac{1}{2} \times 27\frac{1}{4}$ in. (90.2 $\times$ 69.2 cm.)
The National Portrait Gallery, London

An idealized study of factory children, 1814, lithograph by Ernst Kaufmann after George Walker – from *The Costume of Yorkshire,* 1885 Collection Sir Arthur Elton, Bart.

His activities as an international figure fall well outside our Regency limits, but one source of prejudice against him, then and later, must be mentioned. He was fanatically anti-religious, and never hesitated anywhere to denounce religion as the enemy of rational progress. A genuinely benevolent man, he came to be dreaded as a bore because he would discuss his own ideas and nothing else. He was not politically minded, but through his insistence upon co-operation he became the father of what Marx and Engels, much later, denounced as 'Utopian Socialism'. But it can be argued that in the long run it was Owen rather than Marx who had the more lasting influence on British as distinct from Continental Socialism.

William Cobbett agreed with Owen on many matters, but never hesitated to ridicule him. He never hesitated to ridicule or attack anybody. He was easily the most powerful journalist and pamphleteer of the Regency. His *Political Register* would now be considered required reading. This is what Hazlitt says of him:

> As a political partisan, no one can stand against him. With his brandished club, like Giant Despair in the *Pilgrim's Progress*, he knocks out their brains: and not only no individual, but no corrupt system, could hold out against his powerful and repeated attacks. But with the same weapon swung round like a flail, with which he levels his antagonists, he lays his friends low, and puts his own party *hors de combat*. This is a bad propensity and a worse principle in political tactics, though a common one. If his blows were straightforward and steadily directed to the same object, no unpopular minister could live before him; instead of which he lays about right and left impartially and remorselessly, makes a clear stage, has all the ring to himself, and then runs out of it, just when he should stand his ground . . .

(top) William Cobbett (detail), anonymous British artist
oil on canvas
35 × 27 in. (89 × 68.6 cm.)
The National Portrait Gallery, London
(above) William Hazlitt (detail), 1825, by William Bewick
chalk
22¾ × 14¾ in. (57.8 × 37.5 cm.)
The National Portrait Gallery, London

PLATE XVIII. The Waterloo Cherry – named after the Battle and raised by the first English plant breeder Thomas Andrew Knight of Downton, Herefordshire, from Volume II of the *Transactions of the Horticultural Society of London* (now the Royal Horticultural Society), 1817 – the Society was founded in 1804
Collection Mr C. P. Norbury

This is well said except that, strictly speaking, Cobbett had no party to put *hors de combat*. He was his own party. What is central in him is his unwearying devotion to rural life and pursuits, rooted in his childhood as a farmer's son in the 1760s. His masterpiece, both of minute observation and a superbly plain prose style, *Rural Rides*, came later than the Regency.

Cobbett was often thought of as a typical John Bull, but he could be compared simply to a bull itself, putting its head down and charging any red rag in sight. His apparent inconsistencies turn on the fact that he was outside the usual party divisions, and can only be described as a conservative radical. (It is a type not uncommon in England.) He attacked the Court, the Lords, the unrepresentative and reactionary Commons, the hocus-pocus of legal and financial jugglery, the *Thing*, because he was a militant radical. He detested the new Scots philosophers and economists, the steam-engine educators and extreme rationalists, the whole

The Waterloo Cherry.

Louis Spohr (detail) from Paine's
Famous Composers, 1891
The British Museum, London

March of Progress, because he was deeply conservative in his values and deep-seated beliefs, having always in mind some uncorrupted rural scene, almost a dream of some harvest home long ago. Cobbett lived in America from 1792 to 1800 and then from 1817 to 1819, when he wrote *A Year's Residence in America*, an account, closely observed but very lively, of agricultural life on Long Island and in Pennsylvania.

However, so far in this chapter we have had a great deal of discord and little harmony, so now I am happy to record that in 1813 the Philharmonic Society came into existence. This is an event of some importance to anybody who cares about music. The Society, now the Royal Philharmonic, still exists, and in fact it is the second oldest concert organisation in the world. It has commissioned many great works, including Beethoven's Ninth Symphony.

Musically the Regency hardly seems to exist, chiefly because such composers as it had – Clementi, William Shield, Vincent Novello, for example – seem so many dim dwarfs when compared with the giants abroad. However, London's fashionable society was not completely indifferent to music. Consider Haydn's twelve Salomon Symphonies, all composed first for London audiences. But performances suffered from amateurishness, a lack of any professional organisation. The Concert of Ancient Music had been established as far back as 1776, but it was a snobbish amateur society, which gave performances, we are told, that 'were directed in turns by an archbishop, dukes (royal and otherwise), lords, and a member or two of the commonalty who had blue blood in their veins'–clearly not a society prepared to do justice to masterpieces.

The Philharmonic Society was a different affair. Its founding members were experienced professional musicians. Its object, as it announced at once, was 'to promote the performance, in the most perfect manner possible, of the best and most approved instrumental music'. There were some rather odd restrictions at first, vocal solos and duets and even concertos not being allowed; but vocal items were permitted in 1816, and by 1819 the strange ban on concertos was lifted. The Society was immediately successful. Writing thirty years after its foundation, Henry F. Chorley, a well-known critic, was almost lyrical in praise of it:

> Never was a society formed in a better spirit and with a more commendable aim than the Philharmonic. It began where it ought; it was governed as it ought. There was no hunting after titled patrons or subscribers; no weak subserviency to mere rank. The most eminent members of the profession took the whole affair into their own hands, and entered upon their duties strong, and justly strong, in their own strength. They merged all claims of rank and precedence in one great object – the love of their art.

PLATE XIX. Walking Dress, April 1817,
from *La Belle Assemblée*
Collection Mrs Doris Langley Moore,
London

The Prince of Pleasure

The Philharmonic Society's
Programme for 19 June, 1820 – this
was the occasion when Louis Spohr
first used the baton
The Royal Philharmonic Society,
London

Grand pianoforte, *c.* 1819, by John
Broadwood
The Colt Clavier Collection,
Bethersden, Kent

After two successful seasons, the Society had £1,300 to invest
and was now able to commission new works. At the end of 1814
Cherubini accepted £200 to provide 'a symphony, an overture, an
Italian Vocal Piece for not less than three voices with complete
orchestral accompaniment, to be composed expressly for the
Society' – which may suggest that the Philharmonic was asking a
lot for its money, until we remember that £200 was a substantial
sum in 1814. The next year, the Society bought three of his minor
overtures from Beethoven, and in 1817 it offered him three hundred
guineas if he would come to London and bring with him two new
symphonies that would be the property of the Society. However,
Beethoven demanded four hundred guineas, with one hundred
and fifty of them paid in advance, and this was thought to be
excessive. There were further efforts to persuade Beethoven to
visit London, and in 1819 he promised that he would certainly
come; but he never did. And by the time the Ninth Symphony was
commissioned our Prince had been George IV for some years.

The composer who did accept the Philharmonic Society's
invitation, arriving in 1820, was Louis Spohr. He is almost forgotten
now (though I have a fairly recent recording of his Nonet in F),
but during the first half of the nineteenth century he was regarded
as the equal of Haydn, Mozart and Beethoven. As well as being a
prolific composer, Spohr was a fine solo violinist and an experienced
conductor. It was in this last capacity, giving his third concert
with the Society in 1820, that Spohr made musical history in
London. Up to this time – and indeed for some years afterwards –
orchestras had not had conductors. They were under a clumsy dual
control by the leading violin and a pianist who had the full score

110

in front of him. And we can well believe George Hogarth, Dickens's father-in-law, when he tells us that 'Neither of these functionaries could efficiently perform his duties separately, and they could not perform them jointly without interfering and clashing with each other.' It was Spohr – at least for London – who changed all this.

Let him explain what happened:

I then took my stand with the score at a separate music-desk, drew my conducting baton from my coat pocket, and gave the signal to begin. Alarmed at such a novel procedure, some of the .directors protested against it at first; but after I had begged them to grant me at least one trial, they became mollified. The symphonies and overtures to be rehearsed were well known to me, and I had conducted them in Germany. Immediately after the first movement of the symphony, the orchestra testified to their acceptance of the new method of conducting, thereby overruling all further opposition on the part of the directors . . . In the evening, the results were even more brilliant than I could have hoped. The audience, it is true, were at first startled by the innovation and could be seen exchanging whispers; but when the music began and the orchestra played the well-known symphony with unusual power and precision, the general approval was demonstrated at the end of the first movement by long-sustained applause . . .

And so, as the Regency was ending, there began the reign of the conductors, ranging from men of the highest musical talent to all manner of capering charlatans.

Now we must return to the autumn of 1813, when, no doubt, the happy Philharmonic Society was beginning to plan its next season's programme. Suddenly it seemed easier to make plans, all

The Vauxhall Fête held in honour of the victory of the Battle of Vittoria, 1813, by George Cruikshank
The British Museum, London

manner of plans, than it had been earlier, for the war against Napoleon and his Empire that had gone on for years and years, and had looked as if it might go on yet for years and years, dramatically changed its character. Wellington, after his decisive stroke at Vittoria in June, had gone back to his usual cautious form and had been creeping towards the French frontier. But then he defeated Soult's counter-offensive in the Pyrenees; and on 8 October his redcoats were actually in France, where they would move steadily forward. Napoleon was still capable of a few brilliant strokes, but he was slowing up. He had an army chiefly made up of raw recruits, and his marshals and senior officers had never recovered from the Russian disaster and its ordeals; and now he fought and lost the Battle of Leipzig. His Empire was falling apart. The French were beaten in Italy by the Austrians; they were expelled from Holland; and they had to retreat across the Rhine. In December, Napoleon was offered generous terms, which even allowed him the left bank of the Rhine, but he refused them just as he refused to believe that his 'star' was fading and sinking, though an Austrian army was now descending into France through Switzerland, and Wellington was moving towards Bordeaux. All the news that reached London by the end of the year was good, but the city itself was shivering in a spell of intense cold, which began on 29 December, and brought with it an unusual fog that lasted eight days. So 1813 went out and 1814 came in, both almost in darkness.

The Battle of Vittoria, 21 June 1813, from *Wellington Victories*, c. 1815, drawn and etched by William Heath, aquatinted by J. C. Stadler
The British Museum, London

1814

Parades and Fireworks

It is rather odd that this year, which was to see so much parading and flag-waving and public rejoicing, should have begun by gripping London in the longest and hardest frost it had known for centuries. However, whatever their faults Londoners are usually able to cope cheerfully with a crisis, making the best of it in a lively fashion. And this is what they did with the Great Frost. By February, as Lord William Pitt Lennox tells us in his *Recollections*, the Thames between London Bridge and Blackfriars became a thoroughly solid surface of ice. There were notices at the ends of all the local streets announcing that it was safe to cross the ice, and, as in the time of Elizabeth I, full advantage was taken of this new area and the public's interest in it. As before, there now sprang up a Frost Fair. The people moved across the river by way of what was called Freezeland Street. On either side, crowded together, were booths for bakers, butchers, barbers and cooks. There were swings, bookstalls, skittle alleys, toyshops, almost everything that might be found in an ordinary fair. There were even gambling establishments and 'the wheel of fortune, and pricking the garter; pedlars, hawkers of ballads, fruit, oysters, perambulating pie-men; and purveyors of the usual luxuries, gin, beer, brandy-balls and ginger-bread.' (Ah – what we have lost! Oh – to have gone to Frost Fair, to have eaten oysters at a few pence the dozen, and brandy-balls and ginger-bread, and then to have tried pricking the garter!) And, surely strangest of all, we are told that 'a dozen printing presses were erected on the Grand Mall, which extended from bridge to bridge'; though what they printed – hardly 'hot from the press' – was of little consequence.

Apparently the Great Frost was followed by a tremendous fall of snow 'which was general throughout the three kingdoms and continued without intermission for six weeks'. These were strange times. Beyond that curtain of snow, Napoleon's Empire was in ruins. Now out of touch with reality, he refused a peace offer based on the old French frontiers of 1792, struggled on and lost everything. Schwarzenburg marched his Austrians and Blücher his Prussians into Paris; Wellington defeated Soult at Toulouse; Napoleon abdicated and left for Elba; and Louis, who had grown old and fat in exile, was now King of France, Louis XVIII.

(above) Fanny D'Arblay Burney, by
Edward Francis Burney
oil on canvas
30 × 25 in. (77.3 × 63.5 cm.)
The National Portrait Gallery,
London

(opposite top) The Fair on the
Thames, 4 February 1814
engraving
The British Museum, London

(opposite middle) An example of the
printing that was carried out on the
ice, 1814
The London Museum, London

(opposite below) View of the Thames
off Three Cranes Wharf when frozen
31 January to 5 February 1814
The London Museum, London

(below) Louis XVIII, King of France,
before 1824, by Pierre Narcisse
Guérin
oil on canvas
Château de Versailles

It was April; the snow had gone; the war was over; there were
tremendous rejoicings, with the white cockades, tokens, flags of
the Bourbons shown everywhere, and *fleurs de lys* sprouting all
over Carlton House. But not everybody wanted to cheer London's
new French King. Byron kept to his rooms in Albany as the grand
procession went by, and said in a letter to Tom Moore: 'At this
present writing, Louis the Gouty is wheeling in triumph into
Piccadilly . . . the Most Christian King "hath no attractions for
me.".' Fanny Burney was less critical. She went to Grillion's Hotel,
where Louis was holding a levée. A very large chair had been put
in place for him, and 'an avenue had instantly been cleared from
the door to the chair, and the King moved along it slowly, slowly,
slowly, rather dragging his large body and weak limbs than
walking, but his face was truly engaging; benignity was in every
feature.' (Possibly; but soon, back in Paris, he was to prove that yet
another Bourbon had learnt nothing.) The Regent, prompt to make
the most of these occasions, invested Louis with the Order of the
Garter, and graciously buckled the Garter round a leg even fatter
than his own. Indeed, he said later, 'When I clasped his knee it was
exactly as if I were fastening a sash round a young man's waist.'

On 20 April *The Times* announced to the world that 'The Prince
Regent and Louis XVIII have each in his sphere done their duty
before God and man. They have merited and have obtained the
applause of mankind' – from which we can only conclude that at
least one editor, in the spring of 1814, could believe anything. One
of the Regent's courtiers tells us: 'Nothing can be more agreeable
and good natured than he is. In excellent spirits and looking, in
health and beauty, better than I have seen him for years. He wears
a certain new sort of darkish coloured wig, without powder, that
particularly becomes him.' However, there were other opinions,
held by dissenting, low, disloyal and unpatriotic types. For example,
'Peter Pindar' (John Wolcot), whose topical satirical verses
delighted everybody except their victims, had this to say:

> And France's hope and Britain's heir
> Were, truth, a most congenial pair;
> Two round tun-bellied, thriving rakes,
> Like oxen fed on Linseed cakes.

Nothing could be more typical of this age, running so often to
extremes, than the three passages I have quoted above – the sycophantic bosh and the savagely insulting verse of the radical
satirist.

When Louis left London for Paris, half the rank and fashion of
Britain followed him. Once the British have been denied Paris for
a few years, they cannot wait to return there as soon as the way is

open. Even by the end of April it was reported that Paris had twelve thousand British visitors. There was even a popular song: 'All the world's in Paris'. Fashionable ladies went to discover what was being worn there. The dandies and rakes went to look the women over. Older men went with their mouths watering for French food and wine. Artists and connoisseurs went to examine the art treasures that Napoleon and his marshals had looted. Hostesses like Lady Oxford were already giving 'charming *soirées*, at which were gathered the *elite* of Parisian society'. Even the great Duke of Wellington himself could be found there, having been appointed ambassador to the new kingdom.

(above left) Princess Charlotte Augusta of Wales, *c.* 1815, by Thomas Heaphy
watercolour
19½ × 15¼ in. (49.5 × 38.7 cm.)
The National Portrait Gallery, London

(above right) *La Famille Anglaise à Paris,* engraving from *Le Suprême Bon Ton No. 11*
Collection Mrs Doris Langley Moore, London

Meanwhile, in London all arrangements had been completed for the state visit in June of the Czar Alexander and King Frederick of Prussia, with various minor royalties in their suites; the Emperor of Austria had also been invited but had declined. This ought to have been the happiest time the Regent had ever known. A tremendous victory was to be celebrated, and though the Regent had not been near any battlefields himself, he felt that over and above all that his country had done to help defeat Napoleon (the naval blockade, Wellington's campaign, all the subsidies to the Allies) he himself, in some mysterious fashion, had made an immense personal contribution to the victory. 'He attributes every wonderful event now passing in the world to his own great talent,' one lady wrote. The prestige of Britain had never been higher, and, after all, the Regent could remind himself, he represented Britain.

Moreover, a state visit on this scale would involve many things in which our Prince of Pleasure could take a passionate interest.

Duty and enjoyment could for once go down the same highly decorated road. Splendid uniforms could be worn; there would be processions and illuminations; vast state banquets would be in order; and the crowds that cheered these victorious monarchs would surely have a few cheers to spare for *him*. So he might well have argued. But he remained dubious. Not only was he still completely separated from his wife, Princess Caroline, but their relations were worse than ever. If she could embarrass him, she would. And the London mob was on her side. Though he might ignore her, almost pretend she did not exist, she was after all the niece of George III and the daughter of the Duke of Brunswick. The visiting monarchs and all their attendant princelings, many of them related to her in one way or another, could hardly forget her existence just because the Regent could not endure the mere sight of his wife. So his guests might arrive feeling embarrassed. The Regent might – and indeed did – do all he could to fête them on the grandest scale. But what might have been, in more propitious circumstances, a blissful prospect of processions and dining, was clouded by these doubts.

A Russian advance guard arrived as early as March, in the shape of the Czar's sister, the Grand Duchess Catherine of Oldenburg. At this time the Regent was anxious for a match between his daughter, Charlotte, and the Prince of Orange; and as such an alliance, which would add the Dutch fleet to the British, was regarded with alarm in St Petersburg, it was believed that the Grand Duchess had been sent to London so early on a diplomatic mission. What is certain is that when the Regent first called on her at Pulteney's Hotel – he arrived too soon and she was not dressed – they took an instant dislike to each other. And the Regent did not like her any better when he heard that she had gone to inspect Whitbread's Brewery and had been shown round by Samuel Whitbread himself, one of the most radical of the Whig M.P.s who had denounced the war against Napoleon time after time. On her part, Catherine – the Czar's 'platter-faced sister', as Lord Clancarty called her – must have sent to St Petersburg an extremely unfavourable account of the man who was to be her brother's host in June. So the Russian half of the state visit did not promise well.

The Czar Alexander and King Frederick of Prussia landed at Dover on 6 June. Alexander delighted the crowd by declaring in his enthusiastic fashion: 'God be praised! I have set foot upon the land that has saved us all.' But – a blow to the Regent – he refused to stay at St James's Palace and insisted upon joining his sister at Pulteney's Hotel. Even King Frederick, a bluff soldierly type, did not fall in completely with the Regent's arrangements. He went to Clarence House but ignored the suite of satinwood furniture installed specially for him, and demanded a spartan camp bed in

The Czar of Russia and his sister the Grand Duchess Catherine of Oldenburg and friends on the balcony of Pulteney's Hotel, anonymous watercolour
5 × 3½ in. (12.7 × 8.9 cm.)
The British Museum, London
(Crace Portfolio X, No. 84)

(opposite) Covent Garden programme for 13 June 1814, the occasion when Queen Caroline made her unwelcome entrance
The Victoria and Albert Museum, London

place of the splendid state bed. It was all beginning badly. For the first evening, the Regent had arranged a magnificent banquet at Carlton House, but Alexander would have none of it and dined at their hotel with his sister.

The relations between Alexander and the Regent during this visit belong to ironical comedy. The Czar was a complex character, who combined almost extreme progressive ideas with various pseudo-mystical notions, and was regarded with suspicion and some alarm by reactionary foreign ministers like Metternich and Castlereagh, who thought him half-mad. So here was the Czar of All the Russias, the most powerful absolute ruler in all Europe, coming to London and demanding to meet Whig leaders, the very men the Regent had discarded in favour of severely reactionary Tories. It was the Czar who defended liberal views, and even criticised the Regent for not including men who held such views in his government; and it was the Regent, who had spent years surrounded by Whig leaders, who had to defend a narrowly-based government from which these man and their like had been excluded. It was Alexander, too, who was the enthusiastic crowd-pleaser, showing himself everywhere, while the Regent kept out of sight in his carriage. And Creevey was told: 'Alexander grumbles at the long dinners of the Regent's.' Again, when the Regent introduced his favourite, Lady Hertford, the Czar (very much a lady's man himself) bowed, said nothing to her, and then turned away muttering 'She is mighty old.' And his sister, Catherine, who disliked music, coolly stopped it at a Guildhall banquet. Finally, the pair of them kept asking about Caroline, Princess of Wales. But they saw her soon enough, too soon for the Regent.

It happened at a gala night at the theatre, when Caroline achieved

118

Theatre Royal, Covent-Garden

This present MONDAY, June 13, 1814, will be produced
In COMPLIMENT to OUR ILLUSTRIOUS VISITORS,
an ALLEGORICAL FESTIVAL, called The

Grand Alliance.

With appropriate Musick, new Scenery, Dresses and Decorations.
The ALLEGORICAL SCENE by Mr. Pugh and Assistants.
The DECORATIONS by Mr. Bradwell. The Dresses by Mr. Flower and Miss Egan.
Marshal of *England*, Mr. INCLEDON,   Marshal of *France*, Mr DURUSET,
Marshal of *Russia*, Mr. TAYLOR,   Marshal of *Germany*, Mr. BROADHURST,
Marshal of *Prussia*, Mr. SINCLAIR,   Marshal of *Sweden*, Mr. NORRIS,
Marshal of *Holland*, Mr. HIGMAN,   Marshal of *Spain*, Mr. TINNEY,
Officers of the different Nations,
Mess. Crumpton, Everard, Higman, Lee, Little, Linton, Montague, J. Taylor, Terry, Tett,
S. Tett, Watson, Williams
Genius of *England*, Miss STEPHENS,   Genius of *Russia*, Mrs BISHOP,
Genius of *Germany*, Mrs STERLING,   Genius of *Prussia*, Miss MATTHEWS,
Genius of *Sweden*, Mrs WATTS,   Genius of *Holland*, Miss LOGAN,   Genius of *Spain*, Miss ADAMI,
After which, 6th time, the revived Historical Romance of

Richard Cœur de Lion.

With new Scenes, Dresses and Decorations.
The Overture composed by WINTER—the rest of the Musick by GRETRY.
Richard   by   Mr. SINCLAIR,
Blondel by Mr. BARRYMORE,   Florestan by Mr. DURUSET,
Sir Owen Mr. TAYLOR, The Seneschal Mr. NORRIS, Antonio, Miss RENNELL,
Guillot, Mr Simmons,   William, Mr. Menage,   Old Matthew Mr. Williams
Cavaliers, Pilgrims, Peasants, &c.
Mess. Brooke, I. Brown, Duruset, Everard, Higman, Lee, Little, Linton, Montague, Norris, J. Taylor, I. Terry, Tett,
S. Tett, Watson, Williams, &c.
Matilda by Miss STEPHENS,
Lauretta by Miss MATTHEWS,   Collette by Miss CAREW,
Dorcas, Mrs COATES,   Julie, Miss WORGMAN,
PEASANTS, Mesdames Adami, Carew, Coates, Davies, Findlay, Grimaldi, Herbert, Hibbert, Iliff, Norman, Whitmore.
In act III. a DANCE incidental to the Piece,
In which will be introduced
A grand Pas de Deux by Monf. Soissons and Mrs Parker,
and a *Pas de Trois* by Mr. LE CLERCQ, Miss BRADWELL, & Miss WORGMAN.
With (by permission of the Proprietors of the Theatre Royal, Haymarket) the Comick Farce of

DEAD ALIVE.

Sir Walter Weathercock, Mr. BLANCHARD,   Dennis, Mr JEFFERIES,
Degagee, Mr. MENAGE,   Coachman, Mr. ATKINS,   Hannibal, Master PARSLOE,
Edward by Mr. SINCLAIR,
Motley by Mr. MATHEWS, *in which he will introduce the favourite Comick Songs of*
"*Manager Strut,*" and '*Bartlemy Fair.*'
Miss Hebe Winterton, Mrs DAVENPORT, Comfit, Mrs GIBBS, Caroline, Miss MATTHEWS.
To which will be added (28th time) a New Grand Asiatick Spectacle, called

Sadak & Kalasrade

Or, The WATERS of OBLIVION.
(The Characters as before)

Printed by B. Macleish, 2. Bow-Street.   Vivant Rex & Regina

Tomorrow, for the Benefit of Miss STEPHENS, the Opera of The CABINET.
Floretta (first time) by Miss STEPHENS.
With the Farce of KATHARINE and PETRUCHIO.
On Wednesday for the Benefit of Mr & Mrs LISTON, the Comedy of WHO WANTS a GUINEA,
Previous to which, (for the first time) a New Comick Extravaganza, called
BROAD BUT NOT LONG; or, How to Damn a New Piece.
With (2d time) the Farce of CATCH HIM WHO CAN.
On Thursday, for the Benefit of Mr. BLANCHARD, the Drama of The EXILE.
To which will be added the Melo-drama of the MILLER AND HIS MEN.
On Friday, for the Benefit of Mr. TAYLOR, the Comick Opera of The WOODMAN.
After which, an Interlude called *The Quarter Deck; or, Saturday Night.*
With the Farce of *The SLEEP WALKER.*

a very neat bit of exact timing. Here is one account of it, from the Hon. Mrs Robinson to Lord Fitzharris:

> It was full to overflowing, and we had many fainting and fatigued persons twisted through our box. The drawing up of the curtain and singing 'God Save The King' was very fine, and the Emperor, the Regent, and a large portion of the audience joined in the chorus. The acclamations were great, and just as the sovereigns were seated, fresh shouts of applause were heard directed towards the Princess of Wales's box, and there she appeared in a black wig and many diamonds; the Emperor rose and bowed, I think, to her; the Regent bowed also, I think to the applause; the King of Prussia also bowed, and it passed off very well . . .

That is her opinion; it could not have been the Regent's; he must have cursed his wife's sense of the dramatic; there was something very pointed about the way in which the audience rose, turning their backs to him to applaud Caroline's arrival. A loyal admirer of the Regent, Mrs Robinson goes on:

> Reports say these sovereigns mean to negotiate a reconciliation between the Regent and his wife . . . I hear he was hissed going home . . . The Emperor is, I am told, rather flippant in his conversation sometimes, and lectured the Regent the other day on toleration, when the Regent replied that it might be very well in his Imperial Majesty's dominions to admit people of all degrees into offices and power, but that if he was thoroughly acquainted with our constitution and habits he would know that it could not be. I give H.R.H. credit for so wise and spirited an answer. This is a piece with the Emperor's sending for Lords Grey, Grenville and Holland . . .

(above) Count Platoff, 1814, by Sir Thomas Lawrence
oil on canvas
106 × 70½ in. (269 × 179 cm.)
The Royal Collection, Windsor Castle

(below left) The Reception of the Prince Regent in the High Street, Oxford, 14 June 1814, by George Jones
oil on canvas
28 × 18 in. (71.2 × 45.8 cm.)
Magdalen College, Oxford

(below right) Conferring degrees on the Czar of Russia and the King of Prussia in the Sheldonian Theatre, Oxford, 14 June 1814, engraving by F. Dighton
The Royal Collection, Windsor Castle

Frederick William III, King of
Prussia, 1814–18, by Sir Thomas
Lawrence
oil on canvas
106¼ × 70¼ in. (270 × 178 cm.)
The Royal Collection, Windsor Castle

The Whig leaders, in fact. The good lady cannot see even a glimmer
of irony in a Czar of Russia coming to England to lecture its Prince
of Wales, doing duty for a constitutional monarch, on the virtues
of toleration and liberalism.

The Regent came out badly when compared with his famous
guests. Thus, one typical comment: 'The contrast between their
natural manner and the artificial and manufactured appearance
of our Regent is most striking.' But the poor man was doing
everything in his power to make the visit a success. He commissioned Lawrence, now the most fashionable portrait painter in
Britain, to paint portraits of Alexander, Frederick, Blücher and
Count Platoff, who commanded the Cossacks that harassed
Napoleon's army on its retreat from Moscow. Up to this time the
Regent had ignored Lawrence, probably because Lawrence, some
years before, had exhibited a portrait of Caroline and her daughter
at the Royal Academy and was thought to be a member of Caroline's
circle; but now the Regent promised to sit for a portrait himself
and from this time onwards was Lawrence's best patron.

On 14 June the Regent took his visitors to Oxford, where he had
recently founded two university readerships. There in the evening
there was 'a sumptuous dinner' in the Radcliffe Camera, where
spectators were admitted to the gallery, to gaze down on all the
gold plate shining in the candlelight and on Blücher, who liked to
drink strong beer and cognac, obviously very drunk. Four nights
later they were dining at the Guildhall with the Corporation of
London. The procession there was said to be a magnificent
spectacle: first, the escort of Light Dragoons; then seven of the
Regent's carriages with officers of his household and foreign
generals; state carriages of the Royal Dukes and the Speaker,

The Banquet given by the
Corporation of London for the
Prince Regent and guests in the
Guildhall, 18 June 1814, by George
Clint
oil on canvas
50 × 75 in. (127 × 191 cm.)
The Guildhall Art Gallery, London

121

followed by members of the cabinet and a troop of Horse Guards; then a state carriage-and-six for the Regent's officers of state, six royal carriages for the suites of the foreign sovereigns, a hundred Yeomen of the Guard, the band of Gentleman Pensioners, the heralds, and finally the Regent's own state carriage for himself and his regal guests. At the Guildhall they tried the first turtle of the season, ate a baron of beef, among other things, and drank fifteen toasts, which probably meant that poor old Blücher, who was sinking under all these festivities, was again very drunk.

Blücher was easily the crowd's first favourite. Alexander might stand up in his open carriage, raising his hat and bowing to the ladies, and always be enthusiastically received; but it was Prussia's old soldier whom the English hero-worshipped. This was not unreasonable. They had had no chance yet of seeing Wellington, who was still in Paris. Blücher was not a great general but he was energetic, courageous, tough, had been always resolutely opposed to Napoleon, and was chiefly responsible for the drive towards Paris. (It was he who, on his first sight of London, cried 'What a city to sack!') Lady Frances Shelley notes in her diary: 'Blücher came to the door to please the mob, who had been drawing him about the streets all morning. Lord Burghersh had accompanied him; and it was all they could do to get Blücher safe into the house as he was nearly crushed to death. He told Lord Burghersh that he had never been so frightened.' Lady Malmesbury met him at an inn in Henley, when he was on his way to Oxford, and wrote:

(below) The Prince Regent, the Czar of Russia and the King of Prussia and courtiers riding in Hyde Park, 20 June 1814, drawn and etched by Alexander Sauerweid
The Royal Collection, Windsor Castle

(opposite above left) General Blücher, 1814, by Sir Thomas Lawrence
oil on canvas
106¼ × 70¼ in. (270 × 178 cm.)
The Royal Collection, Windsor Castle

(opposite above right) Blücher greeted by his numerous friends in the park
The British Museum, London

(opposite below) Alexander I, Czar of Russia, 1814–18, by Sir Thomas Lawrence
oil on canvas
107½ × 70½ in. (273 × 179 cm.)
The Royal Collection, Windsor Castle

He is a very fine old man, handsome and fair, without a wrinkle, but feeble on his legs, talks a tolerable French gibberish . . . We drank his health, and he ours, and then went to the window and drank to the people. You never heard such a scream of delight. He complained he was fatigued to death – had had no sleep for three nights – with all the festivities, but was much gratified at his reception, which is far beyond any of them. I don't believe he is ever allowed to be drawn by a horse anywhere . . .

If Huish, the Regent's spiteful biographer, is to be believed (and he always raises doubts in me) there is a melancholy sequel to this story of his triumphant reception. He and his Russian colleague, Platoff, stayed on in London after their respective monarchs had departed. Blücher was as fond of gambling as he was of drinking – an unfortunate combination of tastes – and Huish tells us that he lost at least £25,000 gambling at Carlton House and finally left England (to come to Wellington's rescue next year at Waterloo) almost destitute. Huish declared the Regent knew what was happening and encouraged the fleecing of the poor old soldier, rather as if Carlton House were being turned into a clip joint.

There were some odd little consequences of this state visit. 'No milk sometimes,' we read, 'as the cows are all frightened out of the Green Park by the constant huzzas, and many people cannot get their clothes washed, as the washerwomen work for Princes and Kings.' And the waltz was *in* at last. It had been swinging round the edge of good society for some time, in spite of prejudice and much determined opposition. Then, during this visit, Alexander danced it at Almack's – and now, as Gronow observed, 'the waltzing mania, having turned the heads of society generally, descended to their feet, and the waltz was practised in the morning in certain noble mansions with unparalleled assiduity.' Perhaps they were getting ready for the Congress of Vienna.

The Regent had had no luck with the state visit, when he was said to be looking 'fagged and fatigued' and 'tired of the whole thing' and never had any spontaneous cheering all for himself. But he tried again, after Wellington had arrived at last, giving a very elaborate fête in his honour at Carlton House on 21 July. Nash built a special hall, with a diameter of 136 feet, for this occasion. Guests passed through the house into this structure, which was entirely draped inside with white muslin and had an umbrella-shaped roof painted to look like muslin. There was a temple in the centre of the room that concealed two bands, which played behind a mass of artificial flowers. There were covered walks leading to various supper tents, and their walls were lined with allegorical transparencies representing such subjects as *The Overthrow of Tyranny by the Allied Powers, Military Glory, The Arts in England*, and there might well have been another one representing *The Mad Extravagance of a Prince already heavily in Debt*. The party lasted until 6 a.m.

The crowds could not join in these festivities, and so, to celebrate the peace and to please his subjects, the Regent gave orders that from 1 August great celebrations must be held in Hyde Park, St James's Park and Green Park, though this was reserved for fireworks. Oriental temples, towers, pagodas, bridges, sprouted in the parks. There was to be a mimic naval battle on the Serpentine. And even more important than the balloon ascents and the fireworks was a grand transformation scene, a hundred-foot-high Castle of Discord 'with all its horrors of fire and destruction' being

A group of waltzers, 1 February 1817, engraved for *La Belle Assemblée* The Victoria and Albert Museum, London

(above) The Temple of Concord, Green Park, erected for the display of a Grand Firework, 1 August 1814
The British Museum, London

(right) The Chinese Bridge illuminated, St James's Park on the night of the celebration of Peace, 1814, engraving by M. Dubourg after John Heaviside Clark
The British Museum, London

finally obliterated by smoke, which thinned out to reveal a delightful Temple of Concord. The effect was contrived by Sir William Congreve, who had to employ about fifty men reversing the structure on wheels while they were hidden by the smoke. The crowds were enthusiastic, but more sophisticated persons deplored the extravagance and poor taste of the celebrations. And not only in the radical press; even *The Times* was severely critical: 'The public will first gape at the mummery, then laugh at the authors of it, and lastly grumble at the expense. We are chiefly sorry on account of the contemptible light in which it will exhibit us as a people to foreign nations . . . Alas! Alas! to what are we sinking?'

The whole character of Hyde Park must have been changed immediately, to cater to the crowds, because it was only on 9 August that Charles Lamb wrote this characteristic letter to Wordsworth:

Save for a late excursion to Harrow and a day or two on the banks of the Thames this Summer, rural images were fast fading from my mind, and by the wise provision of the Regent all that was countryfy'd in the Parks is all but obliterated. The very colour of green is vanished, the whole surface of Hyde Park is dry crumbling sand (Arabia Arenosa), not a vestige or hint of grass ever having grown there, booths and drinking places go all round it for a mile and a half I am confident – I might say two miles in circuit – the stench of liquors, *bad* tobacco, dirty people and provisions, conquers the air and we are stifled and suffocated in Hyde Park.

Order after Order has been issued by Lord Sidmouth in the name of the Regent (acting in behalf of his Royal father) for the dispersion of the varlets, but in vain. The *vis unita* of all the Publicans in London, Westminster, Marylebone, and miles round is too powerful a force to put down. The Regent has rais'd a phantom which he cannot lay. There they'll stay probably for ever. The whole beauty of the Place is gone – that lake-look of the Serpentine – it has got foolish ships upon it – but something whispers to have confidence in nature and its revival –

at the coming of the *milder day*
These monuments shall all be overgrown.

Meantime I confess to have smoked one delicious pipe in one of the cleanliest and goodliest of the booths – a tent rather, 'O call it not a booth!' – erected by the public Spirit of Watson, who keeps the Adam and Eve at Pancras (the ale houses have all emigrated with their train of bottles, mugs, corkscrews, waiters, into Hyde Park – whole Ale houses with all their Ale!) in company with some of the guards that had been in France and a fine French girl (habited like a Princess of Banditti) which one of the dogs had transported from the Garonne to the Serpentine. The unusual scene in H. Park, by Candlelight in open air, good tobacco, bottled stout, made it look like an interval in a campaign, a repose after battle, I almost fancied scars smarting and was ready to club a story with my comrades of some of my lying deeds.

After all, the fireworks were splendid – the Rockets in clusters, in trees and all shapes, spreading about like young stars in the making, floundering about in Space (like unbroke horses) till some of Newton's calculations should fix them, but then they went out. Any one who could see 'em and the still finer showers of gloomy rain fire that fell sulkily and angrily from 'em, and could go to bed without dreaming of the Last Day, must be as hardened an Atheist as *****.

By the autumn, London's high jinks were well over and half-forgotten, and it was now the turn of Vienna, where the famous Congress was formally opened on 1 November, 1814. Most of the Allied sovereigns were there, but the Regent stayed at home and was represented first by Castlereagh and then by Wellington. The interminable deliberations of the Congress were rudely interrupted by the news, on 7 March, 1815, that Napoleon had left Elba for

(opposite) The Congress of Vienna 1815, engraved in 1819, Jean Godefroy after Jean Baptiste Isabey
– key by Gottfried Engelmann after Jean Baptiste Isabey
The British Museum, London

126

Noms des Ministres
du
CONGRÈS DE VIENNE.
en 1815

Madame La Duchesse D'Abrantes, engraving by Thierry Frères
The British Museum, London

France. Probably the Prince de Ligne made the best comment on it when he declared, '*Le congrès ne marche pas, mais il danse.*' And Madame Junot, Duchesse d'Abrantes, wrote in her memoirs: 'Vienna was at this period a place of enchantment and delicious pleasure; *fêtes,* joy, love, ambition, all were written on the golden and perfumed pages of enchantment.' (What the Regent, just the man to turn these pages, was missing!) There have been many more useful international conferences, but not another to match the Congress of Vienna in social gaiety. There were excited accounts of the brilliance of the city, thronged as it was 'with crowned heads, ambassadors, ministers, and general officers'; of the hunting, shooting, drives and promenades, vast dinners, evening assemblies, balls, *petits soupers,* plays and operas; of the staging of a medieval joust by younger members of the nobility in the Imperial Riding School; of processions of sledges going through the streets of Vienna out to the Palace of Schönbrunn, and returning, after a performance of *Cinderella,* by torchlight. No wonder there was a film called *Congress Dances.* Such political consequences as it achieved were in the main disastrous and brought much misery. But its glittering gaiety had one odd result. It gave Vienna – a fine but rather sombre city, with not a particularly happy history – a curious glamour, a touch of magic, determinedly exploited by writers and composers of operettas and the like, that refused to vanish until after the First World War, when even the ghost of the Congress stopped dancing.

However, it is time we remembered that the true glory of the Regency shines in its literature. And 1814 saw not only parades and fireworks but also the first appearance of Wordsworth's major long poem, *The Excursion*, a work that made no concession whatever to popular taste in verse, rhymed tales of corsairs, exotic slave girls, lovesick Eastern princes. It is a treasure house of poetic wisdom:

> We live by admiration, hope, and love;
> And even as these are well and wisely fixed,
> In dignity of being we ascend.

When we bear in mind that during the next ten years Keats, Shelley and Byron were to die, there is something curiously prophetic about those lines in *The Excursion*:

> The good die first,
> And they whose hearts are dry as summer dust
> Burn to the socket.

On 7 July, 1814, the first of what soon came to be called the 'Scotch Novels', *Waverley*, was published. It reached its sixth

PLATE XX. Prime Bang-up at Hackney or a Peep at the Balloon 12 August (1811), coloured engraving published by Thomas Tegg showing a balloon ascent of Mr James Sadler
12 × 9 in. (30.5 × 22.9 cm.)
The Royal Aeronautical Society, London

PLATE XXI. (overleaf) A View of the Naumachy, Fireworks and Fair in Hyde Park in Honour of Peace that took place on 1 August 1814 (detail) hand-coloured engraving
14½ × 18 in. (36.8 × 45.8 cm.)
Collection George Rainbird Limited

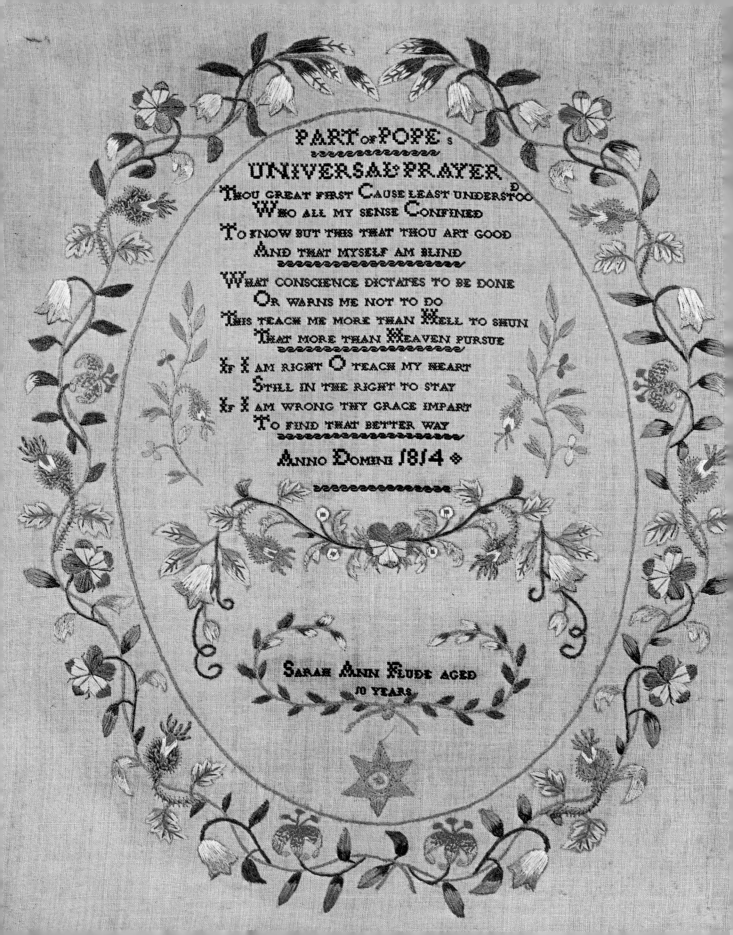

PART OF POPE's

UNIVERSAL PRAYER

THOU GREAT FIRST CAUSE LEAST UNDERSTOOD
WHO ALL MY SENSE CONFINED
TO KNOW BUT THIS THAT THOU ART GOOD
AND THAT MYSELF AM BLIND

WHAT CONSCIENCE DICTATES TO BE DONE
OR WARNS ME NOT TO DO
THIS TEACH ME MORE THAN WELL TO SHUN
THAT MORE THAN HEAVEN PURSUE

IF I AM RIGHT O TEACH MY HEART
STILL IN THE RIGHT TO STAY
IF I AM WRONG THY GRACE IMPART
TO FIND THAT BETTER WAY

ANNO DOMINI 1814

SARAH ANN FLUDE AGED
10 YEARS

edition before the end of the year. Scott had begun the story some time before and chanced to find the unfinished manuscript when he was looking for some fishing tackle. It seemed to him more promising than it had done earlier, and he needed some extra money, so he quickly finished the story and offered it to Constable, the publisher, on the understanding that his name should not appear on the title page. Constable bid £700, a small sum compared with what Scott had previously demanded for his immensely popular narrative poems, but Scott refused to part with the copyright and insisted upon half profits, shrewdly remarking that £700 was too much if the book failed and too little if it succeeded. And he was adamant about anonymity, not only for this first attempt but also, following its great success, for the other novels that soon came after it, all of them described as being 'By the Author of *Waverley*'. And Scott himself, when he found it impossible to be evasive, as suspicion grew, actually went to the length of denying – and more than once – that he was the author of these novels.

I have admired Scott both as a writer and as a man for well over half a century, but this determined masking of himself as a novelist seems to me discreditable. His motives were entirely snobbish, part of a rather affected and idiotic Toryism that did some damage to his otherwise manly and upright character. He had an almost sycophantic admiration for our Prince of Pleasure, whereas if this man had not been Regent and then George IV, Scott would have regarded him with contempt. Scott could openly combine his official status, as a legal man, and his popular reputation as a poet. And now that he had made money, not only out of his poetry but also as a very hard-working critic and editor, he saw himself not as a professional author but as the gentlemanly open-handed host, Scott of Abbotsford. His attitude towards his fiction was that of a pimp; he took the money without acknowledging its source. And the irony was that while only comparatively few people, and not all of them very bright, saw him as Scott of Abbotsford, itself a bogus affair, all Europe was beginning to admire and revere 'the Wizard of the North'. And not only Europe, for, writing long afterwards, Mark Twain, who disliked Scott, declared that the spurious chivalry and semi-feudal affectations of society in the Southern States came from a regular early diet of Scott's romances. His purely literary influence, during at least the first half of the nineteenth century, was immensely wide and deep.

The sharp decline in Scott's reputation, both among critics and the general public, is partly due to the fact that his work is not properly considered. People tend to think of him first – because that is how they first met him, probably at school – as a medieval romancer. But this is to judge him by his later and weaker work, often written under stress and against time. He is best regarded not

PLATE XXII. Sampler, 1814, signed Sarah Ann Flude worked in silk, in satin, chain and long and short, and stem stitches on a woollen canvas 16 × 13½ in. (40.7 × 34.3 cm.) The Victoria and Albert Museum, London

Mary Wollstonecraft Shelley (detail),
1841, by Richard Rothwell
oil on canvas
29 × 24 in. (73.7 × 61 cm.)
The National Portrait Gallery,
London

as the storyteller of romantic old tales, *Ivanhoe* and the rest, but as a novelist, and a Scots novelist, whose mind and heart really belong to the eighteenth century, in which he spent the first twenty-nine years of his life, and not to the Middle Ages. In all his fiction, the closer Scott is to Scotland and to the eighteenth century – and perhaps to the Edinburgh advocate he was once – the stronger and more convincing and engaging he is, with an unusually sane, robust, essentially masculine feeling for variety of character and action, with a Shakespearean breadth if not depth. Readers who are not too impatient should try Scott again, chiefly concentrating on the earlier novels that delighted so many readers during the Regency. Even Hazlitt, who loathed Scott's Toryism, was enchanted by them, crying: 'All is fresh, from the hand of nature . . .'

Even fresher from the hand of nature was that atheistical and revolutionary young poet, Percy Bysshe Shelley, whose opinions, which he always boldly declared, had already shocked his wealthy, solidly-established family and had got him expelled from University College, Oxford. And now he confirmed everybody's worst suspicions, being already a married man and a father, by eloping, in the early morning of 27 July, 1814, with Mary, daughter of William Godwin. They were accompanied by Claire Clairmont, often described as Mary's half-sister though in fact she was the daughter of the second Mrs Godwin by an earlier marriage.

Those who shook their heads were convinced that such dreadful behaviour was only too typical of this circle of unbelievers. Wasn't William Godwin himself some sort of philosophical anarchist? And hadn't Mary's mother been Mary Wollstonecraft, the notorious feminist? And now here was young Shelley, bringing shame upon his decent squire's family in Sussex, deserting his poor wife and child, behaving like a cold-hearted sensual blackguard, and even having the audacity, it was rumoured, to invite his wife to join him and his mistress somewhere, anywhere, on the Continent. That is how the story ran – and was to run for some time. Not only was the truth very different, but we can see now, in spite of the tragedy of Harriet's suicide, that it glitters with comic irony.

First, the comedy of Shelley's relations with William Godwin. Still not of age and in a fever of excitement about injustice everywhere, Shelley read Godwin's *Inquiry Concerning Political Justice*, first published in 1793. Its denunciation of all authority and its demand for the abolition of marriage aroused Shelley's enthusiasm and he wrote from the country to Godwin to tell him so. They exchanged letters for some months before actually meeting in London. Godwin enjoyed the young poet's admiration, which was all the better because it came from a youth with a wealthy family behind him. What Shelley did not know then was that Godwin's publishing and bookselling business was doing badly. Shelley

William Godwin (detail), by Henry
William Pickersgill
oil on canvas
26½ × 23½ in. (67.3 × 59.7 cm.)
The National Portrait Gallery,
London

Claire Clairmont (detail), 1819, by
Amelia Curran
oil on canvas
18½ × 14½ in. (47 × 36.8 cm.)
Newstead Abbey, Nottinghamshire

proudly announced that as, like Godwin, he did not believe in inherited wealth he was going to reject the family entail; and then in his innocence he was surprised to find that the great philosophical anarchist did not respond eagerly but uneasily to this news, suggesting that Shelley should be more cautious. However, when Shelley reached London in 1813, he made Godwin's acquaintance and soon became almost a member of the Godwin family circle. Mary was away for some time, but when she came home, a striking girl with a mind and will of her own, they soon discovered they were in love. But when Mary told her father he told Shelley to keep away from Mary and the house: hence the elopement.

Meanwhile, Godwin had had over £1,000 from Shelley, who was borrowing money on future prospects, signing *post obits*, at ruinous rates. Later, when Shelley and Mary were able to marry, there was a reconciliation, but from then on Shelley discovered that he had a relentless sponger as a father-in-law. Finally, not long before his death, the unworldly and astonishingly good-natured Shelley rebelled; and this was his last letter to Godwin:

I have given you within a few years the amount of a considerable fortune, and have destituted myself, for the purpose of realising it, of nearly four times that amount. Except for the *good will* which this transaction seems to have produced between you & me, this money, for any *advantage* that it ever conferred on you, might as well have been thrown into the sea. Had I kept in my own hands this £4 or £5000 & administered it in trust for your permanent advantage I should have been indeed your benefactor. The error however was greater in the man of mature age extensive experience & penetrating intellect than in the crude & impetuous boy . . .

It was a bad day when Shelley wrote his first enthusiastic letter to the author of *Political Justice*. True, without meeting Godwin he would never have met Mary. But was Mary the companion-mistress-wife he needed? And would they have ever run away together if Godwin had not forbidden him the house?

When we come to Shelley and his women, the contrast between the contemporary legend and the truth is very sharp indeed. Here it is worth noticing that during the Regency, at least on the upper levels of society, there was a change for a time from the familiar pattern, belonging both to the eighteenth century and to the Victorian age, of male authority and the domination of the masculine principle. It is as if a matriarchy secretly took over for a few years. Country squires might still be seducing parlourmaids, but in London something different was happening. It was the girls who were bold and predatory. So Byron, that notorious seducer,

135

was actually always being seduced. And any idea of Shelley as the enticer of innocent young girls can be dismissed. Harriet Westbrook may have been only sixteen to his nineteen – though here we must not forget her elder sister, Eliza – but their elopement and subsequent marriage were really more her doing than his.

As for Mary Godwin, a strong (and not very agreeable) character, she may be said to have nailed him on sight. His desertion of Harriet, his letter proposing that she should join him and Mary, her suicide two years later, these would seem to amount to an inexcusably sorry tale; but facts rarely taken into account remove much of the blame from Shelley. Thus, Harriet may have been a devoted little wife, but it is a fact that, dominated as she was by Eliza (whom Shelley had come to dislike), she deliberately lived apart from him some time before Mary took charge. His letter to her was truly affectionate, and its odd, but not heartless, invitation must be considered in terms of Shelley's character and beliefs. Finally, Harriet's suicide was not the direct result of Shelley's elopement with Mary. She was far gone in pregnancy by another man, possibly the Alder who testified at the inquest. True, there might have been no loneliness, no dubious affair, no pregnancy, no suicide, if she had been still living with Shelley, but her marriage might not have lasted much longer even if there had been no Mary Godwin.

It seems to me impossible to come close to Shelley without feeling a growing affection for him. Peacock, a very different character, who laughed at his habits and opinions, was genuinely fond of him. Unlike Byron, Shelley was a good friend. He never tried to evade fundamental responsibilities. If he cuts an odd figure in his own time, that is chiefly because he rejects the social values and conventions of that time. He is rather like a sensible, warm-hearted representative of some future civilization, some golden age of freedom and love that he celebrates in his poetry. He was a bad judge of character (Mary was a mistake); he could appear selfishly impatient just because, opinions and conventions apart, he often did not understand what other people were feeling, especially where sex was concerned. Sexual possessiveness was a mystery to him. But this did not mean that he himself wanted a travelling harem, as some of his contemporaries imagined. It is more than likely that the actual sexual urge in Shelley was weaker than in most of the people he shocked. The truth is, he was haunted – as D. H. Lawrence was, a hundred years later – by the romantic-prophetical notion of a select group acting out their beliefs, a kind of illuminati, deliberately taking themselves into exile.

The fact that he apparently fell in love, always at a high pitch of excitement, with one girl (they were all young) after another, has now been given a Freudian explanation. The argument runs that he was really a suppressed homosexual, finding one woman after

Thomas Love Peacock, *c.* 1805,
by P. Jean
ivory
$2\frac{7}{8} \times 2\frac{3}{8}$ in. (7.3 × 6 cm.)
The National Portrait Gallery,
London

another unsatisfactory because his hidden essential need was for a man, and that if, for example, he was willing to share Harriet with Hogg, this was a kind of roundabout substitute homosexuality. This does not seem to me to bring us very close to Shelley. If he is to be explained in terms of depth psychology, we should turn from Freud to Jung. All his most ambitious work, narrative and dramatic poetry, leaves the outer world to explore the depths of the psyche, that Collective Unconscious of Jung's which discovers for us the magical archetypes. One of these is the anima – 'an eternal image of woman, not the image of this or that definite woman, but rather a definite feminine image . . . fundamentally an unconscious, hereditary factor of primordial origin' – magical in its effect, just because it arises from the mysterious depths of the unconscious. Literature, especially romantic literature, offers us scores of anima figures. And as Jung pointed out more than once, when a man projects the anima on to a real woman he finds her irresistible while the magic lasts. This is what Shelley did, and might have continued doing for some time if he had lived.

Shelley was really the opposite of a sensual, over-sexed man who wants new physical adventures, or of the Don Juan type who must pursue woman and 'possess' them just because he despises or hates the opposite sex. He was really the victim of the ancient enchanters of his own inner world, into which his poetry always took him. What he called 'love' was not a fully conscious attachment to and understanding of another person, the relationship that most women want, nor was it simply an overpowering desire for yet another woman: it was a kind of spiritual excitement, making the world seem magical again, created by the projection of the anima. When the white flame faded, and the enchantment was gone, he was not contemptuous and heartless as another sort of man might have been (and as Byron often was), but considerate and affectionate. He was not a cad with convenient theories, nor yet an angelic being lacking humanity, not yet again a suppressed homosexual, but a good, if odd, human being who took the risk of exploring the depths of his inner world and brought us news of it in poetry.

In the summer and early autumn of this year, the fashions from Paris, adopted by the girls at Vauxhall and other places, in the thinnest muslin, offered glimpses of breasts and legs to ardent young men. These delighted the eye but troubled the mind and heart of a very young surgeon's apprentice, enticing him to write more and more verses, though he knew that as yet these were too much like other men's verses. And when he realised this, he felt almost suicidal, and even declared that unless he could turn himself into a real poet, life would not be worth living. He was a rum little fellow, though quite good company at times – this young John Keats.

Russian Mantle, Pelisse and Bonnet from *La Belle Assemblée*, 1 November 1814
The Victoria and Albert Museum, London

137

1815

The Year of Waterloo

There could hardly be any other title for this chapter. Waterloo may not have been the most important battle in British history – Trafalgar, for example, saved us from being invaded by the finest army Napoleon ever had – and it was not the most glorious, for though Wellington's men fought hard, they were saved by some bad French tactics and the obstinate courage of Blücher; but the use of its name in London and throughout the country proves that at home it was our most famous victory. So this chapter's title is amply justified. Yet in many ways 1815 is an anticlimax after 1814, which was when the long, long war really came to an end. What 1815 saw was the end of the confused Hundred Days and Napoleon's last despairing bid for power, with an army in which most of his best marshals refused to serve. However, his defeat meant that the British could take him as far away from Europe as St Helena, and the Bourbons and their friends could safely return to Paris, where they proceeded to behave very badly indeed, all manner of ugly proscriptions and prosecutions culminating in the execution of Ney. Napoleon's insatiable ambition, combined with his increasing lack of judgment, made his distant exile well-deserved, but the Europe on which he had to turn his back, dominated as it was by the new Holy Alliance of Russia, Prussia and Austria, and with a savagely reactionary government in Westminster, was no better – perhaps worse – than his Empire before 1812. There was not more freedom for anybody except kings and princes. Progress in some shape or form there was bound to be, but neither international nor national politics made any contribution to it in 1815.

Even if we agree that some battles may be romantic, Waterloo can hardly be considered one of them. It was a mixture of commanders at crosspurposes (both Ney and Grouchy behaved stupidly), messages miscarrying, and some desperate fighting at close quarters, with few prisoners but a great many casualties. Nevertheless, we see it in a romantic light. And this is worth some explanation.

By 1 June, 1815, Napoleon had raised an army largely composed of veterans. Wellington and Blücher were holding Belgium while the Austrians and Russians were moving towards France's eastern frontier. The headquarters of Wellington's Anglo-Dutch army was

(opposite) The Duke of Wellington at the Battle of Waterloo, 18 June 1815 (detail), from *Wellington Victories*, *c.* 1815, drawn and etched by William Heath, aquatinted by J. C. Stadler
The British Museum, London

in Brussels, and as there seemed to be plenty of time before Napoleon could move, Brussels was filled with officers' wives and those fashionable London types who had to be *in* at everything, as if a campaign were a kind of extended First Night. Writing about Wellington, William Pitt Lennox says, 'During the period that preceded the operations in the field, his Grace was daily occupied with matters connected with the shortly expected campaign; but these did not interfere with his entering into and joining the society then assembled at Brussels . . .' And on 15 June, the more important – or the more fortunate – members of that society attended a ball given by the Duchess of Richmond. It is that ball which encourages us to see the Battle of Waterloo through a romantic haze.

All the diarists and writers of military memoirs who were in Brussels then make much of this ball; but it was the literary men who made it famous. So we have Byron:

> Did ye not hear it? No; 'twas but the wind,
> Or the car rattling o'er the stony street;
> On with the dance! Let joy be unconfined,
> No sleep till morn, when Youth and Pleasure meet,
> To chase the glowing Hours with flying feet –
> But hark! – that heavy sound breaks in once more,
> As if the clouds its echo would repeat;
> And nearer, clearer, deadlier than before!
> Arm! Arm! it is – it is – the cannon's opening roar.

Thirty years later, in *Vanity Fair,* Thackeray took all his chief characters to Brussels, Amelia and her George and the faithful Dobbin, Becky and Rawdon Crawley and Mr Jos, and devoted much space to the ball and the hurried departure of the officers, ending the whole episode with what is probably the most famous and the finest passage he ever wrote: 'No more firing was heard at Brussels – the pursuit rolled miles away. Darkness came down on the field and the city; and Amelia was praying for George, who was lying on his face, dead, with a bullet through his heart.' Born in 1811, Thackeray had to take his Regency from books and the talk of elderly survivors of it. He can rarely be faulted on historical details, yet, reading these *Vanity Fair* chapters again when my own mind is filled with the Regency, its characters and atmosphere, I cannot help feeling that the genuine tone and taste of these earlier years escape him, that *Vanity Fair* still suggests an Early Victorian world. But even so, with Byron he helps to increase the fame and the romantic glamour of the Duchess of Richmond's ball and the battle that followed it.

The ball itself was nothing like so large and grand as most of us imagine it to have been. It was an informal affair, held in a house

The Duchess of Richmond's Ball, or Intelligence of the Battle of Ligny, from *Wellington Victories*, c. 1815, drawn and etched by William Heath, acquatinted by J. C. Stadler
The British Museum, London

rented by the Richmonds, and we are told that not more than 223 persons attended it. But at least fifty-three of the officers there were shortly to be dangerously wounded or killed. One account of it was given long afterwards by Georgiana, daughter of the Duchess and then aged twenty:

My mother's now famous ball took place in a large room on the ground floor, on the left of the entrance, connected with the rest of the house by an ante-room. It had been used by the coachbuilder, from whom the house was hired, to put carriages in, but it was papered before we came there; and I recollect the paper – a trellis pattern with roses . . . When the Duke arrived rather late, at the ball, I was dancing but at once went up to him to ask about the rumours. He said very gravely 'Yes, they are true; we are off tomorrow.' This terrible news was circulated directly, while some of the officers hurried away, others remained at the ball, and actually had not time to change their clothes, but fought in evening costume. I went with my eldest brother (A.D.C. to the Prince of Orange) to his house, which stood in our garden, to help him to pack

141

up, after which we returned to the ballroom, where we found some energetic and heartless young ladies still dancing . . . It was a dreadful evening, taking leave of friends and acquaintances, many never to be seen again . . .

Another observer tells us:

The ball was at its height when the Duke of Wellington first received the *positive* intelligence that Napoleon had crossed the Sambre with his whole army and taken possession of Charleroi. The excitement which ensued, on the company being made acquainted with Napoleon's advance, was most extraordinary. The countenances which, a moment before, were lighted up with pleasure and gaiety, now wore a most solemn aspect. The Duke of Brunswick, sitting with a child (the present Prince de Ligne) on his knees, was so affected, that in rising he let the prince fall to the floor. The guests little imagined that the music which accompanied the gay and lively dance at her Grace's ball, would so shortly after play martial airs on the battlefield, or that some of the officers present at the *fête* would be seen fighting in their ball dresses, and, in that costume, found amongst the slain . . .

Another, calling himself a 'Near Observer', describes a scene that Brussels had known before and was to know again in our time:

It was past midnight, and profound repose seemed to reign over Brussels, when suddenly the drums beat to arms, and the trumpet's loud call was heard from every part of the city. It is impossible to describe the effect of these sounds, heard in the silence of the night. We were not long left in doubt of the truth. A second courier had arrived from Blücher: the attack had become serious; the enemy were in considerable force; they had taken Charleroi, and had gained some advantage over the Prussians, and our troops were ordered to march immediately to support them: instantly every place sounded with martial preparations. There was not a house in which military was not quartered, and consequently, the whole town was one universal scene of bustle: the soldiers were seen assembling from all parts in the Place Royale, with their knapsacks on their backs; some taking leave of their wives and children; others sitting unconcernedly on the sharp pavement, waiting for their comrades; others sleeping upon packs of straw, surrounded by all the din of war, while horses and baggage waggons were loading; artillery and commissariat trains harnessing, officers riding in all directions, carts clattering, chargers neighing, bugles sounding, drums beating and colours flying.

A most laughable contrast to this martial scene was presented by a long procession of carts coming quietly in, as usual, from the country to market, filled with old Flemish women, who looked irresistibly comic, seated among their piles of cabbages, baskets of green peas, early potatoes, and strawberries, totally ignorant of the cause of all these warlike preparations, and gazing at the scene around them with many a look of gaping wonder, as they jogged merrily along, one after another, through the Place Royale, amidst the crowds of soldiers, and the confusion of baggage waggons . . .

We must take these observers-on-the-spot as we find them, and not, for example, enquire too closely how lumbering country carts could jog 'merrily along' through a square crammed with troops, horses, guns, baggage waggons. As for the battle itself, it belongs to military history and has been too often described to find a place here. We must return to London and the Prince Regent.

During the alarms of the Hundred Days the Regent knighted Lawrence, the portrait painter, and, we are told, 'assured him that he was proud in conferring a mark of his favour on one who had raised the character of British art in the estimation of all Europe' – which was probably true enough so long as we understand that this 'all Europe' really meant various royal circles. The Regent's patronage of the arts must have been widely recognised by this time, for after Waterloo the Pope offered him the sculpture in the Louvre that Napoleon had filched from Rome. It included the Apollo Belvedere. The Vatican must have lost a great deal more than its sculpture, because apparently it could not afford the expense of transporting all these pieces. The Regent replied that much as he would like to own 'some of these inestimable productions, he could not take advantage of the necessity of their owners'. And then he himself paid for their return to Rome. Later in the year he helped the Royal Academy to obtain casts of Italian sculpture.

Antonio Canova, 1822, engraving by Thomson after John Jackson The British Museum, London

Antonio Canova, Marquis of Ischia, now at the height of his international reputation as a neo-classical sculptor, came to London at last. He was said to be astonished – and now he astonishes us – by the beauty of London's streets, squares, bridges, and by the city's cleanliness and general air of prosperity, all of which suggests that there was a great deal of London, especially on the East side, that he never saw. The Regent received him graciously and presented him with a diamond-studded snuffbox – 'containing besides a gift worthy of the donor', whatever that may mean. Then the Regent gave him various commissions, including a group of Mars and Venus and another representing the Three Graces. We also learn that Canova, 'a man of the utmost simplicity, candour, and independence of mind,' highly praised the fine taste, sound judgment, and extensive information about the arts of his royal English patron – as well he might.

One day behaving like a gigantic spoilt child, the next day a gracious patron of the arts, our Prince really was the oddest fellow. Bearing in mind his boozing and guzzling and gambling, his dressing-up and showing-off and toying with oldish plump mistresses, I for one find it hard to imagine him settling down to enjoy the novels of Jane Austen, but it is a fact that he did. In the late autumn of 1815, her brother Henry was ill in Hans Place and was being nursed by Jane. The doctor in attendance was one of the Regent's physicians, and he told her that the Regent greatly admired her novels and kept a set of them in every one of his residences. Then the Regent's librarian, Stanier Clarke, called to invite Miss Austen to Carlton House as he had been instructed to show her the library, the apartments, and be generally attentive to her. Moreover, she was at liberty now to dedicate a novel to His Royal Highness. So on 11 December Jane wrote to her publisher,

Mr Murray: 'The title page must be EMMA, DEDICATED BY PERMISSION TO H.R.H. THE PRINCE REGENT. And it is my particular wish that one set should be completed and sent to H.R.H. two or three days before the Work is generally public.'

Three months later Stanier Clarke sent a letter to Jane Austen that ought to be immortal for its pompous imbecility. After thanking her on behalf of the Regent 'for the handsome copy you sent him of your last excellent novel', the solemn ass (who might have been created by her) continued: 'Perhaps when you again appear in print you may chuse to dedicate your volumes to Prince Leopold: any historical romance, illustrative of the history of the august House of Coburg, would just now be very interesting.' How Jane must have laughed! 'You are very kind in your hints as to the sort of composition which might recommend me,' she replied, not, I think, without a demure glimmer of irony. 'But I could no more write a romance than an epic poem . . . No, I must keep to my own style and go on in my own way; and though I may never succeed again in that, I am convinced that I should totally fail in any other.' The Regency blazed with beautiful and brilliant women, all manner of charming and witty creatures, but most of us would swap them all for an hour at the tea-table with this rather tall and slender spinster, unfashionably dressed and too often wearing a cap, looking older than her years. But under the cap would be those 'bright hazel eyes', missing nothing.

It was all very well for the Regent to be a gracious and generous patron, commissioning groups of statuary and giving away diamond-studded snuffboxes, but he could not behave as if gold pieces rained on Carlton House and the Brighton Pavilion. So in 1815 he ran into trouble again. And the man who raised the question, in Parliament, of the Regent's expenses was the formidable George Tierney, an extreme Whig, a powerful debater, and an authority on finance. He came from a wealthy mercantile family, and though the aristocratic Whig leaders recognised his ability they tended to mistrust him and keep him out of office because, it was said, 'of the social obscurity of his origin'. Now he pointed out that the furniture for Carlton House alone, in under three years,

Jane Austen, engraving after an original family portrait

George Tierney, 1822, by William
Behnes
marble
26½ in. (67.3 cm.) high
The National Portrait Gallery,
London

had cost the country £260,000. Upholstery expenses for the last year had reached £49,000. The average sum per annum for the Regent's plate and jewels was £23,000. There was an item for ormolu of £29,000, for china and glass £12,000. And Tierney declared it was time some responsible persons took charge of the Regent's household expenses. Even Castlereagh had to admit in Parliament that the Regent's debts, over and above the constantly increasing Civil List allowance, now stood at £339,000.

Because we read about millions and millions every day, we may consider the figures above not very impressive. So we must compare them with some other Regency figures. (They date from the previous two or three years, but they were much the same in 1815.) In all the United Kingdom there were about 250,000 people with more than £700 a year – manufacturers, higher officials, shipbuilders, warehousemen, contractors. There were roughly 500,000 shopkeepers who thought they were doing reasonably well if they made £150 a year. About a million farmers, together with the minor clergy, dissenting ministers, and some lucky schoolmasters, were on the £120 level. Two million artisans and the like earned about £55 per annum, which was the approximate dividing line between a respectable living and poverty. For working very long hours in appalling conditions, the miners received about £40 a year; and there were 1,500,000 agricultural labourers who earned about £30. So a miner, spending nothing on himself, would have to work 725 years to pay for His Royal Highness's ormolu for one year. And, in order to meet the expenses of Carlton House and Pavilion upholstery for one year, an agricultural labourer would have to contribute his total earnings for about 1,633 years. And over six thousand artisans would have to give up their wages for a year to begin paying the Regent's overall debts. No wonder so many people thought our Prince of Pleasure a luxury the country could not afford.

That this bitter attack on the Regent's monstrous expenses and extravagance should come in 1815 is significant. So far as there is a division in the brief span of the Regency, we find it here. Perhaps because Napoleon had vanished at last, because the war that really went back to the French Revolution was over and could be forgotten, because Britain was now free to trade everywhere and industry expanded, this second half of the Regency is different from the first. There is nothing sharp and dramatic about the change; it is something different in the atmosphere. The aristocrats and great landowners were still in control of the country, almost entirely to their own advantage. By 1816 they had abolished income tax. The people were not better off now there was peace; they were in fact worse off, so that popular discontent only broadened and deepened from 1815 onwards. And the new manufacturing men in the

145

Midlands and the North, no longer committed by the Tory land-lords to the Napoleonic war, began to feel restless and demanded better representation in the government of the country. The government remained more or less the same, but it was aware of this change in the atmosphere and became even more obviously repressive and reactionary. It was afraid and no longer had the excuse of being at war. So we are not about to enter five dull years. On the contrary, the highlights will be sharper, the shadows deeper. The country will be at peace with the world but at war with itself. And this is true of society, which will soon know greater scandals than the previous five years of the Regency could offer it.

Even so, I cannot help feeling that the years 1810-1814 come closer to our *idea* of the Regency than the years from 1815 onwards. The dandies, the eccentrics, the mad gamblers, the women-chasing bucks, the great ladies with their lovers and illegitimate children, begin to quit the scene. This change in the atmosphere is unfavourable to the hell-for-leather Regency of popular romance. The first years, though they had their own tone and character, still had something of the eighteenth century lingering in them, whereas from 1815 there is a sense of looking forward, never back at all; the last traces of the eighteenth century seem to have vanished, and we have arrived in the nineteenth century. I may be guilty of some exaggeration here, but I am not without the facts, as we shall see, to support me. Moreover, there is one grand simple reason why the country should show some changes in 1815. For years and years it had been half-strangled by the war, and though the government itself might be anything but progressive, there were many desirable public projects, either ignored or postponed in wartime, that could now be given official support. And a gifted public-spirited figure like Humphry Davy (though it is true he had been knighted in 1812) could now be seen as at least the equal of most admirals and generals.

We have discovered already, in the fourth chapter, that the mining industry was in desperate need of an adequate safety lamp. In 1815 the Society of Coal Owners asked Davy to solve the problem for them, and Davy paid a visit to the Tyne coalfield and then returned to his laboratory to make the necessary experiments. At this very time, George Stephenson, the engineer, was already working on a safety lamp and testing his ideas – often rather hazardously – in the mines themselves. So these two very different men – the rough, badly educated Stephenson, working by trial and error, and the famous Sir Humphry Davy, depending on scientific theory – set out almost simultaneously to solve the same problem, and came up with safety lamps that were not widely dissimilar.

The chief feature of Davy's lamp was a cylinder of wire gauze that absorbed and conducted away the heat of the flame, preventing

Sir Humphry Davy, Bart. (detail)
1822, by Thomas Phillips
oil on canvas
36 × 28 in. (91.5 × 71.2 cm.)
The National Portrait Gallery,
London

the gas outside from exploding. Stephenson, who had noticed that the gas ignited at the base of the flame, believed that if he increased the velocity of the draught of air to the flame, which he did finally by using a number of small holes, the gas would not ignite. Both lamps worked, but whereas Davy's was greeted with great acclaim, both in London and among the mine owners, and he was presented with £2,000 for 'his invention of the safety lamp', poor Stephenson received a casual pat on the back and a mere hundred guineas as a very modest consolation prize. This infuriated Stephenson's friends and supporters on Tyneside, and they gave him a public dinner in Newcastle, an inscribed silver tankard and the balance of the £1,000 that had been raised. And a controversy began that lasted long after both men had died. But in the immediate dispute, reaching its height in 1817, it was the rough Stephenson who preserved a dignified silence and the famous Sir Humphry, awarded a baronetcy next year for his services to industry, who wrote some haughty and foolish letters and received several sharp snubs.

But then, Humphry Davy (1778-1829), considered as a scientist, was an odd fish. Though his discoveries, especially in the relation between chemistry and electricity, were of great service to the nineteenth century, he often seems, as he darts at one problem after another, to be the last and most gifted of the eighteenth-century amateur scientists. In his youth he was extraordinarily brilliant, making original chemical experiments all day and writing verse half the night. Coleridge and Southey, young themselves then, met him in Bristol, became his close friends, and admired him enormously. Southey said of him: '. . . A miraculous young man . . . he is not yet twenty-one, nor has he applied to chemistry more than eighteen months, but he has advanced with such seven-leagued strides as to overtake everybody . . .' Coleridge, when asked how Davy compared with the clever young men in London, declared: 'Why Davy could eat them all . . . Every subject in Davy's mind has the principle of vitality. Living thoughts spring up like turf under his feet.' And to one of his youthful discoveries many of us owe something, for after many experiments he was able to purify nitrous oxide gas so that it could be safely inhaled, as it has been since in innumerable dental surgeries, where, if we are lucky, as I have been twice, it may show us a wonderful metaphysical universe. But it is quite possible that young Davy, doing so much dubious inhaling during his experiments, permanently injured his health.

The newly founded Royal Institution was of immense service to Davy, who at twenty-two was appointed its assistant lecturer in chemistry (promoted next year to chief lecturer and then professor) and also director of its laboratory. His public lectures, which he gave for many years, were a great success, and Davy could be

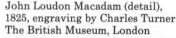

Michael Faraday (detail), 1830,
engraving by Samuel Cousins after
Henry William Pickersgill
The British Museum, London

John Loudon Macadam (detail),
1825, engraving by Charles Turner
The British Museum, London

described as the first – and perhaps the best – popular expositor of science in London. Between his own private researches and experiments he would throw himself enthusiastically into the work demanded by commissions and enquiries that came to him from industry, agriculture, ship-building and so forth. His prestige, both at home and abroad, was enormous. But I feel that the best of him belongs to his glorious youth. In 1812 he made a rather foolish marriage, for his wife, who as a well-to-do widow had been Edinburgh's chief hostess, was too restless and gregarious. His health was bad. Not all of his solutions of the problems submitted to him were acceptable. Always tending to be irritable, he became increasingly touchy. But he never lost his enthusiasm, nor indeed his devotion to writing verse. The value of his experiments I am not competent to assess, but he certainly made one very important contribution when he befriended a bookbinder's apprentice and took him into the Royal Institution. This youth's name was Michael Faraday. Finally, there is one episode in Davy's life we might remember when ready to boast about progress. When Napoleon was First Consul he founded a prize of three thousand francs for the best experiments with galvanic fluid. In 1807 the Institute of France awarded Davy this prize – and France and Britain were officially at war.

It was in 1815, significantly, that both Telford and Macadam were fully engaged in public work. They were alike in being Scots and civil engineers, but not in their backgrounds and circumstances. Thomas Telford, a very remarkable man, began as a self-educated artisan and it was by sheer ability, a capacity for hard work combined with a wealth of ideas, that he became the civil engineer whose services were in demand everywhere, so that he left his impression on roads, canals, bridges, harbours, throughout Britain. He cared little about money – a deputation of engineers once called on him to implore him to put up his charges – but a great deal about serving his country. He was also a very attractive character socially. For over twenty years he had used a certain hotel (he was a bachelor) as his London headquarters. Returning to it to announce he had now a London residence of his own, he found himself facing a new landlord, who was quite indignant with him: 'What – leave the house! Why, sir, I have just paid £750 for you!' Even as a small boy in Dumfriesshire, when he herded cattle to help his widowed mother, he was known to the local farmers as 'Laughing Tam'. He was buried in Westminster Abbey, and a very remarkable amount of perseverance, intelligence, public spirit and cheerfulness was buried with him.

John Loudon Macadam enjoyed a good income, and his experiments in road-making began as a private hobby. He believed that roads, then generally in an appalling condition, could be enormously improved by raising their level and draining them, and by constructing their surface out of thin layers of hard stone broken into very small pieces, not one weighing more than six ounces. Such roads would not be affected by rain, would be durable, and because of the continual pressure of the traffic on them would soon be comparatively smooth. His idea worked, and it was not very long before the verb 'macadamising' became almost a synonym for any improving or modernising process. And it was in 1815 that Macadam was appointed surveyor-general of the Bristol roads and so encouraged to put his theories into practice. The full effect of 'macadamising' throughout the country was not reached until a few years after the Regency, when the last and greatest era of coach services began. But between 1815 and 1820 a lot of people enjoyed much smoother and less hazardous journeys by coach.

Travel in the Regency was no longer as badly organised and slow as it had been. But it still had its dangers, apart from frequent upsets. We think of the highwayman as an eighteenth-century figure, but in fact highway robberies continued well into the Regency, open lonely places not far from London, like Hounslow Heath and Finchley Common, being especially dangerous. The new mail coaches, being faster and carrying a mail guard, were safer than the stage coaches. De Quincey loved the mail coaches and could rhapsodize on this subject, years afterwards:

George IV driving a phaeton, 1830, engraving published by J. Dickenson The Royal Collection, Windsor Castle

The Prince of Pleasure

Seated on the old mail-coach, we needed no evidence out of ourselves to indicate the velocity. The vital experience of the glad animal sensibilities made doubts impossible. We heard our speed, we saw it, we felt it as a thrilling; and this speed was not the product of blind insensate agencies that had no sympathy to give, but was incarnated in their fiery eyeballs of the noblest among brutes, in his dilated nostril, spasmodic muscles, and thunder-beating hoofs . . .

Now that we commonly fly as far in a minute as these coaches travelled in an hour, we seem to have mislaid the eloquence that might celebrate our superiority.

The standard of comfort and performance offered by the mail coaches compelled the grumbling proprietors of ordinary stage coaches to make some improvements: the outside seats were at last made more secure; there was room for parcels and baggage in the 'boots' at the front and rear of the coach; they offered cheaper fares and more comfort; but they did not try to compete with the mail coaches in speed. The extra pace cost too much. The average life of a horse pulling a coach at about eight miles per hour was six

Mail Coach in a Thunder Storm on Newmarket Heath, 1827, engraving after James Holland
The London Museum, London

years; at ten miles per hour or over, possible on good roads, a horse lasted three years. Early in the Regency, the mail from London to Chester took about 28½ hours for the 180 miles. The mail from Shrewsbury to London, via Oxford and Uxbridge, took 23 hours for the 162 miles, but delays were frequent, and, as a contemporary observes, the odds 'were not ten to one that she had not been overturned on the road'.

The fares, by Regency standards fairly stiff, varied with the coaches, with day or night travel, with sitting inside or outside. Fast stage travelling by day, sitting inside, cost about fourpence to fivepence a mile, outside about twopence to threepence. Tips to coachmen, ostlers, etc., usually came to about a quarter of the total fare. In a mail coach each coachman, who usually had a thirty-mile shift, would expect a shilling tip, and the guard, going the whole way, would be given half-a-crown. Both the mail and stage coaches carried only four inside passengers, but while the mail could seat no more than three outside, the stage coaches sometimes had space outside for as many as eleven. A journey by coach was rarely the jolly affair we have seen in illustrations and on Christmas cards. First, there was the danger of accidents: Pitt Lennox wrote, long afterwards: 'I could fill a volume with casualties caused by overturns, violent driving, horses proceeding without drivers, drunken coachmen, overloading, breaking down, and racing.' The outside passengers faced all these, together with all the rain, snow, freezing cold. And the four inside passengers were not much better off, especially in the mail coaches, so small inside, Pitt Lennox recollected, 'that the occupiers appeared trussed like fowls. It was not very pleasant to make one of four, the other three consisting of a stout farmer, rude both in health and manners, a fat nurse with a squalling child, and an elderly invalid who insisted upon having both windows up.' While the larger and often famous old coaching inns were usually good, they were also very expensive; and most of the smaller inns were bad. And often not sufficient time was allowed to sit at ease and enjoy a meal.

Private travel was immensely varied, beginning with the poor, who either walked or rode in stage wagons, which might have four to eight horses, in the charge of a carter, but moved no faster than a healthy pedestrian. When we leave the poor for the respectable and the gentry, we find a great deal of snobbery and status nonsense hard at work in private travel. William Howitt wrote:

How the man who drives his close carriage looks down upon him who only drives his barouche or phaeton; how both contemn the poor occupier of a gig. I have heard of a gentleman of large fortune who, for some years after his residence in a particular neighbourhood, did not set up his close carriage, but afterwards feeling it more agreeable to do so, was astonished to find himself called upon by a host of carriage-keeping people, who did not seem previously aware of his existence; and rightly deeming the calls to be made upon his carriage, rather than himself, sent round his empty carriage to deliver cards in return.

The taxation of private carriages was quite severe, though, like many Regency arrangements, it hurt men of moderate means rather than the rich and the great. In 1814 the tax on two-wheeled carriages was £17, on four-wheeled £21. The owner of one horse had to pay £5 tax, of two £8 tax, of three £9. So a man who owned a two-wheeled carriage and three horses would be paying £30 a year in tax. To this must be added the initial cost and upkeep of the horses and carriage, and the wages of a coachman, possibly a footman, both of them servants who generally wore quite expensive uniforms. As for the stage (as distinct from the mail) coachmen, they were usually spoilt fellows, often of enormous bulk and neither quite drunk nor quite sober but 'muzzy' from too many tankards of strong ale at the wayside inns. Dickens's account of the elder Weller and his friends in *Pickwick* is probably not inaccurate.

Strictly private travel, covering several hundred miles and taking a family and two or three servants, could be appallingly expensive, and whenever somebody like Walter Scott travelled in this style from Edinburgh to London, it must have cost him – in our money, not his – about a thousand pounds. Foreign travel in your own vehicles, though you would probably take fewer people and might not spend so much along the road on accommodation, food and drink, could present you with some formidable bills. Sea passages – say, from Plymouth to Genoa or Naples – might be much cheaper, but as the sailing ships were largely at the mercy of the winds, there could easily be some intolerable delays, sometimes lasting weeks. Small and very slow paddlewheel steamers appeared during the Regency, but they were not taking passengers to Mediterranean ports. When we consider the expense of travel and its discomforts, sometimes turning into downright hardships, after reading the memoirs of the period we can only wonder at the amount of travel there was.

Just before 1815 arrived – to be exact, on 29 November 1814 – *The Times* carried the following announcement:

> Our journal of this day presents to the public the practical result of the greatest improvement connected with printing since the discovery of the art itself. The reader of this paragraph now holds in his hand one of the many thousand impressions which were taken off last night by a mechanical apparatus. A system of machinery, almost organic, has been devised and arranged, which while it relieves the human frame of its most laborious efforts in printing, far exceeds all human powers in rapidity and despatch . . .

PLATE XXIII. Stage Coach Setting Off (detail), 1816, engraving published by Robert Pollard, Holloway
12½ × 17½ in. (31.8 × 44.5 cm.)
The London Museum, London

with much more to the same effect, glorifying this wonderful new

William Hone (detail), by George Patten
oil on canvas
29¼ × 24½ in.
(74.3 × 62.2 cm.)
The National Portrait Gallery, London

machine. And indeed *The Times* could now go to press later and publish earlier than its rivals, while the whole process was more economic. The credit for this innovation must go to the John Walter who in 1812 took over the newspaper from his father. He entered into negotiations almost at once with Frederick Koenig, whose steam printing press, first patented in 1810, was being further developed and improved. By 1814, Koenig and his friend Bauer had been given premises next to the office of *The Times*, and there they set up their machinery. This was supposed to be done in great secrecy, but news of it must have leaked out because we are told there was so much opposition from *The Times's* workmen that one week Koenig and Bauer had to go into hiding for three days.

John Walter had an anxious day and night when the printing machine was first used. His printers were suspicious; they had already threatened destruction to any invention that might cut down their employment; so Walter told them there was a delay because he was expecting important news from the Continent. Then about 6 a.m. he went into the pressroom with the astounding news that the paper had already been printed – by steam. He added that he had made arrangements to suppress any attempt at violence by force, and that if they behaved sensibly their wages would be continued until they had found similar employment. By this adroit move he put *The Times* well out in front. During the next seven years its circulation more than doubled, probably reaching a figure of about 10,000.

By 1815 there were 250 or so newspapers in the United Kingdom, though most of them were limited to their own locality. But also in 1815 the stamp duties imposed on the press were raised to fourpence a copy, so that the price of respectable law-abiding newspapers went up to sevenpence. This had some effect on sales, but on the other hand there was soon much better distribution and an increasing revenue from advertisements. These stamp duties were regarded by the radicals – and they were quite right – as part of a Tory government plot to keep dangerous news and hostile propaganda well away from the mass of the people, who could only afford cheap newspapers. The inevitable result was a kind of large 'black market' press, risking evasion of the stamp duties and almost always violently radical, like Cobbett's *Political Register* or Thomas Jonathan Wooler's *Black Dwarf*. William Hone's satires moved briskly in this underworld of unstamped newspapers, odd sheets and pamphlets, and he is supposed to have sold about 100,000 copies of his parody of the Anglican Liturgy.

No doubt a great deal of what was published on this level, intended for the common people, was extremely virulent and often grossly libellous, and there were many prosecutions and prison sentences. (The Regent himself was the favourite target.) But all

PLATE XXIV. Exhibition Stare Case, 1811 (?), coloured engraving by Thomas Rowlandson
15⅛ × 10⅜ in. (38.4 × 26.2 cm.)
The British Museum, London

these Tory tactics were shortsighted and stupid. They could turn some men of poor ability and dubious character into martyrs in the cause of free speech. And by forcing up the price of newspapers and so cutting off the mass of readers, making it almost impossible to bring out respectable and accepted radical papers, they helped to create a disreputable press, depending often on the sheer virulence of its language. So the gulf between the government and its people was widened. As a Victorian chronicler of the press observed: 'Much appeared in the journalism of those times which no lady of delicate mind would read aloud, and which no gentleman, however gay he might be, would dare to read in the hearing of a lady.' Incidentally, as early as 1811 London had eight morning and eight evening papers. Two or three were short-lived and a few others represented special interests – commerce, auctioneering, the wine-and-spirits trade – but even so, sixteen remains an impressive total for one city.

On 1 June, this year, James Gillray died. If this great caricaturist had been still working, it would have been as if the army of the radicals had at one blow lost all its heavy artillery. But by the end of 1811, though still only in his middle fifties, he was already half out of his mind, the victim of hard drinking and the terrific pressure of work that drove him to the bottle. Nevertheless, he is so strongly associated with the Regency that he cannot be ignored. He was a withdrawn, silent and lonely man, greatly slandered in his lifetime probably by his victims and their friends. He worked in such a fury of creative energy that even his acquaintances, years before his breakdown, wondered if he might be part-demented. He was so popular that there were often queues at the print shop, above which he worked, waiting for his latest cartoons and caricatures. At once the most ferocious and most brilliant caricaturist of his time, Gillray had a genius for turning public figures into monsters that were yet recognisable, his wild exaggeration being itself a criticism of their personalities. To this must be added a wealth of comic ideas, political and social, though he was never at his best except as a caricaturist, the most savage and fearless London has ever known.

Both as an artist and as a man, Thomas Rowlandson was very different from Gillray. He came from the comfortable middle class, had some art training in Paris in addition to the time he spent at the Royal Academy school, and he began as a painter of serious subjects and portraits. But even after inheriting money, he lived so carelessly and lost so much at the gaming tables that he ran into debt. He had to work his way out of it by turning to caricature, satirical cartoons, and illustrations of writers like Smollett, Goldsmith, Sterne. During most of the Regency he was chiefly busy illustrating the popular *Dr Syntax* series, written by William

(opposite) The Universal Advertising Sheet (detail) in *La Belle Assemblée* for 1 November 1811
The Victoria and Albert Museum, London

157

Sea Side Bathing Dress invented by
Mrs Bell from *La Belle Assemblée,*
1 August 1815
Collection Mrs Doris Langley Moore,
London

Combe. Rowlandson had nothing of Gillray's genius for caricature,
and his topical drawings were broadly satirical social comments.
But his range – in subject matter, not treatment – was unusually
wide, and he brought to it, almost always using a reed pen and
adding charming washes of colour, the rhythmic line and delicate
sense of colour and space of a fine artist. His crowds, his absurd
men, his plump women showing their legs, may suggest coarseness,
but there is nothing coarse about his pen-and-wash technique.
And I for one have long had an affection for Rowlandson even in
his capacity as a social satirist. There is in him a healthy, zestful,
rollicking *fatness*, a rich amplitude of physical life, that has made
me long at times to have been one of his contemporaries.

I cannot say that about the third and youngest of the Regency
caricaturists, cartoonists and illustrators, George Cruikshank,
who was coming up just when Gillray was going down – and they
actually worked together for a short time. He too brought crowds
to the printshop windows, and, later, both Ruskin and Thackeray
were among his enthusiastic admirers. Cruikshank's work lacks
Gillray's tremendous force and Rowlandson's charm and eupeptic
quality, and there is to me something fundamentally unattractive,
rather *mean*, about his wiry line, heavy shading, and standardised
faces. He is most successful, I feel, when he is being determinedly
sinister – as in some of his illustrations, much later, to *Oliver Twist*.
He was already successful by 1815, while only in his early twenties,
and he lived until 1878, after about fifty years of aggressive tee-
totalism. I refuse to accept him as a Regency character, even
though it was his cartoons that were the most effective during its
later years.

The Napoleonic Era – a British
comment on the situation in Europe.
Napoleon is shown as Belshazzar
when the prophecy of his downfall
was on the wall, 1803, by James
Gillray

1816

The Byron Scandal

While the Regent longed for popularity and was distressed by his obvious lack of it, there was some perverse element in his nature that encouraged him to make more and more unpopular moves. Having had his debts and extravagant domestic expenditure brought to light in Parliament and then sharply denounced the previous year, if he had been a reasonable man he would have laid low and kept quiet in this year, 1816, especially as there was much distress throughout the country. But an imp of perversity was at work on him. So it was announced in Parliament that he was going to erect in Rome a monument, designed by Canova, in memory of the exiled Stuarts. At once the Whig members boiled over in their wrath. What infuriated them was not the expense of the monument – it was to be paid for by the surplus of the French Government's contribution to the cost of removing the looted statues from Paris to Rome – but its celebration of the Stuarts, a family that might seem glamorous to Highland Tories and Walter Scott but did not inspire any nostalgic affection among English Whigs. The most vociferous and tireless of them, Brougham, in his huge harsh voice, declared: 'Much better would it be instead of doing honour to that Family to profit by its example, to recollect that by thwarting the prejudices, opposing the wishes and pressing on the sore places of this nation, they were at length ousted from the throne . . .' And he went on to suggest at length – Brougham was given to length – that what had gone on under the Stuarts was comparatively harmless and innocent when compared with what was happening now – the utter disregard of an oppressed and insulted nation, one wasteful expenditure after another, a royal association with the most profligate of human beings – with much more to that effect, sadly unwelcome in Carlton House or the Brighton Pavilion.

However, the imp, still hard at work, decided that the Regent should now have a kind of love affair with the Stuart family. It appears to have lasted the rest of his life, for near the end of it he asked Scott to preside over a new commission to examine and edit Stuart papers. Meanwhile, long before this, he had acquired a mass of Stuart papers from the executor of the Countess of Albany, and various Stuart documents from Italy; he had sponsored the publication of a new biography of James II; he had given permission to

Monument to the Exiled Stuarts,
c. 1819, by Antonio Canova
marble
St Peter's, Rome

open an unidentified coffin found in St George's Chapel, Windsor, because it might be the secretly-buried coffin of Charles I, and indeed it was. Among his new treasures were now Van Dyck's triple portrait of Charles I, the sword Charles had left at Wistow on his way to the battle of Naseby, and the collar of the Garter worn by James II. Characteristically he offered a pension to Bonnie Prince Charlie's heroine, Flora MacDonald, and characteristically he forgot to give it to her.

It was as if at any moment he might announce his belief in the Divine Right of Kings. However, there is another explanation that appeals to me. He could not help identifying himself with the Stuarts, though probably unconsciously, not because he wanted to break the bonds of constitutional monarchy, to undo the Revolution of 1688, for unlike his father he was not in fact politically-minded, but because he was intensely and wretchedly aware of his own increasing unpopularity. He was fascinated by the Stuarts – those ultra-romantic glamorous figures – because they had in the end lost everything except a legend. And as he stared at the sword of Charles I and fingered the Garter-collar worn by James II, he may have wondered what might happen in the end to him.

If this seems fantastic it is largely because we are now a hundred and eighty years away from the French Revolution, whereas the Regent and Lord Liverpool's government in 1816 were only twenty-seven years away from it. Many a country squire and magistrate could imagine his stables on fire and a mob shouting outside his bedroom windows. Even these men knew the times were bad; harvests had been poor; and so many small manufacturers, with no more war contracts, had been dismissing their workmen. This vague but disturbing fear of sudden violent revolution was still there on the deepest level. On another level, belonging to the daylight, was the fear of Parliamentary reform, threatening the whole Tory supremacy. This left Lord Liverpool and his Home Secretary, Lord Sidmouth, in a very tricky situation. How far could they secretly encourage revolutionary talk and rioting without setting the whole country alight? They had two good reasons for thinking it worth trying. If the more extreme radicals, often far from sober, threatened a revolution, the more moderate radicals and the responsible Whigs would withdraw from any alliance with them, thus weakening the whole movement for reform. Secondly, the wilder the talk and the meetings, the noisier and rougher the marches were, the easier it was, with a middle class beginning to feel alarm, to hurry through all manner of repressive measures, behaving like a totalitarian state. This largely explains why even a modest Reform Bill – the least that most liberal-minded men had been asking for and far less than what the extreme radicals were demanding – would in 1816 take another sixteen years.

But how was this tricky game to be played and won? (Not only then, but for many years afterwards.) The government had two high trump cards up its sleeve. The first was the employment of spies among the extremists who also acted as *agents provocateurs*. These fellows, scum to a man but often adroit, wormed their way into the councils of the fiery radicals, paid for another round of drinks and then proposed the most daring toasts, shouted for a march here, a gigantic meeting there, denounced the cautious as being half-hearted, and whenever the temperature was falling would promptly heat it up again. The second device of the government was to treat any really large meeting, where the crowds gathered to hear their favourite speakers and pass a heady resolution or two, as if it were actually a menacing mobilisation of rioters, who had to be confronted by a small army of police or even the military themselves. This encouraged scuffles, which could be gravely reported by the government's own press, while at the same time it easily prevented any real outbreak. It was an artful stratagem but dangerous, ending sooner or later in a catastrophe – as, in 1819, it did.

The Spa-fields Orator – Hunting for Popularity to Do-Good!, 1817 – incident 1816, by George Cruikshank The British Museum, London

What 1816 saw, in its last months, were three confused affairs, never reliably reported or explained, known as the Spa Fields riots. The extreme radical movement was now widespread and very active, but it consisted of a number of 'Clubs' and local groups and had no national organisation and no centre. It was inspired largely by Cobbett's thundering articles and by the visits of fiery demagogues of whom the most important was 'Orator' Hunt, a vain and extravagant man with a magnetic influence on any large crowd. Far more extreme than Cobbett or Hunt was a comparatively small group of men who saw themselves as real revolutionaries, English Jacobins. They formed a committee and among its members were a Dr Watson and his son and one John Castle. It was common knowledge in 1816 that not only was there great distress in the provinces, but that conditions now in London were no better. The city was crowded with demobilised soldiers and sailors; East End districts like Spitalfields had tens of thousands of half-starved unemployed; the workhouses and debtors' prisons were crammed full. So the committee of neo-Jacobins helped to organise a great radical demonstration at Spa Fields in London, the more desperate of them hoping for a mass rising. Well-known radicals were asked to be there on 15 November, but most of them (including Cobbett) stayed away, and it was only at the last minute that Hunt agreed to speak. He did this very successfully, ranting away to a huge crowd, far larger than had been expected, from a window overlooking the fields.

It was decided to hold another meeting-cum-demonstration on 2 December. Hunt described later how the triumphant extremists, far more revolutionary than he was, gave him dinner, at which the committee-member called Castle, the wildest Jacobin there, proposed the toast 'May the last of kings be strangled with the guts of the last priest.' Within a few days a revolutionary 'committee of trades' was set up in London, and there was wild talk of attacking the Bank, the Tower, and the prisons. A man named Thomas got himself elected Chairman of this committee, in which Castle, strangler of kings, was soon very active, and it was Castle who put a few weapons in a cart that went to Spa Fields on 2 December. I bring out these details to prove a point I made earlier. Both Castle, the fieriest enthusiast, and Thomas, Chairman of the London committee, were government spies acting as *agents provocateurs*. They were on the spot – and there must have been others like them in the provinces – to urge these innocent blusterers to threaten and to riot, and then to inform the authorities of any plans that may have been made.

On 2 December the younger Watson, who is said to have been drinking hard, ran a sideshow of his own, making an inflammatory speech from a cart to the wilder and less sober element in the crowd.

PLATE XXV. Miss Mary and her loving Cousin; or single Gloucester preferred to German sausage, 1816, by George Cruikshank – allusion to the wedding of Mary, the Regent's sister, to the Duke of Gloucester The British Museum, London

Principal Characters in the Grand Melo-drama

of the

BROKEN SWORD

as Performed at the Theatre Royal Covent Garden

in 2 Plates   Plate 1.st

Estevan   Stella   Pablo

London Published 4 Nov 1816 by W West Exeter House Exeter Strat Strand

Myrtillo   Rosara   The Baron

Then he led some hundreds of them into the City, where they split up and looted some shops. But any idea of storming important buildings had to be abandoned, the government having taken elaborate precautions to protect them. The actual damage that was done was probably just enough to frighten respectable citizens and give the government its case. Cobbett understood these tactics when he wrote in this same December: 'They (the authorities) sigh for a PLOT. Oh, how they sigh! They are working and slaving and fretting and stewing; they are sweating all over; they are absolutely pining and dying for a plot!'

There was a third and even larger Spa Fields meeting before the end of the year, but now young Watson had gone into hiding (to be smuggled to America later) and many of his rioters were under arrest, so the affair was less eventful. The extreme radicals won no victory at Spa Fields, which left them more disorganised and confused than ever. On the other hand, the government with the help of its spies and *agents provocateurs* had split the broad radical movement, by making sure that the wild men alienated the moderates, and now they had a fine excuse for adopting the most repressive measures. This method, planting men in a peaceful movement to make it seem disorderly and dangerous, did not begin or end with the Regency: years later it was used successfully to discredit the Chartists. And I would not care to bet that something like it was never used in Britain during political and industrial disputes in the 1920s and 1930s.

In July of 1816 Richard Brinsley Sheridan died, and was buried with great pomp in Westminster Abbey. It was time for him to die, for his astonishing career had already come to an end. He had quarrelled with his old boon companion, the Regent; he was no longer one of the Whig leaders; he could spend money but not earn any; and all too often he was rolling drunk. Even the Regency, a gallery of odd characters, cannot show us anybody more extraordinary than Sheridan. While only in his twenties he had written the two best comedies of the age, *The Rivals* and *The School for Scandal* – and a third, *The Critic*, which has been fairly often revived and is still extremely funny. Yet apart from one indifferent melodrama, *Pizarro*, he never wrote for the stage again. While still in his thirties, at the impeachment of Warren Hastings he made one of the greatest orations of his or any other time, and he continued to be one of the most brilliant, admired, rewarding speakers in the House of Commons. Yet for all his prominence and genuine devotion to Whig party politics, he never achieved more than a few minor offices. He was renowned for being incorruptible in his public life while at the same time he could be reckless, dissolute and rather unscrupulous in his private life. There is a good entry in Tom Moore's diary on this subject:

PLATE XXVI. Toy Theatre characters for *The Broken Sword* by W. Dimond as performed at the Theatre Royal, Covent Garden, published 4 November 1816 by W. West
The Victoria and Albert Museum, London

The Prince of Pleasure

Richard Brinsley Sheridan, 1788,
by John Russell
pastel
23½ × 17½ in. (59.7 × 44.4 cm.)
The National Portrait Gallery,
London

Had a good deal of conversation with Lord Holland in the evening
about Sheridan. Told me that one remarkable characteristic of S., and
which accounted for many of his inconsistencies, was the high, ideal
system he had formed of a sort of impracticable perfection in honour,
virtue etc., anything short of which he seemed to think not worth
aiming at; and thus consoled himself for the extreme laxity of his practice by the impossibility of satisfying or coming up to the sublime theory
he had formed. Hence the most romantic professions of honour and
independence were coupled with conduct of the meanest and most
swindling kind; hence, too, prudery and morality were always on his
lips, while his actions were one series of debauchery and libertinism . . .

There is something in this, but it does not completely account for
Sheridan's extraordinary career.

His early success, unequalled in the history of English drama,
was really his undoing. Vain, rather lazy, unsure of himself, he
stopped writing because his fear of failure was far greater than
any urge he might have to write. His younger self was his successful
rival. Again, this early success gave him the management of Drury
Lane Theatre, which he subsequently owned. He understood the
theatrical part of it, but he was never a man of business and was
always in trouble. In 1791 Drury Lane had to be rebuilt; then in
1809 it was completely gutted by fire. We are told that an acquaintance found Sheridan outside a neighbouring tavern, a drink in his
hand, staring at the blazing theatre, and said he was surprised to

Captain Manby's invention, 1816
The Fire Protection Association,
London

see Sheridan there. 'Why?' said Sheridan, 'Can't a man take a glass of wine at his own fireside?' This seems to me heroic wit.

It may be objected that we cannot call a man lazy if he managed a great theatre and was at the same time a leading politician. But unless a man held high office – and Sheridan never did – political life was fairly easy-going then. It was pleasanter drinking with Whig cronies and talking to a few playwrights (Sheridan disliked actors) than sitting alone with pen and paper. Sheridan could take trouble when he had to prepare a speech for a great occasion: 'His habit,' wrote Dr Tierney, 'was on these emergencies to rise at four in the morning, to light up a prodigious quantity of candles around him, and eat toasted muffins while he worked.' He gave a clue to his own character in some observations he made to Lord Holland: 'They talk of avarice, lust, ambition, as great passions. It is a mistake; they are little passions. Vanity is the great commanding passion of all. It is this that produces the grand and heroic deeds, or impels to the most dreadful crimes. Save me but from this passion, and I can defy the others. They are mere urchins, but this is a giant.' Like many other writers, he was a bad judge of his own work. He thought so much of *The School for Scandal* that he delayed publication of it for nineteen years, in the hope of polishing it to perfection. On the other hand, he always said *The Rivals* was one of the worst plays in the language, and he would have given anything not to have written it. I believe that now most critics and playgoers would agree with me – and I cannot recall how many times I have seen both these plays – that *The Rivals* is the better of the two, its bubbling fresh humour outlasting the rather forced wit and elaborate contrivances of *The School for Scandal*.

Sheridan's two comedies first appeared in the 1770s, and so did Goldsmith's *She Stoops to Conquer*. It is a remarkable fact that for over a century these three were the only plays written in English to have unfailingly held the stage, to be revived over and over again. It is not that able writers turned away from the Theatre. Indeed, throughout the nineteenth century, the greatest of the poets, from Coleridge, Byron, Shelley in its earlier years, to Tennyson, Browning, Swinburne and then on to Yeats, all wrote plays. But not one of them really succeeded on the stage; they were great poets but indifferent dramatists – unlike Shakespeare, a great poet *and* a great dramatist. However, in the Regency the writers, fashionable society, and the people in general, were all intensely aware of the Theatre. The lectures and critical essays of Coleridge and Hazlitt brought a new depth to the appreciation of Shakespeare and the best of the older poetic dramatists. The popular feeling for the Theatre was in fact far greater than it is today. In the provinces there were so many playhouses of a sort – many of them very small and uncomfortable – that various regions like the North-West or

(opposite) The Drury Lane Theatre
taken from Westminster Bridge
during the Conflagration on the night
of 24 February 1809, engraving
published by Robert Wilkinson 1811
The Fire Protection Association,
London

East Anglia would have their own 'circuits' able to keep actors employed for months. Edmund Kean, years before he conquered London, learnt how to dominate audiencies in towns that have never seen a theatre in our own time.

The two great London theatres were Drury Lane and Covent Garden. They were the only two licensed as proper playhouses. The other metropolitan theatres were officially mere places of entertainment, in which there had to be a certain amount of singing and dancing, no matter how anxious the manager (a fine actor like Elliston, for example) might be to produce straight plays. This limitation did much harm, though it also encouraged the production of ballad-operas, a characteristic English form, at its best in

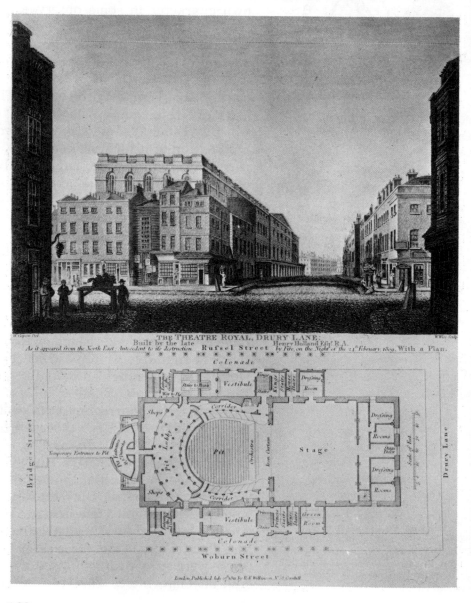

The Theatre Royal, Drury Lane, built by Henry Holland before its destruction by fire in 1809, published by Robert Wilkinson 27 July, 1811
The Victoria and Albert Museum, London

The Publick are respectfully informed that the

THEATRE ROYAL, DRURY LANE,
WILL OPEN
This present SATURDAY, OCTOBER, 10, 1812,
WITH AN OCCASIONAL ADDRESS,
To be spoken by Mr. ELLISTON.

In order to prevent disappointments, the publick are respectfully informed, that every seat in the Boxes has been taken for some days past, for this Evening.

After which their Majesties Servants will act Shakspeares Tragedy of

HAMLET,
PRINCE OF DENMARK.

Claudius, King of Denmark, Mr. POWELL,
Hamlet, Mr. ELLISTON,
Polonius, Mr. DOWTON,
Laertes, Mr. WALLACK, Horatio, Mr. HOLLAND,
Rosencrantz, Mr. CROOKE, Guildenstern, Mr. FISHER, Osrick, Mr. PALMER,
Marcellus, Mr. MILLER, Bernardo, Mr RAY, Francisco, Mr. EVANS,
Priest, Mr. CARR, First Actor, Mr. MADDOCKS, Second Actor, Mr. W. WEST,
First Grave-digger, Mr. WEWITZER, Second Grave-digger, Mr. PENLEY,
First Sailor, Mr. CHATTERLEY, Second Sailor, Mr. WEST,
Ghost of Hamlet's Father, Mr. RAYMOND.
Gertrude, Queen of Denmark, Mrs. BRERETON,
Ophelia, Miss KELLY,
Actress, Miss TIDSWELL.

The Scenery designed and painted by Mr. GREENWOOD, Mr. MARINARI. Mr. DIXON,
Mr. LATILLA, Mr. DEMARIA, Mr. GENTA, Mr. SMITH, and by Mr. CAPON, and
their assistants. The Dresses by Mr. BANKS and Miss REIN, and their assistants.
The Machinery by Messrs. UNDERWOOD, DRORY, &c.
The Decorations by Mr. MORRIS, Miss ROBINSON, &c. &c.
Leader of the Band, Mr. SMART.

After the Tragedy will be performed a musical Farce, called the

DEVIL TO PAY;
OR, THE WIVES METAMORPHOSED.

Sir John Loverule, Mr. J. SMITH,
Butler, Mr. MILLER, Doctor, Mr. MADDOCKS,
Cook, Mr. SPARKS, Coachman, Mr. WEST, Footman, Mr. EVANS,
Jobson, Mr. DOWTON.
Lady Loverule, Mrs. HARLOWE,
Lettice, Miss TIDSWELL, Lucy, Mrs. CHATTERLEY,
Nell, Miss MELLON.

The Doors to be opened at Half past Five o'Clock, to begin at Half past Six.
Boxes Seven Shillings—*Second Price,* Three Shillings and Sixpence.
Pit, Three Shillings and Sixpence—*Second Price,* Two Shillings.
Lower Gallery, Two Shillings—*Second Price,* One Shilling.
Upper Gallery One Shilling—*Second Price,* Sixpence.

Boxes and Places to be taken of Mr. SPRING, Box Book-keeper,
at the Office in Little Russell Street, from Ten till Four,
and from Ten in the Evening until the Doors are closed.

The Box Entrances are in Brydges Street *only.*
The Pit Entrances are in Russell Street and Woburn Street.
The Lower Gallery Entrances are in Russell Street and Woburn Street.
The Upper Gallery Entrance is in Woburn Street *only.*

All Persons claiming Right of Free Admission to the Theatre, having complied with
the Notice given by publick Advertisement, to sign their Names in the book kept by the
Secretary to the Committee, at the Treasury Office in Drury Lane, and having made good
their Title of such Free Admission three days at the least, previous to the exercise of such
Right, will be admitted Free to the Theatre on all nights of Theatrical Representation or
Musical Performance, under the following Regulations and Conditions.

Every Person claiming to be admitted Free, will be required to sign his or her Name at
the Door, in a Book which will be kept ready for that purpose, and will not be admitted
without such signature.

The right hand door, leading from the hall in Brydges Street, will be opened for Free
Admissions to the Boxes, and confined to them *only,* and no Free Admissions will be pass'd
at any other Box Door of the Theatre: Neither will any person, *not* Free, be admitted to
pass through the Free Door.

Free Admissions to the Pit and Galleries will be received at their respective Doors in
Woburn Street *only.*

The very great frauds which have heretofore been committed upon the Proprietors and
the Publick, respecting Free Admission, have made it necessary for the Sub-Committee
to devise the most effectual Controul in a matter so important to the Interests of the
Company; whose affairs they are called upon to administer, and to those who are really
entitled to the Freedom of Admission. For the present, therefore, they have deemed it
expedient to exact, under the authority of the Act of Parliament, the Conditions above
stated for the prevention of Frauds, which will be strictly enforced.

Stage Manager, Mr. RAYMOND.——*Vivant Rex et Regina.*

Lowndes & Hobbs, Printers, Marquis Court, Drury Lane, London.

Playbill on the occasion of the re-opening of the Theatre Royal, Drury Lane, 10 October 1812
The Victoria and Albert Museum, London

Elevation of the front of the Royal Coburg Theatre (Old Vic) . . . designed by I. T. Serres . . . 1811 The Victoria and Albert Museum, London

the immortal *Beggar's Opera* of nearly a hundred years earlier. Nearly all these theatres – the Surrey, the Royalty, the Strand, the Olympic, the Regency – suffered from frequent changes of management and policies and from various disasters, especially fire. (When the Greater London Council insists today on having even a bunch of artificial flowers on the stage thoroughly fireproofed, it is probably remembering all the theatres that went up in flames from the Regency onwards.)

170

The most interesting of the new theatres in the Regency was the Coburg. It was largely constructed out of the remaining stones of John of Gaunt's old palace of Savoy. The first stone was laid by Alderman Goodbehere for Princess Charlotte's husband, Prince Leopold of Saxe-Coburg, in September 1816; and it opened in May 1818 with a mixed programme – *a new melodramatic spectacle entitled Trial By Battle,* and a *Grand Asiatic Ballet called Alzora and Nerine,* and a *Splendid Harlequinade called Midnight Revelry.* It was immediately popular, as well it might be with such varied delights; but it gradually changed the character of its productions, and finally it changed its name too, opening in July 1833 as the Victoria. Nor was this the end of its history, for there came a time when it was known as the Old Vic – and out of neglect and almost ruin it rose again, to give this century some of the finest Shakespearian players in the world.

There were many connoisseurs of acting among Regency audiences – and superb critics of it such as Coleridge, Hazlitt, Lamb, Leigh Hunt – but they were out of luck in its earlier years. The older members of the famous Kemble family, the stately John and his equally stately sister Sarah, Mrs Siddons, had almost retired and made only occasional appearances, and the theatrical scene began to look rather dull. Then in 1814 Edmund Kean arrived like a fiery meteor. He could only succeed in a very narrow range of parts; he was no Romeo, no Hamlet; he had to be Shylock, Richard III, Iago, Macbeth, the mad miser Sir Giles Overreach; he was small, had a harsh voice, and was as wild off the stage as he was on it; and not everybody appreciated him. Mary Russell Mitford wrote: 'Well, I went to see Mr Kean, and was thoroughly disgusted. This monarch of the stage is a little insignificant man, slightly deformed, strongly ungraceful, seldom pleasing the eye, still seldomer pleasing the ear...' But he excited Hazlitt, terrified Byron, and made Coleridge declare that 'to see Kean act is like reading Shakespeare by flashes of lightning.' Clearly he was one of those actors – and they are very rare indeed – who over and above all technique have a kind of demoniac mastery of an audience (all except the Miss Mitfords), their complete involvement with a part releasing a tremendous force. He made successful appearances, in New York as well as in London, for some years after the Regency had ended, gradually destroying himself by hard drinking; but it was those early performances at Drury Lane, between 1814 and 1820, that fully revealed his astonishing power. Edmund Kean, we may say, was yet another Regency character.

Whilst working on this chapter, I have just read the following paragraph in today's paper:

The Westminster Abbey authorities have given permission for a Byron memorial to be erected in Poets' Corner – 144 years after authority was refused to bury Lord Byron's body in the Abbey. The announcement was made at the Poetry Society's annual luncheon in London yesterday. The Abbey turned down three previous attempts to erect a memorial – two in the nineteenth century and one in 1924.

The extraordinary coincidence here – Jung would have called it an example of his 'synchronicity' – is that I was about to explain the very events that were largely responsible for this refusal to allow a Byron memorial. I had already called this chapter on 1816 'The Byron Scandal'.

The break-up of Byron's marriage and the accusations and recriminations that followed it well deserve more space than I can give them here. Thousands and thousands of printed pages have been devoted to them. And while Byron and his wife, at first, innocently assumed that their domestic affairs were 'confidential', even 'strictly secret', they were already beginning to play their tragi-comedy in full limelight. It was not simply that they provided endless tittle-tattle, with much whispering of terrible rumours, to members of their own high society, a comparatively small society always entertaining or being entertained and always in need of an exciting topic. There was also the more unscrupulous section of the London press, which reported gossip and so spread it among various classes of readers. And at this time Byron's appeal and reputation as a poet were greater than ever. Indifferent narrative poems like *The Corsair*, knocked off during a few all-night sittings with a brandy bottle, were selling ten thousand copies on the day of publication. He was 'news', as we say now. And so appalling was the scandal, the horrified whispers turning into a roar of condemnation, that on 25 April 1816 he left England and never came back, producing his best work in exile. The man generally considered to be the country's greatest living poet (though he was not) could no longer stay in it, with consequences, as we shall see, of both literary and social importance.

The story of his engagement, marriage and separation from his wife has been told over and over again, but it was not until quite recently that Mr Malcolm Elwin, a very thorough and sensible biographer, writing his *Lord Byron's Wife* (published in 1962) was allowed to make use of the Lovelace Papers. This was an enormous collection of family letters and documents assembled by the second Earl of Lovelace, who was Byron's grandson. No previous biographer of Byron or his wife had had access to this collection. Byron's own memoirs – alas – were burnt by Hobhouse, his executor, and Murray, his publisher.

Curious readers should examine *Lord Byron's Wife* for themselves. I have gone through it carefully – it is a very substantial

PLATE XXVII. George Gordon Byron, 6th Baron Byron, by Thomas Phillips
oil on canvas
29½ × 24½ in. (74.9 × 62.2 cm.)
The National Portrait Gallery, London

volume – and I am greatly indebted to it, but in re-telling the story, and condemned to brevity, while I may take my evidence from Mr Elwin, I shall offer judgments and opinions that are mine and not his. We must remember this – that Byron died in 1824 whereas his widow, forever justifying herself, lived until 1860, and this tends to make Byron scholars, as distinct from ordinary readers, severely critical of her, even in her youth as a bride, and rather lenient with his lordship. And though scrupulous in his use of evidence, Mr Elwin does not seem to me entirely free from this bias.

When we left Byron in 1812 he had already proposed in a rather offhand fashion to Annabella Milbanke and had been refused. He was still not free of the wild attentions of Lady Caroline Lamb, and fled from her to enjoy an affair in the country with the forty-year-old but enticing Lady Oxford, who was everything that Caroline was not. He spent little time thinking about Annabella Milbanke, but even so her refusal of him wounded his vanity. Moreover, she was an heiress and he was beginning to be short of money; and she was the niece of his close friend, Lady Melbourne, who was advising him to marry, if only as an escape from entanglements with infatuated married women. A shrewd woman, Lady Melbourne may have guessed that while Byron often liked to pose as a ruthless predatory male, there was a curiously passive element in his relations with women. He tended to give in rather than to pursue and pounce. He could easily become the victim of the deepseated feminine will and obstinacy. Thus, he drifted into a correspondence with Annabella Milbanke – they rarely met as she was often out of London, at home with her parents in Durham – and behind the pompous stilted letters of the period – and his were nearly as bad as hers – they played the ancient comedy of advance and retreat, one going forward if the other went back.

Nevertheless, they were not as yet moving on the same level of interest and involvement. While he was still merely amused, she could write to him in this lofty manner, like a troubled great-aunt:

> My regard for your welfare did not arise from blindness to your errors; I was interested by the strength & generosity of your feelings, and I honoured you for that pure sense of moral rectitude, which could not be perverted, though perhaps tried by the practice of Vice. I would have sought to rouse your own virtues to a consistent plan of action, for so directed, they would guide you more surely than any mortal counsel . . .

But behind this high-faluting stuff was the fixed determination of a spoilt girl of twenty-one to claim this man for herself. Born in 1792, Anne Isabella Milbanke, always known among her family and friends as Annabella, was the only child of Sir Ralph Milbanke, the sixth baronet, and the Hon. Judith Noel. Sir Ralph was an amiable and rather bumbling coal-owning squire, whose long

PLATE XXVIII. Anne Isabella (Annabella) Milbanke, 1812, by Sir George Hayter
watercolour
4⅜ × 3⅜ in. (11.1 × 8.5 cm.)
Collection the Earl of Lytton

stories over the port later set Byron yawning. His wife, Judith, was intelligent and well-read, a sharply determined character, whose one weakness was her blind devotion to her daughter, whom she succeeded in spoiling just as surely as Sir Ralph did. Knowing very well that Annabella now wanted Byron, Judith did all she could to secure the match. However, even before the actual marriage she and Byron began to dislike each other, and later, when Annabella was demanding a separation, she had a formidable ally in her mother.

It is possible that if Judith Milbanke had been rather more detached and tolerant the whole story might have been different. Annabella was no beauty but her face was pleasing enough and

she is said to have had a pretty little figure. She had no fortune herself at this time, but it was well known that she would inherit money from an uncle. Even so, I do not think her various suitors during this period were simply after her inheritance, and we can assume she was reasonably attractive. But having been spoilt at home, she grew up to be egocentric and extraordinarily self-complacent. She was priggish and patronising – living, we might say, above her intellectual income – and was entirely without any sense of humour, a fatal lack in any woman proposing to live with Byron. He saw all this quite early in their acquaintance, and must have often laughed at her pompous solemnity and sermonising tone when discussing her with his close friend, that worldly and experienced dame, Lady Melbourne. She was Sir Ralph's sister and therefore Annabella's aunt; and she was mistrusted and disliked by Judith and some old friends of the family. Nevertheless, in spite of misgivings, Byron found himself drawn towards this strange cool priggish girl, so very different from a Caroline Lamb or a Lady Oxford. It was rather as if he had no will of his own and so was at the mercy of this concentrated feminine wish.

He was feeling restless and dissatisfied. He was not working steadily, only in late-night, brandy-soaked snatches, and he was increasingly worried about money. He had decided to sell his Newstead house and estate but could not obtain what he thought was a reasonable price for them. He was ready, in spite of some misgivings, to take Lady Melbourne's advice, find a serious young wife with money, and settle down. And then he discovered – and the whole story turns on this discovery – his half-sister, Augusta. She was four years older than he was, his father's daughter by an earlier marriage. Byron's mother having died in 1811, Augusta was now the only close relative he had. She had married in 1807 her cousin, Colonel Leigh, an amiable but thriftless sporting type, who spent most of his time attending race meetings in the company of men with far more money to lose than he had. An affectionate, easy-going woman, Augusta was fond of him and was beginning to fill their house at Newmarket, in spite of his frequent absences, with their children. She and Byron had of course exchanged brief visits and letters earlier, but now for the first time they spent a great deal of time together – and the result was at once delightful and appalling.

Augusta was everything that Annabella was not, and Byron should have realised that if he could be entirely happy with one of these women he would never be even fairly contented with the other. Augusta was rather scatter-brained, though not a fool, was tender-hearted and indulgent and not concerned with 'moral guidance'; she was charming and intuitive – and Annabella was not – and she had a lively sense of humour and could tease Byron out of his black moods. Added to all this was their close relatedness:

(above) Augusta Leigh, by Sir George Hayter
pencil and indian ink
5 × 3⅛ in. (12.7 × 7.9 cm.)
The British Museum, London

(opposite) Fare-thee-well, 1816, by George Cruikshank
The British Museum, London

she was 'family', all that was left, as well as being a delightful companion. She released in Byron a fountain of joy and tenderness that no other woman had discovered in him. He did not 'fall in love' with her, but loved her. And for once, I suspect, he did not play a rather passive rôle, accepting rather than demanding a woman's attentions, but was the active dominating male, sweeping away any timid protestations. This is a guess; but it is going beyond guessing to believe – all the evidence pointing that way – that they were lovers, and not merely on a few reckless occasions.

Believing in and depending upon close rewarding relationships, most women are at heart free of the sinister spell of masculine terms like *adultery* and *incest*. It was Byron who in his darker moods was appalled by what he had done – or was doing. The Calvinistic side of him readily accepted guilt, and now, especially when Augusta was not available to tease and enchant him, it loaded on his back this huge sin of an incestuous relationship. Moreover, as he genuinely loved his sister – he always referred to her as his sister, never half-sister – he was afraid that the secret might leak out, ruining her marriage and destroying her socially. Augusta was afraid too, on this level, but had no taunting demons to face, as Byron had.

So now, Byron having found the kind of woman he had always wanted, but being unable to live openly with her (though he did suggest at one desperate time that they went abroad together), the acidly ironic comedy begins another act. Because of Augusta, he was driven nearer and nearer to marrying, if only for safety's sake, her very opposite, the priggish and humourless Annabella, who had fallen in love after a fashion with her *idea* of him. Any intuitive and perceptive girl would have felt there was something strange and chilling in being proposed to not in person but by letter. This was in September 1814 when she was with her parents at Seaham in Durham, and he was at Newstead with Augusta beside him. After being accepted, he was writing to her in this laborious vein:

> I wrote to you yesterday – not very intelligibly, I fear – and to your father in a more embarrassed manner than I could have wished. But the fact is that I am even now apprehensive of having misunderstood you and of appearing presumptuous when I am only happy – in the hope that you will not repent having made me more so than I ever thought to have been again . . .

together with much more of the same, pumped out by a man with no heart and zest in what he was writing. That was on 19 September; and next day, the last before he left Newstead, as Mr Elwin tells us: 'He and Augusta carved their names in the bark of an elm behind the Abbey, with the date, 20th September 1814.' And they probably did it half-laughing, half-crying. But did Byron, now engaged to Annabella, hurry to Seaham to begin carving names on trees? He did not. He went to London and did not go to Seaham until early November.

His excuse was that he had to put his finances in order before his marriage. There was some truth in this, but what really delayed him was a reluctance to face the fact of his engagement. At heart he did not want to see Annabella or her parents, expecially when he would have to live with them for some weeks. It was then that he ought to have called the whole thing off, but, haunted day and night by the thought of his relationship with Augusta (herself not against the marriage; she was already exchanging letters with Annabella), he was incapable of taking a decisive step – he was simply drifting. And when, during his first visit to Seaham from 3 November to the 16th, Annabella at times suddenly found him strange and unaccountably hostile, she was not sufficiently perceptive to realise that this deeply divided man was angry with himself for his passive acceptance. Though Byron tried hard at first to be amiable all round, the visit was not a success. Sir Ralph soon bored him; he disliked his future mother-in-law; and the hours he spent with Annabella were far from easy and lively. And he confided to Lady Melbourne in a letter dated the 13th November:

> Do you know I have grave doubts if this will be a marriage now: – her disposition is the very reverse of *our* imaginings. She is overrun with fine feelings – scruples about herself & her disposition (I suppose in fact she means mine) and to crown all is taken ill every three days with I know not what. But the day before and the day after she seems well, looks & eats well & is cheerful & confiding & in short like any other person in good health and spirits . . . I am never sure of A, for a moment. The least word – and you know I rattle on through thick and thin (always however avoiding anything I think can offend her favourite notions) if only to prevent one from yawning – the least word, or alteration of tone, has some inference drawn from it . . . I have lately had recourse to the eloquence of *action* . . .

It was undoubtedly this *action* that made Annabella suggest they had better separate until immediately before their marriage, so that Byron left Seaham on the 16th. He had had much to do with women, from ardent society ladies to willing housemaids, but they had not been priggish and prudish virgins of twenty-two, and one reason why he had been reluctant to see Annabella was probably because he was not sure how he ought to behave when they were left alone. So, trying *action*, he soon went too far, frightening her and making him feel he had made a fool of himself. His vanity wounded, he was glad to escape from Seaham, going south towards the ease and laughter and tenderness of Augusta.

He returned for the wedding at the end of December, accompanied by his friend Hobhouse, who said of him on their journey north – 'never was lover less in haste.' He and Annabella, both really against their better judgment, were married on 2 January 1815 and went off immediately on their honeymoon, to the Milbanke house in Yorkshire, Halnaby. Byron was in one of his blackest moods and the wretched bride found herself in a kind of long nightmare.

Now there is an understandable prejudice against Lady Byron. During the many years after his death in 1824, in her unattractive character as an embittered widow, she spent too much time justifying herself and persecuting Byron's memory. She piled up charges Byron was not alive to deny. But I for one am inclined to accept most of her account of the honeymoon because it was written fourteen months later. According to her, as soon as they were in the carriage he was all gloom and defiance; the sound of the wedding bells ringing in Durham horrified him and he 'said something very bitter about *our happiness*'; he told her she had better not have married him at all; and, after dinner, he observed in a sinister manner that now he had her in his power and could make her feel it. Then later:

> He asked me with an appearance of aversion, if I meant to sleep in the same bed with him – said that he hated sleeping with any woman, but I might do as I chose. He told me insultingly that 'one animal of the kind was as good to him as another' provided she was young – and that with men, this was not any proof of attachment.

The next scene does not come from Annabella but from Samuel Rogers (not altogether reliable, though; inclined to malice), who was able to read Byron's own memoirs before they were burnt:

> On his wedding night, Byron suddenly started out of his first sleep: a taper, which burned in the room, was casting a ruddy glare through the crimson curtains of the bed; and he could not help exclaiming, in a voice so loud that he wakened Lady B., 'Good God, I am surely in hell!'

But his wife might have felt closer to it than he did.

We can easily share her bewilderment. Byron behaved and spoke from various levels of his complicated personality. On one level he was like a mischievous and rather malicious schoolboy, trying to shock, busy showing off. On the level below, he might be acting to some extent but could be goaded by a solemn self-righteous woman like Annabella (but not Augusta) into being deliberately cruel, patient suffering bringing out the sadist in him. Further below still, where neither woman could reach him nor really understand what he felt, Hell and its demons were waiting for him. He never lost the fears of his childhood. The taper in the bedroom, mentioned above, gives us a clue. Byron was terrified of the dark and always slept in a lighted room. He also kept loaded pistols by him. And sometimes at Halnaby, on this strangest of honeymoons, unable to sleep he would pace up and down the corridor, pistols in hand. But there was something menacing in the dark of his mind that no bullet could destroy – a feeling that he had some invisible but implacable enemy, that doomsday was on its way. If he craved excitement and pleasure, bright lights, amusing women, and a few good fellows round the decanter, it was so that he could forget he was one of the eternally damned, an idea he could dismiss intellectually but could not root out of his personality. And the bewildered and anxious Annabella, one of the righteous, could not keep him company down there.

The honeymoon over, they returned to Seaham, where Byron was well-behaved but soon bored by the Milbanke family games and anecdotes, so that he began to feel depressed. He had agreed to rent the Duchess of Devonshire's house in Piccadilly, really much too large and expensive for them, but on their way there they stayed with Augusta at Newmarket. Between the two women, who formed an alliance to be kind and loving, Byron, infuriated by this alliance and tantalised by Augusta's presence, was at his worst, often behaving like a madman, muttering things that must have roused his wife's suspicion. But she invited Augusta to join them in London, if and when Augusta was free to do so, and this blanket invitation was accepted, most unwisely. However, it looked as if the marriage might work, if only because in the spring Annabella found she was pregnant. (Augusta was always finding herself pregnant too; and indeed it is hard to follow any society women through the Regency without blundering into a trail of pregnancies.) The Byrons' daughter, christened Augusta Ada, was born on 10 December 1815.

Augusta Ada Byron, 1820, engraving by Edward Scriven after L. Ferriere
The British Museum, London

During these months in Piccadilly Byron characteristically swung between extremes, one day behaving as he had done on the honeymoon and in Augusta's house, another day showing his wife consideration, even affection and tenderness. But he had more excuse for behaving badly now. He could not sell Newstead and he was deeper and deeper in debt. Hearing that he had married an heiress, his creditors were closing in on him, dunning him hard without much success so that bailiffs often invaded the house. And for various reasons Annabella had not brought him the financial relief he had expected. He was not writing steadily, so that the explosive force of his personality had no outlet there. He did join the committee that had been formed to run Drury Lane, and worked hard on it – the Theatre always having its own peculiarly enticing urgency – but this took him away from Annabella, offered him some pretty actresses to play with, and too often kept him up late, drinking far too much brandy. His health in fact was not good during these months. His liver was giving him trouble, and the drastic medicaments of the Regency probably gave even more trouble. He began taking laudanum and so alarmed his wife and Augusta that they plotted to water the decanter of it he kept. So what with debts, duns, brandy, calomel, laudanum, actresses who soon became a nuisance, a patiently suffering wife, an Augusta no longer laughing at him or with him, a reactionary European settlement and the Tories worse than ever in Westminster, and not finding it possible to do any serious work, Byron too often behaved at home like a man going out of his mind. And in late-night drunken rages, he would smash things; and with his laudanum and loaded pistols to hand, there seemed always a danger that he might kill himself.

His talk could be very wild; he would go abroad *alone* as soon as he had some money; he dropped hints about having done terrible things. Annabella and Augusta began to wonder together if he was going mad, if he had once committed murder. During the last weeks of her confinement, Annabella found him harsher, more unfeeling, than ever. Just before and after the birth of her daughter, as she said shortly afterwards, Byron's behaviour was so abominably callous that it was hard to believe he was in his right mind. But he now had the bailiffs in below and was wondering where next to turn.

On 15 January, 1816, Annabella departed with her baby for Kirkby Mallory in Yorkshire, where her parents were staying. They had invited her to join them, and Byron had no objection, though he himself was determined to remain in London. While not telling Byron what she had in mind but receiving daily bulletins of his behaviour from Augusta, Annabella set wheels in motion, and some of them took her mother to London, where that energetic and now implacable dame went to-ing and fro-ing between lawyers and doctors; and more and more letters (most of them to be found in Mr Elwin's book) were exchanged in that strictest confidence which so often sets rumours flying. By early February Annabella was determined to have a legal separation, and she wrote to Augusta: 'You are desired by your brother to ask if my father has acted with my concurrence in proposing a separation. He has.' The anxious and bewildered wife had suddenly acquired a face of stone.

Byron seemed now even more bewildered than she had ever been. He began writing in this strain:

Dearest Bell – No answer from you yet – perhaps it is as well – but do recollect – that all is at stake – the present – the future – & even the colouring of the past. The whole of my errors – or what harsher name you choose to give them – you know – but I loved you – & will not part from you without your *own* most express and *expressed* refusal to return to or receive me . . .

But if she had any feeling for him, she hardened herself against it – a process more easily available to the proud self-righteous than it is to the frail and faulty. The same obstinate will that had drawn him into marriage was now rigidly fixed to end it, whatever the consequences. And these would be bad because she was soon busy – together with family friends and lawyers – justifying herself. This meant there would be more and more whispering in corners, with rumours reaching the Tory politicians (who detested Byron) and their ladies, and the press – and finally the mob, that never really knew what it was all about but was ready to hiss that villainous Byron in the street or the theatre. There were even coloured cartoons in the print shops showing Lord B – in various nasty situations, almost all imaginary. Throughout March and early April, there was a general conspiracy, to which the English lend themselves in a degrading fashion every generation or so, to claw down this former insolent handsome favourite. It was during these days that Claire Clairmont, who had come back from abroad with Shelley and Mary, forced herself upon Byron's acquaintance and then determinedly seduced him, so that she afterwards bore him a daughter.

On 8 April his few remaining women friends in high society made a last attempt to bring him back into it. They gave a large party at Almack's and asked Byron and Augusta (no longer living under the same roof) to attend it. The result was disastrous; Augusta was ignored and then the room emptied as soon as Byron arrived in it. Now legally separated from his wife and child, ostracised by society, hooted in the streets, two weeks later Byron left England, never to return.

Without attempting to examine and then digest the huge mass of print on this marriage and its partners, I will risk a few guesses. Byron should never have married Annabella Milbanke and ought to have broken off the engagement, instead of allowing himself to drift along. He knew he was making a mistake, and then he projected on to her his anger and disgust with himself. Wanting a husband she could reform, not one to understand and enjoy, Annabella was the wrong woman for Byron. Nevertheless, I feel that if he had not behaved so badly, from the first moment they were alone as husband and wife, she might have borne him several children, lost some of her egoism and priggishness, and had a marriage as good as many another in Regency society. (Below the level of mere posing, Byron, I believe, had possibilities as a family man.) Any woman would have resented such treatment, and Annabella was still in her early twenties, had been spoilt, and

Parisian Walking Dress from *La Belle Assemblée*, 1 August 1816
Collection Mrs Doris Langley Moore, London

183

thought much of herself, so that her vanity, together with her self-respect, was deeply wounded. Then the fear of losing her child hardened her will – and Byron was doomed.

But the case she built up against him – and for years and years too – seems to me to have been quite false. Its secret basis was that he had proved to be an inconsiderate and unappreciative husband, unworthy of such a wife as herself: wounded vanity was still there. And it was *not* that he was a madly wicked man, guilty of incest, homosexuality, all manner of abominations. This was feminine humbug, to startle and impress doctors, lawyers and the like. If he had been a good husband, she would have shrugged away his wicked past. While she was confiding in Augusta and exchanging affectionate letters with her, she must have already guessed what Augusta's relations with Byron had been, but so long as Augusta had put a stop to them – and this is more than likely – Annabella was probably ready to pretend even to herself, as many women are adept at doing, that this relationship had never existed. As for the rumours of homosexuality – and the supposed fright Byron once gave her – she would have swept them away too if the marriage had been shaping well. Even to a pious woman like Annabella a ruined relationship, a scornful rejection of what she had to offer a husband, was the great sin.

Certainly Byron behaved badly. We have to admit so much, even when bailiffs, brandy and a liver complaint are taken into account. But the argument, now becoming all too familiar, that behind the cover of his womanising he was really homosexual, I for one cannot accept. There is a fair amount of evidence that at certain times, trying anything, he indulged in homosexual pastimes, but it was on a low level, without any real emotional involvement. I may be told that his relations with Augusta were a disguised homosexuality, that she was the woman he wanted because he ought not to want her, as if she were a man; but what strikes me in this relationship is his essential *boyishness*, adoring a playful and indulgent older sister. There is something very young, too, in his loud contempt for women in general, based largely on his fear of their deep desire for a mature and lasting relationship, which so often frightens youths merely in search of sexual adventure. It is true that in spite of his pose as a ruthless predatory male, as we have noticed already, he was often strangely passive, drifting into an affair as if half-hypnotised by the woman's obstinate will to have him; but if this turns him into a homosexual, the same argument would turn his various women into disguised lesbians, and all is nonsense. The real explanation, I believe, is to be found in his sexual and emotional immaturity. And even in his Don Juan, for all its wit, cynicism, air of extreme sophistication, there is a suggestion of a brilliant boy showing off, ablaze with excitement.

Dover was filled with women trying to obtain a last glimpse of the poet. He was already world-famous; there were grey hairs creeping into his dark chestnut curls; yet Byron when he left England for ever was only twenty-eight. He was on his way towards his best work. Nevertheless, he paid heavily for his exile. London might be detestable, but it was still magical, whereas Switzerland and Italy soon bored him. However, it can be argued that the London that turned him out paid a heavier price still. It lost the man other nations regarded as England's greatest living poet, the man soon to be accepted as the gigantic symbolic figure of the Romantic Age. The society that rejected him and drove him out began to acquire a European reputation for being stupid, insensitive, smug, hypocritical. This was a country whose poets had to leave it. So Victorian England, taken in a pejorative sense, might be said to have made its first appearance as early as 1816.

The Elgin Marbles, or John Bull buying stones at a time his numerous Family want Bread, 1816, by George Cruikshank – Lord Castlereagh addresses John Bull, the price £35,000 The British Museum, London

185

Table De S.A.R. Le Prince Régent
Servie au pavillon de Brighton Angleterre
15 Janvier 1817
Menu de 36 entrées

Quatre Potages
Le potage à la Monglas
La garbure aux choux
Le potage d'orge perlée à la Crecy
Le potage de poissons à la Russe

Quatre Relevés De Poissons
La matelote au vin de Bordeaux
Les truites au bleu à la Provençale
Le turbot à l'Anglaise, sauce aux homards
La grosse anguille à la régence

Quatre Grosses Pièces Pour Les Contre-Flancs
Le jambon à la broche, au Madère
L'oie braisée aux racines glacées
Les poulardes à la Périgueux
Le rond de veau à la royale

Trente-Six Entrées, Dont Quatre Servent de Contre-Flancs
Les filets de volaille à la maréchale
Le sauté de merlans aux fines herbes
La timbale de macaroni à la Napolitaine
La noix de veau à la jardinière
Les filets de volaille à l'Orléans

Le Jambon à la Broche
La darne de saumon au beurre de Montpellier
Le sauté de faisans aux truffes
La fricassée de poulets à l'Italienne
Le turban de filets de lapereaux

Les Truites au Bleu
Les boudin de volaille à la Béchamel
Le sauté de ris de veau à la Provençale
Les ailes de poulardes glacées à la chicorée
Les galantines de perdreaux à la gelée

L'Oie Braisée aux Racines Glacées
Les petites canetons de volaille en haricots vierges
Les poulets à la reine, à la Cherry
Les petites croustades de mauviettes au gratin
Les côtelettes de mouton à l'Irlandaise
Les filets de bécasses à la royale
Les filets de sarcelles à la Bourguignotte
Les petits poulets à l'Indienne
Les petites pâtés de mouton à l'Anglaise
L'épigramme de poulardes, purée de céleri
Le faisan à la Minime, bordure de racines

Les Poulardes à la Périgueux
L'aspic de blanc de volaille à la ravigote
Les filets de perdreaux à la Pompadour
L'émincé de poulardes au gratin
La côte de bœuf aux oignons glacés

Le Turbot à l'Anglaise
Le sauté de poulardes à la Provençale
Le salmis de cailles au vin de Madère
Les escalopes de volaille aux truffes
La salade de filets de brochets aux huîtres

Le rond de Veau à la Royale
Le pain de carpes au beurre d'anchois
Les côtelettes d'agneau glacées à la Toulouse
Le vol-au-vent de quenelles à l'Allemande
Les ailerons de poulardes aux champignons
Les pigeons à la Mirepoix financière

Pour Extra Dix Assiettes Volantes de Friture
5 De filets de soles
5 De filets de gelinottes à l'Allemande

Huit Grosses Pièces De Pâtisserie
La brioche au fromage
Le nougat à la Française
La ruine d'Antioche
L'hermitage Syrien
Le biscuit à l'orange
Le croque-en-bouche aux pistaches
L'hermitage chinois
La ruine de la mosquée turque

Quatre Plats De Rôts
Les coqs de Bruyères
Les canards sauvages
Les poulets gras bardés
Les gelinottes

Trente-Deux Entremets
Les truffes à la cendre
La gelée d'oranges moulée
Les épinards à l'essence

La Brioche à Fromage
Les homards au gratin
Les petits pains à la duchesse
Les schals au beurre
Le pouding de pommes au muscat
Les miritons aux citrons

Les Canards Sauvages
Les bouchées perlées aux groseilles
Les œufs brouillés aux truffes

Le Nougat à la Française
Les pommes de terre à la Hollandaise
La gelée de punch renversée
Les champignons à la Provençale
Les navets glacés à la Chartre

Les Coqs de Bruyères
Les gâteaux glacés aux abricots
Le fromage bavarois aux avelines
Le purée de haricots

L'Hermitage Chinois
Les petits panier aux confitures

Les Poulets Gras Bardés
Les génoises glacées au café
Le charlotte à l'Américaine
Les choux-fleurs au Parmesan

L'Hermitage Syrien
Le céleri en cardes à l'Espagnole
La crème française à l'ananas
Les petits soufflés d'abricots

Les Gelinottes
Les gâteaux de feuilletage praliné
Les huîtres au gratin

Les Croques-en-Bouche
La gelée de liqueurs de isles
Les concombres à la Béchamel
Les Biscuits de Fécule à l'Orange
Les Laitues farcies à l'essence
Les petites carottes à la Flamande
La gelée de citrons moulée
Les truffes à l'Italienne

Pour Extra Dix Assiettes Volantes
5 De petites soufflés de pommes
5 De petites soufflés au chocolat

1817

The Line Breaks

This year, 1817, was on the whole a melancholy one. It would end very badly indeed for the Regent, but then it did not begin well either for him or for his people. He was now so unpopular that when he opened Parliament in January he had to drive through a very hostile crowd. On his return to Carlton House, according to Robert Peel, then Secretary for Ireland, the crowd was 'amazingly increased both in numbers and violence. Opinions are much divided as to the fact of a shot having been fired from an airgun. The general spirit of the country is worse, I apprehend, than we understood it to be . . .' There is no doubt that gravel and stones were thrown at the royal carriage, and some windows broken. The Regent said he had felt a stone or bullet pass his face, and certainly there was a small neat hole in the window. The Regent may or may not have felt panic-stricken – if there is evidence either way, I have not found it – but Lord Liverpool's government soon behaved as if there had been barricades in St James's Street and the rattle of musketry along Piccadilly. They may have been genuinely alarmed or they may have seized upon a good excuse to be repressive, but what is certain is that they rushed through a number of deplorable measures, which could hardly have been worse if half the towns in England had been in flames.

The Habeas Corpus Act was suspended, which meant that anybody under suspicion could be thrown into gaol and kept there. An unrepealed Act dating back to Edward III was brought out, dusted, set in motion, giving magistrates everywhere the power to send to prison any persons they thought likely to commit an act prejudicial to public order. As most men on the Bench in 1817 were not inclined to be tolerant in their dealings with the lower orders, anybody caught pulling a face or making a rude noise was in danger of being thrown into gaol. And it was no use trying to march to Westminster to present a petition against all this abuse of power, because there was an Act prohibiting meetings of more than fifty persons within a mile of Westminster Hall. So too there were strong measures against *Seditious Libel,* a great catch-all for anything a reactionary government disliked. There were of course a few wild men ready to preach violent revolution. The trick was to equate everybody who protested with these fellows, and so sweep all

(opposite) Menu for Dinner on the 15 January 1817 at The Royal Pavilion, Brighton

reformers into one net. Thus, the so-called 'Blanketeers', who began a march in Manchester, were for the most part decent people who wanted to protest against the suspension of Habeas Corpus, but they were halted at Stockport as if they wanted to set fire to all Westminster. By the end of March, 1817, when these various Acts were law (including one to protect the King and the Regent by declaring any act against them treasonable), and when Lord Sidmouth had sent a circular to magistrates encouraging them to suppress all 'seditious publications', which could be anything in print that Sidmouth disliked, the mass of discontented people and the middle-class radicals (not too many) who sympathised with them were asked to submit to being gagged and almost fettered. These people who had helped to defeat Napoleon were now probably worse off than they would have been if he had been victorious.

The war had piled up an enormous National Debt. Only an increase in direct taxation, the income tax that Pitt had introduced as a wartime measure, could have coped with it. But direct taxation – on the ground that it was never meant to outlast the war – had been almost abandoned, with the result that indirect taxation, not only on luxuries but on necessities, had to bear the burden. Tea, sugar, beer, soap, candles, paper, for example, were all heavily taxed. The Corn Laws still protected the landowners and the farmers who could grow plenty of wheat. So the rich were richer and the poor were poorer, and a man was liable to be prosecuted for saying so. This was very much a year in which too many people ate too little, and a few people ate far too much. Among the latter, of course, were our Prince of Pleasure and his friends. He had secured the services at this time of the famous French chef, Carème, who must have been responsible for the *Menu de 36 entrées*! – reproduced on p. 186 – at a dinner party given by the Regent at his Brighton Pavilion on 15 January, 1817. If we add a constant flow of wine, with a high proportion of fortified wines like Madeira and Port, to this gigantic menu, then we can imagine how bilious or nearly stupefied many of the guests must have been after dinner. No wonder we are told that "the principal entertainment after dinner was provided by the Prince's private band, composed only of wind instruments.' Wind instruments indeed!

Now we can no longer afford to ignore a young woman who has been kept waiting too long to make her entrance on our stage. She is Princess Charlotte, the Regent's only child, now in this year happily married to Leopold of Saxe-Coburg and about to have a child of her own, who would, like its mother, be in a direct line of succession to the Crown. Though Charlotte has been kept in the background until her marriage, she has captured the imagination of the people. They are as ready to admire her as they are to dislike

(opposite) The Music Room showing the Prince Regent's wind band (detail), from John Nash's *Brighton Pavilion*, 1820–25
The Royal Institute of British Architects, London (Drawings Collection)

Christian Friedrich, Baron Stockmar,
1874, engraving by F. Holl after Franz
Winterhalter from Theodore Martin's
*Life of His Royal Highness the
Prince Consort,* 1875, Vol. I
The British Museum, London

her father, the Regent, whose coach they have been pelting with gravel.

The Regent's own attitude towards his daughter, frequently condemned, is not easy to explain. He was fond of children in his easy negligent fashion, and just after she was born, we are told, he received her 'with all the Affection possible'. His sisters used to write to him giving him the smallest details of her progress as a baby. The little princess divided her time between old Queen Charlotte and her aunts at Windsor and various governesses and ladies-in-waiting at Warwick House. This was not unreasonable because her father's Prince-of-Pleasure establishments at Carlton House and down at Brighton were hardly suitable for a curious growing child. But then he saw very little of her himself and, playing dog-in-the-manger, gave strict orders when she was already in her middle teens – as we noticed in 1812 – that she must not meet her mother in private. She had no great affection for her mother, but the Regent's odd behaviour provided them with a common bond of antagonism towards him.

Charlotte, a blonde type, was quite a good-looking girl, but she had some unattractive mannerisms – 'Her hands generally folded behind her,' Stockmar noted, 'her body always pushed forward, never standing quiet, from time to time stamping her foot, laughing a great deal, and talking still more . . .' Possibly the Regent, nothing if not elegant, winced at the sight and sound of this boisterous hoyden. (It was also said that she strode about with her drawers conspicuous.) Perhaps her presence reminded him of his disastrous marriage. Also, it was common form in this Hanoverian line to dislike the heir. The Prince had had his daughter brought up to be a Whig and something of a rebel, and now the Whigs were his bitter enemies and anyhow he wanted no rebels around him. Early in 1813 Brougham told Grey that the Regent was jealous of his daughter 'to a degree of insanity', and that the Duke of Cumberland and Lord Yarmouth had been telling the Regent he could get rid of his daughter by divorcing his wife. This seems far-fetched – though Cumberland *was* far-fetched – but in spite of Brougham's heavy bias against the Regent there was probably something in this jealousy story. The Regent wanted to be popular and wasn't, whereas young Charlotte undoubtedly was – and without taking too much trouble about it.

The question of her marriage was now coming up. She was a fairly susceptible girl, and at seventeen was showing an increasing interest in the young Duke of Devonshire. But the Regent thought him definitely unsuitable as he lacked royal status. The Regent's choice was the Prince of Orange, and Castlereagh, busy scheming, also wanted this match because a future alliance with the Netherlands, once Napoleon had lost his Empire, would be very useful to

The Archbishop of Canterbury, Dr John Moore, 1794, by Sir Thomas Lawrence
oil on canvas
50 × 40 in. (127 × 101.6 cm.)
The Art Gallery, Southampton

Francis Horner, 1812, by Sir Henry Raeburn
oil on canvas
49½ × 39¼ in. (126 × 100 cm.)
The National Portrait Gallery, London

England. As a husband and not an alliance the Prince of Orange, known as 'Slender Billy', was no great catch: Wellington said he was 'a dissolute untidy and stupid young man'. However, Charlotte, after many a backward look at the Duke of Devonshire and much coaxing at Carlton House, finally accepted the Prince of Orange. We are now into 1814.

Then in the glittering high summer of that year of state visits, Charlotte changed her mind, summoning the Prince of Orange to Warwick House to tell him so. Her ostensible reason was that no provision had been made for her to live in England after this marriage, and she did not want to leave her mother. But the truth was, she was now infatuated with Prince Augustus of Russia, who had come to London in the suite of Frederick William III of Prussia. The Regent was very angry, not only having lost Castlereagh's future Dutch alliance but feeling strongly that his daughter might be jeopardising her chance of making a good match. Because he believed her ladies-in-waiting had probably encouraged her, he summarily dismissed them all. Now equally furious, the headstrong Charlotte rushed out of Carlton House, took the first free vehicle and gave the driver a guinea to take her to her mother's house in Connaught Place. There were now consultations between Caroline, the Archbishop of Canterbury, the Dukes of York and Sussex; finally wilful young Charlotte was persuaded to return to her own home, Warwick House. But the news was out; there was a huge scandal; and the Regent was the villain of the piece. Brougham asked, 'Why again is the Princess to be treated as a state criminal? Why are we to have a Queen so brought up? Out of Turkey is there anything so barbarous?' And Francis Horner, a Whig M.P., declared that a Prussian Corporal could not have behaved worse than the Regent. It is hard to be a Prince of Pleasure and yet to have a wayward daughter and a possible royal marriage on your hands, and the Regent, after talking for an hour to a friend about his deep affection for Charlotte, burst into tears – something he was apt to do on emotional occasions, when fine feelings might be added to fine wines.

However, Caroline angered her daughter by departing for Europe, and gradually throughout the later months of 1814 Charlotte's relations with her father improved. By Christmas Day she was able to take him into her confidence. She confirmed to him many of the scandalous rumours about her free-and-easy mama, and included some items he felt he could not repeat. An odd way of spending Christmas Day – but then this was an odd family. She also described how Caroline had locked her in a bedroom with Captain Hesse, believed to be the illegitimate son of the Duke of York, telling her to amuse herself. 'And God knows,' cried Charlotte, 'what would have become of me if he had not behaved with so much respect towards me.' And she added that she had never been able to understand if Hesse, who had sailed to the Continent with Caroline, was to be her lover or her mother's. These 'melancholy and frightful disclosures' – as the Regent described this Christmas treat – brought father and daughter closer; and in February 1815 she was able to tell him, 'Happily for me we are now on the most comfortable terms possible. We have broken through the awkwardness of talking upon one subject, which is a very delicate and painful one, and I should grieve if there was anything left to make us less open with each other.' But however wide open they were, there was still the question of Charlotte's marriage to be decided.

Now there arrives on the scene, with modest but firm tread, Leopold of Coburg. He was the third son of Prince Francis of Saxe-Coburg, a tiny and impoverished German principality that seemed to have as its chief industry marrying into much wealthier royal families. He was a handsome young man, with fair hair and hazel eyes, only in his earlier twenties but carefully well-behaved, pleasantly attentive, though inclined to be calculating and somewhat priggish. (He was afterwards that Leopold, King of the Belgians, who insisted upon giving his young niece, Queen Victoria, rather more advice than she needed from him. And Victoria's Prince Consort was his nephew.)

Leopold had come over in the summer of 1814 in the suite of the Emperor Alexander, and not being allowed to accept the hospitality of Carlton House and having very little money he had had to lodge above a grocer's shop in Marylebone High Street. He had been presented to Charlotte that summer, but she was still fascinated then by Augustus of Russia. But when 1815 arrived and there was

(below left) The Princess Charlotte of Wales and Prince Leopold of Coburg returning from the altar after the marriage ceremony, from *La Belle Assemblée*, 1 July 1816
The Victoria and Albert Museum, London

(below right) A Brighton Hot Bath, or Preparations for the Wedding, 1816, by George Cruikshank
The British Museum, London

A sofa table made ensuite with three others for the wedding of Princess Charlotte and Prince Leopold, *c.* 1816; English
amboyna and kingwood
veneer with brass inlay and gilt mounts
The Victoria and Albert Museum, London

no chance of her marrying Augustus, she was able to write that she 'had perfectly decided and made up my mind to marry, & the person I have decidedly fixed on is Prince Leopold ... At all events, I know that *worse off,* more unhappy and wretched I *cannot* be than I *am now,* & after all if I end by marrying Prince L., I marry the *best* of all those I *have seen,* & that is some satisfaction.'

Like many another girl before or since, Charlotte, after making a rather cool choice, began to warm towards it and gradually fell in love. The Regent was dubious at first but allowed himself to be persuaded by the Duke of York. In January 1816 Castlereagh wrote to Leopold telling him that the Regent intended to give him the hand of the Heiress Apparent, and inviting him to England. Towards the end of February he was the Regent's guest at the Pavilion in Brighton, very different from that room above the grocer's in Marylebone High Street. A month later, Charlotte could say to Lady Lindsay, 'Nothing you can utter in the Prince of Coburg's favour is too much.' The wedding took place on 2 May. 'When the ceremony was over,' Lady Liverpool reported, 'the Princess knelt to her father for his blessing, which he gave her, and then raised her and gave her a good hearty, paternal hug that delighted me.' Our Prince was unsatisfactory in many ways, far too many, but at least he could rise to these occasions.

It was a happy marriage. Charlotte and Leopold complemented each other neatly. If he was soon less of a solemn young stick, she was soon less of a noisy and rebellious hoyden. Patiently attentive and careful, Leopold was able to calm his wife while improving her manners, for which the Regent, who had so often winced at them, was duly grateful. In the autumn of 1817 the happy pair, now living outside London at Claremont, were expecting a child. Before the middle of October, when the Regent visited Claremont, the nurses and Sir Richard Croft, the obstetrician, were in residence. The latter describes how the royal couple 'leave us at about half past ten, and he reads to her every night till twelve, and I think you will agree with me they are very reasonable people'. There were still little daily excursions, Charlotte going 'to view the Gothic Temple, which was building in the Park', and Leopold taking his guns into the grounds. Nevertheless, the people were anxious, the papers printing frequent bulletins. And old Queen Charlotte, now failing, had been ordered to rest at Bath and so could not be with her namesake grand-daughter. She left on the very day, 3 November, that Charlotte's labour began. Meanwhile, the Regent had gone off to Suffolk, to shoot with the Hertfords. So neither her father nor her grandmother was there when, on 5 November, Charlotte gave birth to a stillborn son, or when, at 2.30 in the morning of the 6th, she died.

She was only twenty-one, the people loved her, and her death made appalling news. One correspondent wrote: 'No description

Claremont, the seat of H.R.H. Princess Charlotte and H.R.H. the Prince of Saxe Coburg, 1817, engraving by Thomas Sutherland after Clavert Dely
The Royal Pavilion, Brighton

(above) Benjamin Robert Haydon,
by himself
millboard
9 × 6½ in. (23 × 16.5 cm.)
The National Portrait Gallery,
London

(below) The Funeral Procession of
Princess Charlotte, 1817
The Royal Collection, Windsor Castle

in the papers can exaggerate the public sympathy and the public sorrow ... The nation would have resigned all the rest of her family to have saved her.' Haydon, the painter, declared: 'The loss of the Dear Princess Charlotte to us is irreparable. She was our rallying point, our hope ...' And this was Southey's theme: 'Low our Tree of Hope is laid!' Suspicion and anger followed grief. Why was 'no relative watching over a young woman about to bring forth her first born, and the expected heir to a kingdom?' What had been happening at Claremont? What about that famous obstetrician, Sir Richard Croft? (He, poor fellow, though commended by the Regent and Leopold for his care and attention – and incidentally exonerated since by our own medical researchers – committed suicide three months later.) And, above all, what about that fat libertine of a father, the Regent?

He was careless, not callous. A more thoughtful man, less devoted to the pleasure principle, would have put off the Hertfords and their Suffolk shoot, if only to be within reasonable call of Claremont. But there seemed to be plenty of time. As soon as he was told that Charlotte's labour had begun, he left Suffolk at once. If he was late that was because there had been a delay of twenty-four hours in sending off the message to him. At least, this was Croker's story. (John Wilson Croker, Tory M.P., was a great sneerer at romantic poets in the *Quarterly Review:* not one of my

(above left) John Wilson Croker,
c. 1812, by William Owen
oil on canvas
24 × 19½ in. (61 × 49.5 cm.)
The National Portrait Gallery,
London

(above right) The Hombourg Waltz
with characteristic sketches of family
dancing, 1818, by George Cruikshank
– A satire on a royal dukes' haste to
marry after the death of Princess
Charlotte, there being no heir
presumptive to the throne, except
the Duke of York – none of the
brothers having legitimate children
The British Museum, London

favourite characters.) The Regent asked at each halt on the road if
there were a message for him, and at one point did learn that the
labour was prolonged. A messenger bringing the news that the
child was dead actually passed him by on the road. He reached
Carlton House in the small hours of 6 November, learnt then that
the child was stillborn, went to bed but shortly afterwards had to
be roused to greet the Duke of York, who had come to tell him that
Charlotte was dead. He was at Claremont by 9 a.m., asked to see
the bodies, and then drove away with the blinds of his coach drawn.
A week later, Croker was writing: 'All his thoughts and conversation turn upon the late sad event. He never stirs out of his room,
and goes to bed sometimes at eight or nine o'clock, wearied out,
and yet not composed enough for rest.' He lived in retirement at
Brighton for many weeks, his dejected appearance noted by the
few who saw him. It was even said he had a severe illness, described
as being 'of the worst nature, founded on religion and despon-
dency'. The pleasure principle works badly at such times.

It was the fashion then in the theatre to have a farce following a
tragedy. Now the royal family and the government between them
improvised a farce. The immediate situation was serious enough;
the direct line of succession to the Throne had been broken; an
heir was urgently needed; but there is something farcical about the
hasty attempts to put an end to this situation. The country was
littered with the illegitimate children of the Royal Dukes and their
various mistresses; but now there must be marriage – on a proper
high level too – and legitimacy. Lord Liverpool, still Prime Minister,
promised increased allowances to the Royal Dukes to encourage
dynastic marriages. But the Duke of Clarence said he would marry

196

(above left) *An Address to British Females on the Moral Management of Pregnancy and Labour,* London: E. Cox, 1817
The Wellcome Institute of the History of Medicine, London

(above right) The drawing room, 50 Albemarle Street, as it was in 1815, painted *c.* 1852 by Jacques Christophe Werner
(left to right) Isaac D'Israeli, John Murray, Sir John Barrow, George Canning, William Gifford, John Wilson Croker, Sir Walter Scott and Lord Byron
– original painting destroyed
Collection Mr John Murray, London

only if the government provided handsomely for his ten illegitimate children and settled his own debts. In December 1817, the Duke of Kent told Creevey, 'It is now seven and twenty years that Madame St Laurent and I have lived together . . . you may well imagine, Mr Creevey, the pang it will occasion me to part with her' – but should the Duke of Clarence do nothing about marrying before St George's Day – 'it will become my duty, no doubt, to take some measures upon the subject myself . . .' The Duke of York was out of the race, being no longer able to father a child, but among his brothers there was much jealousy and some hurried scrambling through possible German princesses, like shuffling and cutting cards. What came out of it, the following summer, were two marriages. The Duke of Clarence, fifty-three, married Princess Adelaide of Saxe-Meiningen – 'hair of a peculiar colour approaching the lemon tint, weak eyes and a bad complexion'. The Duke of Kent, fifty-two, as we saw in the first chapter, did better, got the jackpot, by marrying Leopold's widowed sister, Victoria Mary Louisa of Leiningen. Thus he became the father of another Victoria, the queen who did much to restore a royal prestige damaged by so many years of farcical antics.

Another woman, only forty-one, slipped quietly away a few months before Charlotte died, and was buried in Winchester Cathedral. This of course was Jane Austen, who has probably given more delight to more English-speaking people than any other woman who ever lived. Though she made no stir with the public, it is a mistake to imagine that her exquisite work was not appreciated at all in her own time. The Regent himself, as we have seen, was among her admirers, and so were Scott, Coleridge, Southey, Sydney Smith, Lord Holland; and in the next age Macaulay called her 'a wonderful creature', placed her next to Shakespeare as a creator of character, and at one time wanted to raise a fund to erect a monument to her. And how pleasant it is – and perhaps rather surprising – to read her nephew's description of her! 'In person she was very attractive,' he wrote. 'Her figure was rather tall and slender, her step light and firm, and her whole appearance of health and animation. In complexion she was a clear brunette with a rich colour, she had full round cheeks with a mouth and nose small but well-formed, bright hazel eyes and brown hair forming natural curls round her face . . .' Her novels are subtle works of art, highly selective in their detail, but her letters bring us close to quiet upper-middle-class life in the Regency, to people who were neither fashionable and raffish nor evangelical puritans.

However, 1817 can show us something very different from Jane Austen's quiet vicarages or the Regent's thirty-six entrées and a wind band at the Brighton Pavilion. This year, two parliamentary Select Committees removed the lid from a London, east of St James's and Mayfair, that seemed to belong to an inferno. The first of these two Select Committees was concerned with the police and crime. It had been discovered before – and would be observed again and again for many years yet – that the policing of London was completely ineffectual. It was a kind of antiquated hotch-potch of parish officers, beadles, constables, watchmen and street keepers, far closer to the Watch of Shakespeare's Dogberry and Verges than to any police force today. It was hopelessly out of date in its traditional organisation, belonging to a cluster of parishes and not to a city with a population that had now passed the million mark; and it was ridiculously undermanned. The strongest permanent force, which was that of the City of London itself, had only about forty-five men, directed by two City marshals. The famous Bow Street had only a few more men, chiefly for patrol duties, than the other London magistrates' courts, which had at their disposal only eight to twelve policemen. The forces of law and order must have been hard to find in those hundreds of alleys and narrow, badly-lighted streets.

In Pierce Egan's *Life in London* his heroes Tom and Jerry are arrested after a fight in a coffee house, a low haunt to which they repair at the end of a long night's drinking. And when we look at Cruikshank's illustrations, a notable feature of the book, we wonder how so many guardians of the law could have arrived so promptly on the scene, unless of course they ignored whole areas to keep close to that particular coffee house. Some odd details emerge after the appearance of Tom and Jerry at Bow Street. For example, the watchmen, in order to make sure they had evidence

PLATE XXIX. Sir Walter Scott, 1824, by Sir Edwin Henry Landseer
oil on panel
$11\frac{1}{2} \times 9\frac{1}{2}$ in. (29.2 × 24.1 cm.)
The National Portrait Gallery, London

Parisian Home Costume, from *La Belle Assemblée*, 1 January 1817 Collection Mrs Doris Langley Moore, London

PLATE XXX. Princess Charlotte and Prince Leopold, 1818, by William Thomas Fry after George Dawe stipple engraving painted over in watercolour
17½ × 14 in. (44.5 × 35.6 cm.)
The National Portrait Gallery, London

they had been attacked, carried broken lanterns round with them. And not only was the watchman who brought the charge called Barney O'Brother but the men he had called in to assist him were called Pat Sullivan, Tim Ryan, Roger M'Carthy and Dennis O'Bryan, as if this part of London had become another Dublin. It seems that Pierce Egan here was hinting at an Irish invasion.

Before we return to the police, Pierce Egan and his *Life in London* deserve a little more attention. He was a well-known sporting journalist and the editor of *Boxiana*. The full title of his book is *Life in London or the Day and Night Scenes of Jerry Hawthorn, Esq. and his elegant friend Corinthian Tom in their Rambles and Sprees through the Metropolis.* To which was added: *With Numerous Coloured Illustrations from Real Life Designed by I. R. & G. Cruikshank.* It was first published in 1821 – being suitably dedicated to our Prince, now elevated to 'His Most Excellent Majesty King George the Fourth' – and it was such a success that not only was it often reprinted but various dramatic versions were played throughout the 1820s. The text is irritating because it bristles with slang and coy or leering italics, the stylistic devices of sporting journalists; and Egan is rarely telling the full honest truth about anything, but, like a man boasting of fashionable and sporting life in London to a country cousin, makes everything look rosier and more glamorous than it really was, as if seen through a wineglass – brightly. Nevertheless, though it came out when the Regency proper had come to an end, Egan must have collected his material rather earlier, and so, in spite of his weaknesses, he does bring us fairly close – perhaps closer than anybody else – to the Corinthian Tom style of life in the actual Regency, together with a fairly typical Regency outlook and attitude of mind. Moreover, the Cruikshank plates are more realistic than the text they illustrate.

Now we must return to the London police of 1817. They were badly organised; they were shockingly undermanned; they were also poorly paid. This inevitably resulted in too many of them being dishonest. From the beadles, elected annually and paid about a pound a week, to the constables, one for each watch-house throughout the night, to the 'street keepers' – one to a parish and on duty during the day, to the watchmen who went out after night-fall to tackle the footpads and thieves in the dark streets, they were too often on the make, taking a bribe here, doing a little blackmail there. However, the Select Committee of 1817 obtained sufficient trustworthy evidence from members of the force. Some of it, quoted verbatim, may be found in *A People's Conscience* by Strathearn Gordon and T. G. B. Cock, a book that describes six typical enquiries (1729-1837) by Select Committees of the House of Commons. And as there were two of these enquiries in 1817, I am greatly indebted here to this report of them.

201

Midnight – Tom & Jerry at a Coffee Shop near the Olympic, from Pierce Egan's *Life in London*, 1821 – drawn and etched by I. R. and G. Cruikshank
The British Museum, London

Tom & Jerry in Trouble after a Spree, from Pierce Egan's *Life in London*, 1821 – drawn and etched by I. R. and G. Cruikshank
The British Museum, London

Bow Street, Tom & Jerry's sensibility awakened at the pathetic tale of the elegant Cyprian – the feeling Coachman and the generous Magistrate, from Pierce Egan's *Life in London*, 1821 – drawn and etched by I. R. and G. Cruikshank
The British Museum, London

Tom & Jerry Sporting their 'bits of blood' among the Pinks in Rotten Row, from Pierce Egan's *Life in London*, 1821
The British Museum, London

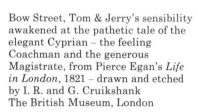

The evidence shows us an inefficient and largely corrupt police force and plenty of crime and criminals. But what shocked the members of the Select Committee will shock us now. It was the existence of what the police called 'flash houses'. Fagin's establishment in *Oliver Twist* was probably a surviving flash house, though Dickens could not describe everything that went on there. The Regency flash house – and there were several of them in St Giles's alone, and up to four hundred slept in one of them – boarded and often trained delinquents in their earliest teens. The boys, gradually becoming expert, went out thieving, picking pockets, pilfering here and there. The girls, who might be only thirteen or fourteen, were prostitutes. They were probably taught where to go and what to do. They often slept with the flash house boys, but this was not by way of business but for comfort and companionship. (When a boy was sent to prison, his favourite girl might visit him, pretending to be a relative.) Many of these youngsters had been abandoned by their parents or were orphans. Apart from thieving or whoring, no other way of life appeared to be open to them. And a boy, arrested for some minor pilfering, could be sent to prison, flogged there, and then turned out without a penny in his pocket. Unless he was prepared to sleep in sheds or under stalls and live on garbage, he had to go back to a flash house, where he would find food and warmth if he agreed to return to thieving.

The young girls were no better off – perhaps even worse off – than the boys. They could only join the crowds of adult prostitutes. It is often suggested that the figures for prostitution and brothels in London, during most of the nineteenth century, have been enormously exaggerated, but in this 1817 enquiry exact numbers were given for several East End parishes and they were horrifying. One witness called by the Select Committee offers us a glimpse of what the young girls might expect when they were grown up:

> It is probable there may be some who remain on the town through inability to get their living in an honest employment; but it is considered, from their early habits of vice, by far the greater part of the prostitutes living in this parish continue their miserable practice from a depraved inclination, aided by the constant excitement of the procuresses, who, receiving the whole of the wretched produce of their prostitution, are necessarily active to prevent the possibility of their reformation; for which purpose they attend them in their nightly and daily walks, especially watching those most recently initiated into their baneful course, and keeping them continually in a state of inebriety, if not in a state of absolute intoxication. The state of slavery in which those unhappy females are held is beyond description or belief; they have not anything they can call their own, but appear to be entirely abandoned, in body and mind, to the service and advantage of the persons with whom they reside, and from whose trammels it is impossible they can escape . . .

But in answering a later question about giving employment to prostitutes who might wish to reform, this same witness shakes his head over 'the present distressed state of the country, and the general stagnation of trade, which has thrown so many honest industrious persons out of employ', thus reminding these legislators, who probably needed reminding, of the interdependence of things.

It was more or less proved that the constables and watchmen or their superiors, by occasionally closing a flash house or brothel, then threatening others, were able to augment their poor pay very considerably. It was also suggested that the owners of such places, mostly women, were able to live well on their profits, keeping their carriages and owning villas in leafy suburbs, where no doubt they were regarded as pillars of respectability. If there is any record of even one of these harpies being carted off to gaol, I have not succeeded in finding it. Other women did well out of a surprisingly large traffic (it was said to employ six hundred agents) in grossly obscene books and prints. No doubt a fair number of bachelors were among their customers, but the best trade was said to be done in boarding schools for young ladies – 'wholesome seminaries of female education'. It was easy for the women agents to gain admission into these schools on one pretext or another, often under the pretence of buying cast-off clothes from the servants. I wonder how many Early Victorian wives and mothers of the upper class tried not to remember what they stared at and giggled over, twenty-odd years before, when they were at school in 1817?

All those half-grown girls in the flash houses were there because the women running the houses had plenty of customers for them. Again, a large number of girls in their early teens must have been working for procuresses who were in the retail trade rather than the wholesale trade. And we know that Harriette Wilson and her sisters were being kept by men of rank and fashion when they were only thirteen or fourteen. All this throws a curious light on male sexuality during the Regency.

The desire for young girls was not peculiar to the Regency; it had existed among men of fashion during the second half of the eighteenth century, and was to continue in London throughout most of the nineteenth. Even in our day *Lolita* has become a best-seller. Clearly, a man with uncomplicated feelings about sex, one who simply wants as much sensual gratification as his money can buy, is likely to prefer a ripe and experienced woman to a half-grown girl. In simple physical terms, regarded as a sexual object, twenty-four is probably better value than fourteen. We can only assume, then, that we are dealing here with a psychological twist, the appeal being really mental and not physical. A natural sexual urge has been warped by the mind into this perverted taste.

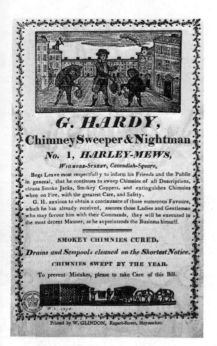

G. Hardy's Trade Card
The British Museum, London

Having a woman at all is regarded as a contemptuous male gesture of conquest, and having one as early as possible, when she is still half a child, is to make the conquest – really of the whole sex – even more complete and contemptuous. These young-girl pursuers and buyers are not lovers of women: they really fear and hate them. They use their sex and their money as instruments of feminine destruction. And clearly there were plenty of their kind in the Regency, though, oddly enough, its most prominent personages – for example, the Regent himself, and even Byron – went to the other extreme, not only ignoring young girls but always finding a fascination in women older, sometimes much older, than themselves, as if they were still looking for some sort of acceptable and loving mother.

Now for the second Select Committee of that year – and another glimpse of Hell. It was appointed in June, 1817, after a petition, well furnished with signatures, had been presented to the House of Commons protesting against the common practice of using small boys to sweep chimneys. The chairman of this Select Committee was Henry Grey Bennet, second son of the Earl of Tankerville, and one of the few aristocratic members of the House who was a genuine reformer, indeed an enthusiastic radical. Protests against the employment of 'climbing boys', as they were called, were not new. There was even a society demanding their abolition that went back to 1803. The society had constantly pointed out that there were good alternative methods of clearing and sweeping chimneys – these were referred to as 'machines', a queer term for what can only have been elongated brushes – but almost all sweeps preferred to send small boys up the chimneys – and the smaller and younger the better. There was an official minimum age of eight, but children of four to six had often been forced into the chimneys. Much of the evidence given to the Select Committee is like a nightmare.

Some of these wretched little boys were the sons of chimney sweeps, not necessarily skilled men but former day-labourers hoping to earn more money. Other boys, probably the large majority, had been sold to sweeps by parents for three or four guineas. A few, as we shall see, had even been kidnapped. As a rule they were badly fed, had to sleep on the floor in some corner, and might go for months, thick with soot, without being washed. No child in his senses wants to inch his way up narrow chimneys and flues – less than the width of two bricks, some of them – with soot and mortar falling, half-blinding and choking him; and this meant that the climbing boys, especially the shrinking new arrivals, were very roughly handled by the sweeps and their apprentices. Often a larger boy was sent up after the small one and jabbed a pin into his bare feet to keep him going. The new boys suffered from

bruises and sores until their knees and elbows were sufficiently hardened, and even then they were always in danger of being burnt by chimneys partly on fire. Occasionally they were driven up by lighting hay or straw below them.

Medical evidence, taken by the Select Committee, showed that the climbing boys nearly always grew up to be stunted and deformed, were more subject to coughs and asthma and inflammation of the lungs than other people, and were often victims of cancer, especially one that attacked the scrotum and was known as 'the chimney-sweeper's cancer'. Even when they had done their climbing, children of eight or nine might be compelled to carry loads of soot and sweeping cloths weighing anything from thirty pounds upwards. Some of them were given nothing to eat by their masters and had to beg or steal food at the houses where they worked. There were altogether too many unlucky children in the early nineteenth century, but the most wretched of them all were the climbing boys. Death – and there were recorded cases of boys having died of exposure, of burns, of suffocation, of beating must have seemed a welcome release.

There was a curious case of a stolen child that suggests popular nineteenth-century story-telling but was entirely authenticated. A well-to-do family in Yorkshire, called Strickland, became interested in a tiny boy, a handsome child, who had come crashing down a chimney and bruised himself very badly. They took him home, the chimney sweeper being glad to get rid of him. When he saw a silver fork, the little boy was delighted and cried, 'Papa had such forks as those.' This happened with many other things he saw: they were like Papa's. He would not get into bed without first repeating the Lord's Prayer, which he had obviously been carefully taught. He had been too young at home to know his surname; still living in a world of Mama and Papa. He did not know what part of the country had been his home, but the Stricklands soon guessed from his accent and various details that it must have been somewhere in the south of England.

Gradually his story came out. It appeared that his Mama was dead and his Papa had been travelling abroad, and he had spent some time with a dearly-loved Uncle George. He had been gathering flowers in Uncle George's garden when a strange woman (probably a gipsy) came in and asked him if he liked riding. When he said he did, she took him away on her horse and then they went in a ship with sails. Eventually they landed in Yorkshire. There, as the Stricklands discovered for themselves, he had been bought from the woman for eight guineas by the chimney sweep. The Stricklands were not able to restore him to his family, though they advertised, but some lady adopted him and saw to his education. When they first discovered him, this little boy was thought to be

(opposite) Two plates from *The Chimney-sweeper's Friend and Climbing Boys Album,* arranged by James Montgomery, 1824
The British Museum, London

Court Dress with the New Hoop, from *La Belle Assemblée,* 1 June 1817 The Victoria and Albert Museum, London

about four years old: he had 'beautiful black eyes and eyelashes, a high nose, and a delicate soft skin'. He was probably only one, the lucky one, of many stolen children, whisked away from parents and gardens to find themselves in the lasting nightmare of the climbing boys.

Bennet, Chairman of the Select Committee, brought in a bill to the House of Commons to abolish the employment of climbing boys. But there was not time to get the bill through, so he tried again in 1818, when it was accepted by the House of Commons but held up in the Lords, where a new official enquiry was demanded. The results of this enquiry did not contradict the report of the original Committee, and early in 1819 Bennet again brought in a bill. The Commons passed it once more, and its chances in the Lords looked hopeful, two peers speaking in favour of it. But then the Earl of Lauderdale, who was not in favour of the bill, made one of those light facetious speeches, frequently punctuated in the report by '(Loud laughter)', that are more deadly than any other kind to any decent humane action by legislators. He kept his fellow peers amused by comparing climbing boys to doses of calomel prescribed by doctors, to the geese sometimes drawn up chimneys in Ireland, and then, after much lordly merriment, killed the bill. For my part I wish the Earl of Lauderdale could have been forced up a chimney, if only for a few minutes, because sheer experience then might have taken the place of the imagination and compassion lacking in him. His facetious half hour sent innumerable little boys up chimneys for years and years to come, and though by 1875 they were no longer used in London and the larger provincial towns, it was not until the Chimney Sweepers Bill of 1875 was passed that the country saw the last of the climbing boys.

This melancholy year asks for at least a little light relief. We can find it in the last Sunday of 1817, when Haydon, the painter, gave a dinner at three o'clock in his studio, the guests being Wordsworth, on one of his occasional visits to London, Charles Lamb, John Keats, and another friend, Monkhouse. For the next three or four hours there was some wonderful talk about poetry, and Keats read part of *Endymion,* after Wordsworth had solemnly intoned some Milton, and Lamb, tipsy now, scattered wit. The party then moved to the drawing room for tea; several friends arrived – and one stranger, who had already asked Haydon if he could call to meet Wordsworth. His name was Kingston; he was deputy Comptroller of the Stamp Office; and for the past four years Wordsworth had been supporting his family by acting as Distributor of Stamps for Westmorland and part of Cumberland. But though Wordsworth was under the supervision of Kingston, acting as deputy Comptroller in London, the two had never met before. Now we must turn

PLATE XXXI. John Keats, 1821, by Joseph Severn oil on canvas 22¼ × 16½ in. (56.4 × 41.8 cm.) The National Portrait Gallery, London

to Haydon's own account of what happened when the two did meet that Sunday evening:

When we retired to tea we found the comptroller. In introducing him to Wordsworth I forgot to say who he was. After a little time the comptroller looked down, looked up and said to Wordsworth, 'Don't you think, sir, Milton was a great genius?' Keats looked at me, Wordsworth looked at the comptroller. Lamb who was dozing by the fire turned round and said, 'Pray, sir, did you say Milton was a great genius?' 'No, sir, I asked Mr Wordsworth if he were not.' 'Oh,' said Lamb, 'then you are a silly fellow,' 'Charles! my dear Charles!' said Wordsworth; but Lamb, perfectly innocent of the confusion he had created, was off again by the fire.

After an awful pause the comptroller said, 'Don't you think Newton a great genius?' I could not stand it any longer. Keats put his head into my books. Ritchie squeezed in a laugh. Wordsworth seemed asking himself, 'Who is this?' Lamb got up, and taking a candle, said, 'Sir, will you allow me to look at your phrenological development?' He then turned his back on the poor man, and at every question of the comptroller he chaunted –

> Diddle diddle dumpling, my son John
> Went to bed with his breeches on.

The man in office, finding Wordsworth did not know who he was, said in a spasmodic and half-chuckling anticipation of assured victory, 'I have had the honour of some correspondence with you, Mr Wordsworth.' 'With me, sir?' said Wordsworth, 'not that I remember.' 'Don't you, sir? I am a comptroller of stamps.' There was a dead silence; – the comptroller evidently thinking that was enough. While we were waiting for Wordsworth's reply, Lamb sung out

> Hey diddle diddle,
> The cat and the fiddle.

'My dear Charles!' said Wordsworth, –

> Diddle diddle dumpling, my son John,

chaunted Lamb, and then rising, exclaimed, 'Do let me have another look at that gentleman's organs.' Keats and I hurried Lamb into the painting-room, shut the door and gave way to inextinguishable laughter. Monkhouse followed and tried to get Lamb away. We went back but the comptroller was irreconcilable. We soothed and smiled and asked him to supper. He stayed though his dignity was sorely affected. However, being a good-natured man, we parted all in good-humour, and no ill effects followed.

All the while, until Monkhouse succeeded, we could hear Lamb struggling in the painting-room and calling at intervals, 'Who is that fellow? Allow me to see his organs once more.'

I know this story has often been told, but here in its proper place, 28 December 1817, it helps us to say goodbye to that melancholy year – with a smile.

1818

Fact and Fiction

Desolated late in 1817 by the loss of his daughter and grandchild, the Regent might well have cried with Falstaff: 'A plague of sighing and grief! It blows a man up like a bladder.' The rumour went round that he had 'left off his stays'. This was confirmed early in 1818. Lord Folkestone wrote to Creevey, who was abroad: 'Prinny has let loose his belly which now reaches his knees: otherwise he is said to be well.' And not long afterwards, the Duke of Wellington, who had just come from England, said in reply to a question of Creevey's about the Regent: 'By God! you never saw such a figure in your life as he is. Then he speaks and swears so like old Falstaff that damn me if I was not ashamed to walk into a room with him.' His talk, so far as it has come down to us, hardly seems Falstaffian, but he was not without a turn of wit. Croker, dining at the Pavilion towards the end of this year, tells us: 'There was a fine boar's head at the side table at dinner. The Prince pressed Lord Hertford to eat some of it. He refused, and the Prince said it was the only kind of bore that Lord Hertford was not fond of: this is good, because Lord Hertford has a real passion for persons whom everybody else considers as bores.'

He was certainly Falstaffian now in girth and tonnage. Even in 1816 *The Times,* in a solemn article about the Regent's state of health, had described how he contrived to ride a little round the Pavilion lawn – the problem being How could he mount his horse?

An inclined plane was constructed, rising to about the height of two feet and a half, at the upper end of which was a platform. His Royal Highness was placed in a chair on rollers, and so moved by the ascent, and placed on the platform, which was then raised by screws high enough to pass the horse under: and finally, his Royal Highness was let gently down into the saddle. By these means the Regent was undoubtedly able to enjoy in some degree the benefit of air and exercise . . .

But by December 1818 he was doing no more riding, as he told Croker:

The fineness of the weather does not tempt him abroad: his great size and weight make him nervous and he is afraid to ride. I am not surprised at it. I begin to fear he will never ride again. He says, 'Why should I?

(opposite) The Kitchen (detail), from John Nash's *Brighton Pavilion,* 1820–25
The Royal Institute of British Architects, London (Drawings Collection)

The Prince of Pleasure

I never had better spirits, appetite and health than when I stay within, and I am not so well when I go abroad.' He seems as kind and gracious as usual to everybody. The etiquette is, that before dinner, when he comes in, he *finds* all the men standing, and the women rise; he speaks to everybody, shakes hands with the newcomers or particular friends, then desires the ladies to be seated. When dinner is announced, he leads out a lady of the highest rank or when the ranks are nearly equal, or when the nominal rank interferes with the real rank, as yesterday, with Lady Liddell and Mrs Pelham, he took one on each arm. After dinner the new dining room was lighted and he took the ladies to see it . . .

(He was vastly proud of his Pavilion; but more of that later.) It was during this same month that the Regent entertained his servants to supper in the Pavilion Kitchen: 'A scarlet cloth was thrown over the pavement,' we are told. 'A splendid repast was provided, and the good-humoured Prince sat down, with a select party of his friends, and spent a joyous hour. The whole of the servants, particularly the female portion, were delighted at this mark of Royal condescension.'

Falstaff's lies were deliberate; he multiplied his men in buckram

The Royal Pavilion, Brighton, from John Nash's *Brighton Pavilion,* 1820–25
The Royal Institute of British Architects, London (Drawings Collection)

to amuse his company. The Regent's sudden departures from anything like the truth were very different. It is hard to discover if he knew he was lying, his mind being such an amiable muddle. For example, our old acquaintance Lady Melbourne died this year, 1818. In 1822, with our Prince now King George IV, Lady Cowper was staying at the Pavilion; and there the King told her that during the last illness of Lady Melbourne 'he had walked across to Melbourne House every day to inquire and sometimes to see her and that she had died in his arms.' But, as Lady Cowper later told Wellington, she had not left her mother's room for the last ten days of her mother's life, and so knew very well that the Regent had never been near, had not even sent to inquire how Lady Melbourne was. Now why this gigantic lie? Was it because he simply wanted to please his guest? Was it because he wanted to show how tender-hearted he was? Or had he persuaded himself by this time that he really had been so attentive and concerned during Lady Melbourne's last illness, just as he may have come to believe that he really had been present at various naval engagements and also at Waterloo? Did he deceive others or did he deceive himself? We lack the evidence that would supply an answer to any such question.

(above left) Monopodium table, design reproduced in Thomas Hope's *Household Furniture*, 1807 mahogany, inlaid ebony and silver The Victoria and Albert Museum, London

(above right) A chair, early 19th century – similar although not identical in design to several in the greek revival style reproduced in Thomas Hope's *Household Furniture*, 1807 The Victoria and Albert Museum, London

Though he might be naturally devoted to pleasure and idleness, the Regent was a ruling monarch in everything but his title and so had many duties from which it was impossible to escape. During Croker's visit to Brighton, already mentioned, he describes how he discovered the Regent hard at work for once: 'He had his table covered with papers for perusal and signature, and he was signing away at full gallop.' These were probably routine matters, reluctantly attended to at the last minute. But he was directly interested in foreign affairs, giving audiences to important personages (he almost always succeeded in charming them), and in making full use of his power of patronage, distributing honours and appointments. He would often go to a great deal of trouble, really exerting himself, to make sure his promise of an appointment, usually to some office of state, was duly kept. There is some evidence too, entirely to his credit, that more than once he reprieved prisoners under the death sentence. On the other hand, he had a habit of neglecting or at least delaying urgent business, to the despair of his cabinet ministers. Anything that gave him momentary pleasure might do the trick. For example, on one occasion, when he was living in Brighton, he called a special cabinet meeting in London to begin at noon. So the ministers, all busy men, assembled at the Treasury, and were relieved to hear that the Regent had already arrived from Brighton. But an hour, two hours, nearly three hours, went by, while they fretted and fumed – but no Regent. They then discovered that 'he was shut with tailors examining different patterns of uniform'. The pleasure principle had intervened.

However, when one of his most enthusiastic courtiers, the Duke of Buckingham, declared that 'The Prince Regent, as the sovereign *de facto*, was exercising a beneficial influence in various directions, particularly in the cultivation of the Arts and Sciences', he was not being entirely carried away by his enthusiasm. At heart the Regent may not have cared deeply for the arts and sciences, but in his official capacity he certainly behaved – as few English monarchs have done – as if he recognised their importance. We have already discovered instances of this behaviour in the visual arts, and now in 1818 it was the turn of literature. The Literary Fund, a society for the relief of distress among authors, was originally founded in 1790 by the admirable David Williams. The Regent had long been one of its patrons and regular subscribers. Now in 1818 he was able to obtain for it a Charter of Incorporation, and allowed the Society to make use of his Crest upon its Arms. (A quarter of a century later, Victoria granted the privilege of using the term *Royal*, so that from then onwards the Society called itself The Royal Literary Fund, but even so it was the Regent who took the first and most important step.) The Royal Literary Fund still exists. Its record is astonishing, beginning with Coleridge, the widow of Robert Burns, and Chateaubriand, in the 1790s, and including among the writers it helped in this century Joseph Conrad, D. H. Lawrence and James Joyce*.

1818 was a good year for the Regent to help the Literary Fund, not only making sure that the society understood it was under his patronage but also enabling it to rent a house as its headquarters. The point is that 1818 was a good year for literature itself. It saw the first publication of Keats's *Endymion,* Hazlitt's *Lectures on the English Poets,* and in Italy Byron had written the first canto of *Don Juan.* Coleridge was giving his last series of lectures. The new fiction included the posthumous publication of Jane Austen's early novel, *Northanger Abbey* and her last, *Persuasion;* Scott brought out, still anonymously, two of his finest stories, *Heart of Midlothian* and *Rob Roy;* Thomas Love Peacock's *Nightmare Abbey* appeared this year, and so did Mary Shelley's *Frankenstein.*

It is time something was said here about Samuel Taylor Coleridge, even though his poetry belongs to an earlier period and he outlived the Regency by fourteen years, during which he wrote little but was famous for his wonderful talk. Our decade belongs to him as a critic, never systematic, chiefly represented by fragments of his

---

*If any readers feel they owe something to English Literature, I suggest they send a donation to The Royal Literary Fund, 11 Ludgate Hill, London E.C.4. Perhaps I ought to add that the Fund gives financial aid to living writers or their dependents under terms of the strictest secrecy.

lectures, but almost entirely original – though influenced to some extent by his German studies – and wonderfully perceptive. Frank and often amusing accounts of Coleridge's lectures can be found in the diary of Henry Crabb Robinson, who knew Coleridge well and greatly admired him, though not always as a lecturer. Robinson was not happy about this last series of lectures in 1818, felt that Coleridge was repeating his favourite ideas too often, that 'his speculations have ceased to be living thoughts', and concluded, 'I fear that Coleridge will not on the whole add to his reputation by these lectures.'

Coleridge's influence on English criticism was enormous. It was he who provided the English romantic movement with its intellectual core. And his influence reached beyond literature. John Stuart Mill, whose background and attitude were very different, declared that Coleridge and Jeremy Bentham between them had supplied the earlier nineteenth-century England with most of its seminal ideas. Coleridge's range of knowledge, thought and feeling was extraordinary; I have been reading him with admiration and gratitude for well over half a century, and my only complaint is that he occasionally lapses into a rather greasy piety, probably because his conscience troubled him. He regarded himself as a dreadful failure; he had let Southey support his wife and family; he had been unable to carry out vast plans for epic poems and volumes of systematic philosophising; he had surrendered himself, though reluctantly and not eagerly, to opium. But he was not a failure, only – as his friend Lamb beautifully put it – 'an archangel a little damaged'.

By the time Coleridge began his last series of lectures in 1818, he had already spent two years – and he was to be there for the rest of his life – as a guest, 'honoured and cherished', of James Gillman (a surgeon) and his wife in their house at the top of Highgate Hill. There, in a room high up at the back, overlooking Hampstead Heath, Coleridge received his friends and young disciples and spun for them his huge glittering webs of monologue. I know that room well because for nearly ten years I used it as my study, having acquired that very house – 3, The Grove, Highgate Village – early in the 1930s. (And nobody need tell me that my friends and I were an anticlimax after Coleridge, Wordsworth, Lamb, Thomas Carlyle, to name no others. I know it. But then in almost any other country a house with such rich literary associations would have been publicly cherished and not left, as I found it, a dilapidated property for sale.) I cannot claim to have listened to Coleridge's ghost – and surely if there could be a talking ghost it would be his – and the point I wish to make now is not one, I think, he would have welcomed.

However, I feel it is too easily assumed that opium undermined

PLATE XXXIII. Samuel Taylor Coleridge, 1814, by Washington Allston
oil on canvas
44 × 35½ in. (111.8 × 85.1 cm.)
The National Portrait Gallery, London

Coleridge's Study at
3, The Grove, Highgate Village
Collection Mr J. B. Priestley

his character and explains all his vacillating and procrastinating. The weakness of will, it seems to me, was always there, opium or no opium. The flaw would have been there, even if laudanum could not have been bought for a few pence at the nearest druggist's. (It was used then more or less as we use aspirin now, and of course it could be dangerous, but nobody can claim it wrecked Regency and Victorian society.) Thomas de Quincey, whose *Confessions of an English Opium-Eater* arrived just after the Regency had ended, was a mere wisp of a man, who probably weighed not half as much as Coleridge. Yet he took opium for most of his life, and at one time was taking enough of it every day to have knocked out ten navvies for a week. He was notoriously eccentric, existing in a highly intellectual dream world, but born in 1785 he lived until 1859, somehow contrived to support a large family, though never sharing the same roof, and his collected works, filled with odd learning, cranky notions and eloquent prose, run to fourteen volumes or so. Opium supplied him with strange elaborate dreams and a kind of heightened writing that did justice to them, but it never destroyed his will to live and work. Coleridge had a far richer personality, had genius where de Quincey had talent, but if he failed his grander projects and his responsibilities as a man, I suggest again the fault was in himself and not in his dependence on the poppy. Incidentally, both men originally took to opium to cope with physical weaknesses, neuralgic and other pains. Medicine during the Regency was still lingering in the eighteenth century.

Coleridge makes a caricatured appearance as Mr Flosky, the

PLATE XXXIV. Romantic Landscape, 1820, by Sebastian Pether
oil on canvas
17½ × 16 in. (44.5 × 40.7 cm.)
Collection Mr John Hadfield

gloomy metaphysician, in Peacock's *Nightmare Abbey*, which arrived this year. (It was in 1818 too that Peacock was appointed an Assistant Examiner by the East India Company, where he remained, with office hours ten to four, for the rest of what we can hardly call his working life.) Peacock's highly original novels consist almost entirely of talk, usually round a heavily loaded dining table in a country house, and it is the wit, humour and genial satire of this talk that have carried these odd books down from one delighted generation to another. They look easy to write, but in fact none of Peacock's imitators has ever succeeded in coming near him. It is not simply a question of literary skill. Peacock found a form that exactly suited his outlook and temperament. Radical in politics but conservative in his tastes, he was sharply aware of ideas, even those of crackpots, but amused himself mocking them. He was a satirist who was never sour and misanthropic; his mockery is never bitter; he *enjoys* the people he is caricaturing. He could laugh at Shelley's wild idealism – as he does in *Nightmare Abbey* – but there is affection behind the laughter; after all, they were close friends. Scythrop Glowry, the ultra-romantic central character of *Nightmare Abbey*, who finds himself divided between two girls, is the absurd side of Shelley taken away from the rest of him, set in motion and given a voice among other caricatures of romanticism. Peacock is much sharper with Byron, who appears as Mr Cypress:

> MR CYPRESS: Sir, I have quarrelled with my wife; and a man who has quarrelled with his wife is absolved from all duty to his country. I have written an ode to tell the people as much, and they may take it as they list.

And a little later:

> MR CYPRESS: I have no hope for myself or for others. Our life is a false nature; it is not in the harmony of things; it is an all-blasting upas, whose root is earth, and whose leaves are the skies which rain their poison-dews upon mankind. We wither from our youth; we gasp with unslaked thirst for unattainable good; lured from the first to the last by phantoms – love, fame, ambition, avarice – all idle, and all ill – one meteor of many names, that vanishes in the smoke of death.

The sting here – and the speech itself is *Childe Harold* turned into neat prose that makes it sound absurd – is that Mr Cypress, for all his despair, is sitting with the others, a good dinner inside him and now ready for another bottle of Madeira and a chorus – as Byron himself, for all his affected pessimism, might easily have been.

Scythrop and his two girls came dangerously close to the Shelley-Harriet-Mary situation, cutting much nearer the bone than any burlesque of romanticism and philosophical anarchy. Peacock must have known that he could depend upon Shelley's good nature and lack of vanity, for he did not hesitate to send a copy of *Nightmare Abbey* to Shelley at Leghorn. And though I suspect that some of Peacock's wit and drollery may have passed unnoticed, Shelley appears to have resented nothing and even wrote: 'I think Scythrop a character admirably conceived and executed.' He said not a word about Mary's opinion of the book, and it is possible that he kept it from her, Mary Wollstonecraft Shelley not being a woman who would enjoy a caricature of herself. Moreover, she was feeling depressed during their stay at Leghorn.

But Mary Shelley was now in print, even though *Frankenstein*, after being rejected by two publishers, Murray and Ollier, first appeared anonymously, in March 1818. The reviewers gave it plenty of space and treated it seriously, even if some of them shook their heads over it. All of them assumed that such a powerful story was the work of a man; they would have been almost as horrified as Frankenstein was by his monster if they had been told it was the first book of a girl of nineteen. In her introduction to it thirteen years later, Mary Shelley describes how it came to be written:

> In the summer of 1816, we visited Switzerland, and became the neighbours of Lord Byron. At first we spent our pleasant hours on the lake, or wandering on its shores; and Lord Byron, who was writing the third canto of Childe Harold, was the only one among us who puts his thoughts upon paper . . . But it proved a wet, ungenial summer, and incessant rain often confined us for days to the house. Some volumes of ghost stories, translated from the German into the French, fell into our hands . . . 'We will each write a ghost story,' said Lord Byron; and his proposition was acceded to . . . I busied myself *to think of a story* – a story to rival those which had excited us to this task. One which would speak to the mysterious fears of our nature, and awaken thrilling horror – one to make the reader dread to look round, to curdle the blood, and quicken the beatings of the heart . . . I thought and pondered – vainly . . .

After listening to a long conversation between Shelley and Byron about 'the nature of the principle of life, and whether there was any probability of its ever being discovered and communicated', she went late to bed but could not sleep. Dreaming half-awake, so to speak, in that state in which images from the unconscious invade the mind, she saw 'the pale student of unhallowed arts kneeling beside the thing he had put together . . . the hideous phantasm of a man stretched out, and then, on the working of some powerful engine, show signs of life, and stir with an uneasy, half vital motion . . .' And there is much more to this effect, all in the style of the Gothic tales of terror.

Mary Shelley, who lived until 1851, wrote other stories but nothing to rival her nineteen-year-old *Frankenstein*. In our time hundreds of millions of filmgoers, who have never heard of Mary Shelley, but who love to sup on horrors and ice cream and chocolates, know about Frankenstein – and the Bride of Frankenstein, the Son of Frankenstein, and so on. It is not her story itself but its central theme – a man destroyed by the huge, unlovable, lonely creature he has created – that reaches us still, after 150 years. Those images floating up from the unconscious did the trick, compelling her to write not just a piece of fiction but a myth. She had in fact, then or later, no great talent as a writer, but stimulated as she was, that night, by the talk of the two poets, between waking and sleeping she plucked an idea from the deep-rooted tree of mythology. And now we feel closer to Frankenstein than Mary, Shelley, Byron, ever felt, for there looms above us, increasingly huge and menacing, the Technology we have been so busy creating. We are now all brides and sons of Frankenstein.

Popular fiction, on a much lower level than *Frankenstein*, flourished during the Regency. The lending or 'circulating' libraries, which had come into existence during the second half of the eighteenth century, multiplied between 1810 and 1820, especially in London. They ranged from libraries with considerable stocks of books, new and old, and charging an annual subscription, to any small bookseller-cum-stationer who might have a few shelves of newish fiction and lent out novels at so much a volume. In the Regency, young ladies and, less frequently, hard-reading boys in their teens, devoured stacks of lending-library fiction, which could hardly have existed if it had had to depend upon book buyers.

Among the hard-reading lads in their teens during most of the Regency – he was born in 1800 – was the soon-to-be-famous Thomas

Dr Syntax and a Bookseller, drawn and etched by Thomas Rowlandson for W. Combe's *Tours of Dr Syntax,* 1812
The British Museum, London

Mrs Maria Edgeworth, engraving by
Mackenzie after Craig
The British Museum, London

Susan Edmonstone Ferrier,
engraving from a miniature by
R. Thorburn
The British Museum, London

Babington Macaulay. He used to take out novels, probably by
the armful, from the Leadenhall Library. Among his favourites,
though his common sense rebelled against them, were a Mrs Meeke
(but he agreed with his sister that the Meeke stories were all alike
'turning on the fortunes of some young man who eventually proves
to be the son of a duke'), and a Mrs Kitty Cuthbertson, author of
Santo Sebastiano or the Young Protector and many other dashing
romances. Young Macaulay, not Mrs Cuthbertson's ideal reader,
made an exact calculation of the number of fainting fits that
occurred in her *Santo Sebastiano* – and they came to twenty-seven,
with a few males added to the females. As, for example: 'One of the
sweetest smiles that ever animated the face of mortal now diffused
itself over the face of Lord St Orville, as he fell at the feet of Julia
in a death-like swoon.' And even at fifteen Macaulay must have
wondered how his lordship contrived to smile and swoon in this
fashion, unless of course the animating sweetness drained the
blood out of his head.

There was a great deal of reading aloud in the evening among the
Regency middle and upper class families. (The working class must
have been glad to stumble to bed.) So – Jane Austen: 'We have got
the second volume of Esprella's Letters, and I read it aloud by
candlelight.' And Tom Moore: 'I pass my day in study or in the
fields, after dinner I read to Bessy for a couple of hours, and we
are in this way at present going through Miss Edgeworth's works.'
But then Maria Edgeworth was a good novelist, writing about the
Irish she knew, and would have been an even better novelist if she
had taken less notice of her father, who wanted her to be didactic
in his own style. It was her novels about Ireland that made Scott
wonder if similar stories could not be written about Scotland. And
it was Scott who encouraged Susan Ferrier – she was the daughter
of a law colleague and friend – to write good Scots novels, and her
first, *Marriage*, published anonymously (reviewers could be hard
on women writers), came out in 1818. And another Scot, John Galt,
tried the regional style, though his best book, *Annals of the Parish*,
appeared just after the Regency. Then an Irishwoman, Lady
Morgan, livelier than Maria Edgeworth but not as solidly based
in her work, wrote novels before, during, and just after the Regency.
And in 1819 the English rural scene came into view when Mary
Russell Mitford contributed the first chapters of *Our Village* to the
Lady's Magazine. It was the regional outlook, the observation of
local types and manners, that gave solidity to all this fiction,
setting it above the lending-library stuff, manufactured by writers
who never thought in terms of real people in real places.

The popular fiction that went in and out of the libraries so quickly
can be divided roughly into three kinds. First, as we have seen, there
was all the snobbish-sentimental-bosh, with the young men who

always turned out to be sons of dukes, the peers swooning at Julia's feet, the very same sort of girls' day-dream material afterwards turned into penny novelettes. Then there was the occasional fiction of the Evangelicals, who preferred issuing penny tracts, which they did on an enormous scale, but were not above offering sinners a few improving novels. One of these, *The Dairyman's Daughter*, is said to have sold two million copies. This highly edifying story, by a Bedfordshire clergyman, is chiefly given to conversions and deathbeds. The deeply pious heroine converts her frivolous sister (who dies), her father the dairyman, and her mother. Then the heroine takes to her deathbed, but is able to write a series of letters to a clergyman about her trials and temptations, and to make some surprisingly long edifying speeches. Finally, as the third popular kind, there were the 'horrid' or Gothic tales of mystery, suspense, horror, now in our time transferred to the cinema. They were usually set in or around fantastic castles in an imaginary Germany or Italy, and dealt largely in vaults and dungeons and secret passages, screams and the clanking of chains coming from dim corridors, haunted chambers, ghosts, spectres, doomed noble families, long-lost heirs. The improbably romantic settings of the 'horrid' novels were reflected in the work of some of the minor painters of the period. The prolific Pether family, for instance, specialised in moonlit landscapes which usually included a Gothic castle or a ruined abbey – sometimes both.

The best-known and most ingenious of the Gothic tales dated from the 1790s, when Mrs Radcliffe, wife of a newspaper editor and proprietor, was bringing out *The Sicilian Romance, The Romance of the Forest* and, her masterpiece, *The Mysteries of Udolpho*, which was still being read during the Regency. She exercised her ingenuity on a favourite device that we cannot afford to laugh at, simply because it has been used over and over again in our time by admired writers of detective or 'mystery' stories. This trick is to suggest

226

Matthew Gregory Lewis (detail),
by George Letheridge Saunders
watercolour
4¼ × 3½ in. (10.8 × 8.9 cm.)
The National Portrait Gallery,
London

that events must be supernatural when in fact, as it turns out, there
is a more or less rational explanation of them.

On a lower but rather livelier level was the first tale by Matthew
Gregory Lewis, always known in society as 'Monk Lewis' because
this tale was called *The Monk*. After spending some time in
Germany, the home of Gothic horrors, witchcraft, and sinister sor-
cery, he returned to England and at the age of twenty dashed off his
Monk in ten weeks. It was widely denounced at once not so much
for its supernatural effects and atrocities as for its sexual im-
morality, and this of course immediately created a huge demand for
it. So young 'Monk Lewis' went into society, and though vain,
fussy, rather pompous, he was on the whole well liked, and is
always turning up in Regency memoirs and diaries. He was one
of the Duchess of York's set at Oatlands, and there is a good story
about him there. Once when the Duchess was leaving a room, she
whispered something to him that brought tears to his eyes. When
asked what was the matter, he replied, 'Oh – the Duchess spoke so
very kindly to me!' And a Colonel Armstrong said, 'My dear fellow
pray don't cry. I dare say she didn't mean it.' Poor 'Monk Lewis',
still only in his early forties, died this very year, 1818.

A late but successful arrival in this Gothic field – perhaps
'graveyard' would be better – *Melmoth the Wanderer*, was first
published in 1820. Its author was Charles Robert Maturin (1782–
1824), a Dublin curate and schoolmaster of Huguenot descent,
who had already produced several Gothic tales and a few plays
in which Kean had acted at Drury Lane. Its basic theme rather
than any literary merit gave *Melmoth the Wanderer* its importance.
Melmoth sells his soul to the devil so that he may live on and on,
then spends his time trying to find somebody, in terrible circumstances, who will take over this bad bargain and so free him from
it. But coming down from one age to another on this dismal quest,
which involves him in all manner of miseries and horrors, Melmoth
cannot find anybody who will release him. Maturin, a rather unstable type himself, could deal powerfully with the miseries and
horrors, but was lacking in constructive skill. He revived – and
then carried to a ridiculous extreme – the tiresome eighteenth-
century device of having a tale within a tale, as Saintsbury points
out:

The Rev. Charles Robert Maturin,
1819, engraving by Henry Meyer after
William Brocas
The British Museum, London

> It has faults in plenty – especially a narrative method of such involution
> that, as it has been said, 'a considerable part of the book consists of a
> story told to a certain person, who is a character in a longer story,
> found in a manuscript which is delivered to a third person, who relates
> the greater part of the novel to a fourth person, who is the namesake
> and descendant of the title-hero'.

But in spite of this absurdity, and chiefly because of his basic theme,
the pact with the devil, Maturin attracted the admiring attention

of Balzac and several of the French Romantics, and has not been altogether without influence on English Literature. So, for example, Oscar Wilde, who had had something to do with the new edition of the story in 1892, wanting a pseudonym after his release from prison, called himself Sebastian Melmoth.

There were plenty of periodicals, as distinct from newspapers, during the Regency, but most of them were either solemnly evangelical in tone, like the *Christian Observer* and the *Child's Companion or Sunday Scholar's Reward*, or were on the level of the *Lady's Magazine or Entertaining Companion for the Fair Sex*. The two heavyweights were the *Edinburgh Review* and the *Quarterly Review*, and they had both reached a circulation of about 14,000 by 1818. The *Edinburgh* arrived first, in 1802, and came out of a meeting in that city of Francis Jeffrey (who became editor), Sydney Smith and Henry Brougham, all young men at that time. It was Whig in politics, could be witty and satirical and was altogether livelier in tone than existing political and literary periodicals. But its purely literary criticism, chiefly in the hands of Jeffrey, was old-fashioned, still cherishing eighteenth-century standards. As Walter Raleigh amusingly observes in his notes for some lectures on the Periodical Reviewers:

Francis Jeffrey, Lord Jeffrey, 1826, by Andrew Geddes
oil on canvas
56 × 43 in. (143 × 110 cm.)
The National Portrait Gallery, London

William Gifford (detail), *c.* 1812, by John Hoppner
oil on canvas
29½ × 24½ in. (74.9 × 62.2 cm.)
The National Portrait Gallery, London

Francis Jeffrey was a shrewd, affectionate, kindly, sensible man. He did not bother his head with poetry. When he read a poem, he had felt he had seen this kind of thing before. He had a loyal heart, and he liked best those poems which exactly resembled those he already knew. He is never tired of appealing to common sense and old usage. A departure from old usage he calls 'mannerism'. Take his quarrel with Wordsworth's characters . . . Wordsworth's treatment of these characters and themes is not identical, Jeffrey complains, with their treatment by others. Jeffrey's standard is very simple and very incurious. His characters are the characters of the stage. If you say *Enter a tramp*, or a schoolmaster, or a schoolboy, or a lover, Jeffrey feels that he knows all about each of them, and is indignant if they are not traditionally dressed. His attitude to human life and thought is curiously *outward*. He seems never to have contemplated the possibility that he might be a tramp, or a schoolmaster, or a lover, himself . . .

This is well worth quoting because it defines the central weakness of a whole school of criticism.

The Tories wanted to counterbalance the aggressive Whiggery of the *Edinburgh*, so in 1809, a group of Tory writers, together with John Murray the publisher, founded the *Quarterly Review*, heavy and ponderous with authority. Its editor was William Gifford, an industrious but extremely narrow and pedantic critic, of whom Hazlitt, who detested him, wrote:

Mr Gifford was originally bred to some handicraft. He afterwards contrived to learn Latin, and was for some time an usher in a school, till he became a tutor in a nobleman's family. The low-bred, self-taught man, the pedant, and the dependent on the great, contribute to form the Editor of the *Quarterly Review*. He is admirably qualified for this situation, which he has held for some years, by a happy combination of defects, natural and acquired; and in the event of his death it will be difficult to provide him with a suitable successor.

I do not deny there are several foul blows here, but they are easier to forgive if we remember how stupidly and often savagely the *Quarterly* reviewed the work of the romantic poets, Keats especially, the chief offenders being Croker and John Lockhart, Scott's son-in-law and biographer and a supercilious and waspish critic.

Lockhart and John Wilson, best known as 'Christopher North', and James Hogg, the 'Ettrick Shepherd', were largely responsible for *Blackwood's Magazine* – often called *maga*. William Blackwood was John Murray's agent in Edinburgh, and he felt that a Scotch monthly magazine, far lighter in tone than the *Quarterly Review* but Tory in its politics, might succeed. The first numbers attracted little attention; something impudently new and rather scurrilous was needed; so Lockhart, Wilson and Blackwood got together and – in Lockhart's words – 'drank punch one night from eight till eight in the morning' and concocted the 'Chaldee Manuscript'. This piece, in a burlesque of biblical language, was college-magazine humour, but it was boldly impudent, ridiculing and attacking all the notables of Edinburgh. It raised a storm of protests, threats of violence and lawsuits, but now in 1817 *Blackwood's* was a success and continued to be widely read throughout the country. Its literary criticism, mostly by Wilson, was fresher and more sympathetic to new work than that of the two older quarterlies; but it kept up a certain sensationalism and scurrility, and there were frequent rude references to 'the Cockney School' of poets and critics, and to 'the pimpled Hazlitt' – all the more annoying to poor Hazlitt because he had in fact a clear pale complexion.

Since the beginning of the century small paddle-wheel steamers, clumsy and experimental, had come increasingly into use for short and sheltered voyages on rivers and canals. Then both in Britain and America, keen rivals in this traffic, larger vessels, using steam and sail, were built for coastal work and channel crossings. Long voyages well away from land were held to be impossible for steamers; their engines – crossing the Atlantic, for example – would demand more fuel than the ships could carry. However, the Atlantic was now crossed from west to east by an American vessel, the *Savannah*, that could claim to be a steamship. But this voyage, though admirable in its enterprise, did nothing

Fancy Mourning Dishabillé, from
La Belle Assemblée, 1 January 1818
The Victoria and Albert Museum,
London

229

P.S. 'Savannah', 1818
model
The Science Museum, London

to shake the belief that it was impossible for a steamship to cross the Atlantic. The *Savannah* was designed for a sailing packet service between New York and Havre, and she was nearly completed before it was decided to instal a single-cylinder engine, driving two collapsible paddle wheels. Steam was clearly a mere auxiliary to sail, only to be used when the winds were unhelpful. And this is how it turned out, for while the *Savannah* took twenty-nine days and eleven hours to reach Liverpool, she had made use of her engine, at intervals, for a total of eighty hours. Even then, her fuel had been exhausted by the time she sighted Ireland. So though the *Savannah* took an honoured place in the annals of shipping, the Atlantic-steamer problem was far from being solved, and it would be many, many years before the North Atlantic could be conquered by steam alone. The next generation or so of the poorer emigrants would find themselves packed into the holds of sailing ships, and might remain there week after week after week, somewhere between Liverpool and New York.

Such figures as we have for emigration during the Regency show an immense leap after 1815. This was the result of bad harvests, the soldiers who had been demobilised and could not find work, and the general depression in trade. Most emigrants, however, came came from rural areas; as yet there was little demand for industrial

230

labour in North America. Official policy was cautious, vague, uncertain, if only because opinion at Westminster was divided about emigration. One side argued that good money could be saved by cutting down the number of the poor who had to be supported, that emigration would improve the economic situation at home, and that with larger populations the colonies could produce more and more surplus food and raw materials that Britain needed. The other side declared it was unwise to deplete our population, and that we had sufficient wasteland here that might be profitably settled. These anti-emigrationists also drew attention to various complaints New York had made against the dumping of indigent emigrants. In 1819 they had a powerful American ally in John Quincy Adams, who published and then distributed throughout various European countries a pamphlet written to discourage emigration to the United States.

The figures I quote below were compiled by customs officials at the larger ports. The actual numbers must have been considerably larger; a great many ships carrying emigrants left from tiny ports, where there were no customs officials to compile statistics.

Year	U.S.	Canada	Other Countries	Total
1815	1,200	680	192	2,072
1816	9,022	3,370	118	12,510
1817	10,280	9,797	557	20,634
1818	12,429	15,136	222	27,787
1819	10,674	23,534	579	34,787
1820	6,745	17,921	1,063	25,729

(What was British North America then, I have called Canada, to avoid confusion.) This table makes the great leap after 1815 quite obvious. The gain in Canadian emigrants from 1817 to 1819 is partly explained by the fact that the British government did try, if only half-heartedly, to make emigration to Canada more attractive. The actual figures for Canada were probably much higher. Scotland did not have the English poor relief system, so that emigration for poorer families became an urgent necessity. Again, Scotland has a long coastline, tempting to cargo ships wanting to evade customs and excise, and many of these ships sailed west with emigrants. So the numbers of many of the Canada-bound Scots do not find their way into our table. And now, we may say, there began that relation between Scotland and Canada which leaves so many Canadians, even today, with a faint melancholy Scots undertone to their almost-American accent. We can also say that by 1819, when the emigration figures take a jump, Britain was a good country to get out of, at least for an able-bodied man with no property, no prospects, just a wife and family.

What do I see. The Briton Saxon Roman Norman amalgamating
In my Furnaces into One Nation the English: & taking refuge
In the Loins of Albion. The Canaanite united with the fugitive
Hebrew, whom she divided into Twelve. & sold into Egypt
Then scatterd the Egyptian & Hebrew to the four Winds:
This sinful Nation Created in our Furnaces & Looms is Albion

So Los spoke. Enitharmon answerd in great terror in Lambeths Vale

The Poets Song draws to its period & Enitharmon is no more.
For if he be that Albion I can never weave him in my Looms
But when he touches the first fibrous thread. like filmy dew

Jerusalem

My Looms will be no more & I annihilate vanish for ever
Then thou wilt Create another Female according to thy Will.

Los answerd swift as the shuttle of gold. Sexes must vanish & cease
To be, when Albion arises from his dread repose O lovely Enitharmon:
When all their Crimes, their Punishments their Accusations of Sin:
All their Jealousies Revenges. Murders. hidings of Cruelty in Deceit
Appear only in the Outward Spheres of Visionary Space and Time,
In the shadows of Possibility by Mutual Forgiveness forevermore
And in the Vision & in the Prophecy. that we may Foresee & Avoid
The terrors of Creation & Redemption & Judgment. Beholding them
Displayd in the Emanative Visions of Canaan in Jerusalem & in Shiloh
And in the Shadows of Remembrance. & in the Chaos of the Spectre
Amalek. Edom. Egypt. Moab. Ammon. Ashur. Philistea. around Jerusalem
Where the Druids reard their Rocky Circles to make permanent Remembrance
Of Sin. & the Tree of Good & Evil sprang from the Rocky Circle & Snake
Of the Druid. along the Valley of Rephaim from Camberwell to Golgotha
And framed the Mundane Shell Cavernous in Length Breadth & Highth

1819

The Year of Peterloo

In an earlier chapter, discussing the radical and reform movements, I declared that the attitude of the authorities would sooner or later be responsible for a disaster. This was because they tended to regard any very large meeting as a mobilisation for riot, or even revolution. The disaster arrived on 16 August of this year, 1819. It took place in St Peter's Fields, Manchester. It was called Peterloo as a companion battle to Waterloo in savage irony, the military exploits of that day consisting in sabreing and trampling down hundreds of unarmed men, women and children. There had been a number of radical meetings and small demonstrations in Manchester, chiefly for Parliamentary reform and the repeal of the Corn Laws. There had even been some drilling with staves, though it is quite possible that a government spy or two, acting as *agents provocateurs*, may have suggested this menacing development. However, what is certain is that the huge mass meeting, organised for 16 August, was as much a holiday affair as a political demonstration. Radical contingents from all around trooped in with bands and banners. The men carried no weapons of any sort, and many of them brought their wives and children. They were there to shout, sing, and listen to Orator Hunt and others addressing them from the hustings. They were no more dangerous to public safety than the annual crowds at Epsom on Derby Day. And, after lively exchanges of greetings between the various contingents, more than sixty thousand of them – and some estimates go as high as eighty thousand – packed themselves into St Peter's Fields at the end of a fine morning.

We shall never know for certain how to divide the responsibility for this day's work between the local magistrates – and several of them were in a house overlooking the meeting, ready to issue orders – and Lord Sidmouth at the Home Office. He must have sanctioned the use of regular troops, the 15th Hussars, then stationed in Manchester, but possibly not the support of squadrons of local Yeomanry, who would be the chief offenders. It is possible that the government, as it afterwards declared, advised the magistrates to proceed with caution, and that the magistrates, quaking at the sight of this monster meeting, gave panic-stricken orders. But it is also just possible – and it has been suggested – that Sidmouth

(opposite) Page from *Jerusalem, The Emanation of the Giant Albion*, 1820, by William Blake
The British Museum, London

233

delivered some top-secret instructions to Manchester. What we do know is that shortly after Hunt began to speak and the cavalry arrived on the scene, men, women and children were charged, sabred, trampled down, with the result that within a few minutes there were nearly six hundred wounded or badly hurt (over a hundred women among them) and at least eleven deaths. A noble victory, this of Peterloo!

There is no lack of eye-witness accounts, of varying reliability. I will briefly sample three, which may be relied upon. Bishop Stanley, who at the time was Vicar of Alderley, close to Manchester, saw everything from a window overlooking St Peter's Fields. He described the beginning of the meeting in some detail, and then went on:

> As the cavalry approached the dense mass of people they used their utmost efforts to escape; but so closely were they pressed in opposite directions by the soldiers, the special constables, the position of the hustings, and their own immense numbers, that immediate escape was impossible. The rapid course of the troop was of course impeded when it came in contact with the mob, but a passage was forced in less than a minute...On their arrival at the hustings a scene of dreadful confusion ensued. The orators fell or were forced off the scaffold in quick succession ... During the whole of this confusion, heightened by the rattle of some artillery crossing the square, shrieks were heard in all directions, and as the crowd of people dispersed the effects of the conflict became visible. Some were seen bleeding on the ground and unable to rise; others, less seriously injured but faint with the loss of blood, were retiring slowly or leaning upon others for support ... The whole of this extraordinary scene was the work of a few minutes ...

He added that he saw nothing that gave him any idea of resistance, no stone-throwing and so forth, only vain attempts by the men holding banners to prevent their being snatched away by the troopers. Now we can jump to an outside view, reported by a man who had left the meeting and gone home some time before the military arrived:

> I had not been at home more than a quarter of an hour when a wailing sound was heard from the main street, and, rushing out, I saw people running in the direction of Pendleton, their faces pale as death, and some with blood trickling down their cheeks. It was with difficulty I could get any one to stop and tell me what had happened. The unarmed multitude, men, women and children, had been attacked with murderous results, by the military.

There were no 'murderous results' visible here, but this account does suggest to me that a large number of minor casualties were never reported at all, so that the semi-official figure could have been much greater.

Morning Dress, from Ackermann's *Repository of Arts,* 1819
Collection Mrs Doris Langley Moore, London

Walking and Morning Dress, from Ackermann's *Repository of Arts,* 1819 Collection Mrs Doris Langley Moore, London

One of the best-known descriptions of Peterloo can be found in the memoirs of Samuel Bamford, a leading radical who had conducted about six thousand people to the meeting. After describing their arrival and then that of Hunt and his party 'preceded by a band of music and several flags', he gives in some detail the first impact on the crowd of the cavalry. Then he concludes, with a certain grandiloquence avoided by the best reporters but not ineffectively:

On the breaking of the crowd the yeomanry wheeled, and dashing whenever there was an opening, they followed, pressing and wounding. Many females appeared as the crowd opened; and striplings or mere youths also were found. Their cries were piteous and heart-rending, and would, one might have supposed, have disarmed any human resentment: but here their appeals were in vain. Women, white-vested maids, and tender youths, were indiscriminately sabred or trampled; and we have reason for believing that few were the instances in which that forbearance was vouchsafed which they so earnestly implored.

In ten minutes from the commencement of the havoc the field was an open and almost deserted space. The sun looked down through a sultry and motionless air. The curtains and blinds of the windows within view were all closed. A gentleman or two might occasionally be seen looking out from one of the new houses before mentioned, near the door of which a group of persons (special constables) were collected, and apparently in conversation; others were assisting the wounded or carrying off the dead. The hustings remained, with a few broken and hewed flagstaves erect, and a torn or gashed banner or two drooping; whilst over the whole field were strewed caps, bonnets, hats, shawls, and shoes, and other parts of male and female dress, trampled, torn, and bloody . . . Several mounds of human beings still remained where they had fallen, crushed down and smothered. Some of these still groaning, others with staring eyes, were gasping for breath, and others would never breathe more . . .

At this point, some readers are probably telling themselves that this Peterloo thing seems a lot of fuss about very little. But it is all a matter of scale. During the last fifty years or so we have lived in a world of gigantic casualty lists and colossal disasters; we have poured out lives as if they were dirty water; men work on our behalf on projects that could wipe humanity and all living things from half the planet; there are now so many of us that our world exists on a huge, reckless and de-humanising scale. To understand Peterloo we must see it against its own background. Or if that does not work, then we must multiply everything by twenty and adjust a few details, and imagine what we would feel if we learnt that tanks had gone grinding into an immense crowd in Manchester, killing 220 innocent persons and wounding about twelve thousand more.

It was generally agreed at the time that it was not the regular soldiers but the local yeomanry who were chiefly to blame. It was also assumed, then and since, that the officers and troopers of the yeomanry, half-trained and poorly disciplined, simply lost their heads when ordered to deal with so great a crowd. (It has long been my opinion, after sitting on a commission of enquiry in the nineteen-thirties, that men on foot are better able to cope safely with a crowd. The use of mounted police, however well-trained, dangerously heightens the temperature.) But this accepted idea of the yeomanry at Peterloo, that they were so confused and scared that they hardly knew what they were doing, was sharply challenged a few years ago by Mr Edward Thompson. He did this in his monumental but carefully documented study of the English working class between 1780 and 1832, *The Making of the Working Class*, 1963. He claims that the strange, quite unjustifiable savagery of the yeomanry's behaviour came out of a class hatred, that of these mill-owners' sons and their friends for the working-class reformers – and indeed for their own workpeople. (If we treat people badly, we begin to dislike them just because we treat them badly. So Hitler, needing a political scapegoat, could start by blaming the Jews, and could end by murdering millions of them.) Mr Thompson quotes a letter from Francis Place, the tailor-reformer, to Hobhouse:

> These Manchester yeomen and magistrates are a greater set of brutes than you form a conception of. I know one of these fellows who swears 'Damn his eyes, seven shillings a week is plenty for them'; and when he goes round to see how much work his weavers have in their looms, he takes a well-fed dog with him . . . He said some time ago that 'The sons of bitches had eaten up all the stinging nettles for ten miles around Manchester, and now they had no greens to their broth.' Upon my expressing indignation, he said, 'Damn their eyes, what need you care about them? How could I sell you goods so cheap if I cared anything about them?'

It was the local men on horseback – from the cotton trade employers, the substantial publicans and shopkeepers – who, unlike the regular officers, felt personally involved, knew many of the radical speakers by name and hated them, and so thrust and slashed to capture the banners, and believed at the end they had achieved a triumph. This is borne out by one of the eye-witness accounts:

> I picked up a Cap of Liberty; one of the Cavalry rode after me and demanded it; I refused to give it up. Two others then came up and asked what was the matter, when the first said, this fellow won't give up this Cap of Liberty. One of the others then said, damn him, cut him down. Upon this, I ran . . . One of the Cavalry cut at Saxton, but his

PLATE XXXV. Greta Bridge, 1810, by John Sell Cotman
watercolour
9 × 13 in. (22.9 × 33.1 cm.)
The British Museum, London

horse seemed restive, and he missed his blow. He then called out to another, 'There's Saxton, damn him run him through.' The other said, 'I'd rather not, I'll leave that for you to do.' When I got to the end of Watson-street, I saw ten or twelve of the Yeomanry Cavalry, and two of the Hussars cutting at the people, who were wedged close together, when an officer of Hussars rode up to his own men, and knocking up their swords said, 'Damn you what do you mean by this work?' He then called out to the Yeomanry, 'For shame, gentlemen; what are you about? The people cannot get away.' They desisted for a time but no sooner had the officer rode to another part of the field, than they fell to work again.

Orator Hunt himself – who may have made immoderate speeches but was strongly against any violent measures – was beaten up by the special constables as he was taken under arrest to the magistrates' house, and a gallant General Clay took two hands to a stick to bash him over the head. And the Law was no more forgiving or even decently tolerant when it was joined with the Church, for it was a clerical magistrate – as reported in *The Times*, 27 September 1819 – who said to one poor wretch brought before him: 'I believe you are a downright blackguard reformer. Some of you reformers ought to be hanged, and some of you are sure to be hanged – the rope is already round your necks.' And I suggest that this – one of at least many hundreds – is the speech of a middle-aged educated man who is temporarily out of his mind; there is boiling up in him a horrible mixture of fear and repressed guilt.

What a chance for popularity at last our Prince of Pleasure missed here, after Peterloo! If, instead of sending his thanks to the magistrates and the military for their 'decisive and efficient measures for the preservation of public peace' (which in fact they alone had disturbed), he had risen in wrath and demanded to know why his innocent subjects had been handled in this fashion, he would have been cheered throughout the country. He was not a hard man, nor yet a complete fool, and while it is possible he was completely humbugged by his ministers, Lords Liverpool, Castlereagh and Sidmouth, it is also possible that the same mixture of fear and guilt was working in him. While his Tory loyalists were congratulating the Manchester Yeomanry as if they had cleaved their way through Napoleon's Old Guard, to most people in the country, of the middle as well as the working class, Peterloo came as a profound shock. Throughout the late summer and early autumn of 1819, industrial workers, especially in the Midlands and around Tyneside, still furiously reacting to the news, were buying sharpened knives to fasten to their staves – and so make pikes. The men were not only arming but organising themselves. If, in the extreme radical movement, there had risen now one leader with a strong magnetic quality, a touch of genius, even a lesser

PLATE XXXVI. San Giorgio from the Dogana, Venice: Sunrise, 1819, by Joseph Mallord William Turner watercolour
8⅞ × 11⅝ in. (22.4 × 28.9 cm.)
The British Museum, London
(Catalogue Number CLXXXI–4)

Cromwell, there would have been open violent rebellion and then civil war. But there was no such man. Cobbett returned from America but ignored the violent extremists; Hunt, the most popular figure, was vain, irresolute, and not an advocate of violence; some local leaders were in prison, those still at liberty could not create any national organisation. All the fiery meetings, the menacing banners, the bitter songs, the knife-sharpening, went for nothing.

In December the government, which had been aware of every move the angry workers had made, came crashing down with its Six Acts. These extended earlier repressive measures. They gave extraordinary powers to magistrates: private houses could be searched without warrants; men suspected of any political offence could be arrested and summarily sentenced; meetings attended by more than fifty persons were prohibited; any whiff of 'seditious libel' – in short, anything a Tory magistrate disliked – could lead to an immediate prosecution; and one of them, Act Four, in some ways the most effective of them all, put up the stamp duty on periodicals so that now they cost at least sixpence. So the Lancashire mill-workers were to be severely punished for putting themselves under the sabres and hoofs of the Manchester Yeomanry. During the following six months, there was hardly anybody prominent among the extreme radicals or 'Old Jacks' (the men originally inspired by the Jacobins: they still called one another 'Citizen') who was out of prison. So the working class found itself severely suppressed, disorganised, helpless. And it was still riddled with government spies. On the other hand, Peterloo united and stiffened the middle and upper class Whigs to combine and campaign, under

A Match Girl, 1819, drawn and engraved by T. L. Busby
Private Collection, London

the leading advocate Lord John Russell, for the reform of Parliament and the whole electoral system. The famous Reform Bill, becoming law in 1832, owed much to this year.

So did the Victorians. The future queen was born on 24 May 1819, and a month later she was christened at an imposing ceremony in Kensington Palace. Crimson velvet curtains were brought from the chapel at St James's, and a gold font from the Tower. A day or two before the christening, there was some difference of opinion about the child's names. Her father, the Duke of Kent, as Greville tells us, 'gave the name of Alexandrina to his daughter in compliment to the Emperor of Russia. She was to have had the name Georgiana, but the Duke insisted on Alexandrina being her first name.' Hearing this, the Regent went into action. He sent for de Lieven, the Russian Ambassador. (His wife, Princess de Lieven, for ever turning up in Regency letters and memoirs, was one of the most important figures in its high society.) The Regent, in his florid fashion, paid many compliments to both the Czar and his ambassador, but told de Lieven firmly 'that the name of Georgiana could

Henry Hunt 'The Orator', by Adam
Buck
watercolour
8¼ × 6¼ in. (21 × 15.9 cm.)
The National Portrait Gallery,
London

be second to no other in this country, and therefore she (the baby) could not bear it at all'. The Regent then announced that he would attend the christening himself – though he disliked his brother, the Duke of Kent, disliked the Duchess of Kent, and could not regard their infant daughter, now a likely heir to the Crown, with much enthusiasm. So it would be he who, at the last moment, would decide upon the names.

It proved an embarrassing ceremony. The Archbishop of Canterbury – and here for once the phrase 'holding the baby' can be used literally – stood there waiting for the Regent to give him the first name. Perhaps the Regent wanted to embarrass the parents, perhaps his mind was wandering, but there was now one of those silences that last twenty-five seconds but appear on ceremonial occasions to be lasting half an hour. Then he gruffly ejaculated 'Alexandrina' and fell silent again. The Archbishop and the baby waited. The Duke of Kent prompted his brother with 'Charlotte' and got a fierce shake of the head: obviously the Regent furiously rejected any suggestion of using the name of his own dead daughter. Though taken aback, the Duke tried again, whispering 'Augusta?' No. no, too much grandeur in that name. But what then – what? At last the Regent broke the silence with a thundering 'Let her be called after her mother', and, we are told, glared at the poor Duchess of Kent, whose elaborate curls and enormous hat shook with her tempestuous sobs. And as the Duchess was called Victoria Mary Louisa, the baby was christened Alexandrina Victoria, and eighteen years later came to the throne as Victoria and stayed there until 1901.

It was in 1819 that Turner went to Italy for the first time, falling at once under the spell of its luminous light. And Venice, of course, might have been created specially for him. His fine watercolour, *San Giorgio from the Dogana, Venice: Sunrise*, 1819, is one of his first steps along a trail that would take him eventually into his own magical world of light and the elements. Though Turner's best work falls well outside the Regency, and Girtin's short but glorious life ended in 1802, we may reasonably claim that the supreme art of the Regent's England was in watercolours. This was not realised at the time, when the watercolour was regarded as a poor relation in the family of the visual arts. Drawing masters, teaching at a school or instructing young ladies, went off to paint watercolours during their holidays. Or if they were tired of teaching, they accepted topographical commissions. To an artist moving around and working quickly, watercolours were much better than oils, less expensive, more portable, drying far more quickly. There had been, too, a rapid improvement in the quality of materials. There was watercolour paper now that stood up to rough treatment

241

– and got it, especially from Turner, who would not only use a sponge with the rest of them but would scratch and scrape, using a knife to suggest broken little highlights.

The tinted drawing, line-and-wash technique, which had served a gifted (and curiously modern) artist like Francis Towne so well, was going out. William Blake still used it, and because of the sheer force of his imagination he must be included among the great English watercolourists. It may be asked why I have taken so long to arrive at Blake, as poet, painter or prophet. Most of his poetry appeared long before the Regency; and after 1809, when he held a public exhibition that was a disastrous failure, he spent the next nine years without a patron and could barely keep himself going. It was not until 1818 that he met John Linnell, a close friend as well as a patron, who brought with him a new set of fellow artists and sympathisers. So Blake set to work again, and in 1820 produced the last of his great symbolic works, *Jerusalem, The Emanation of the Giant Albion*, and the last of his illuminated books. Blake was quite indifferent to society, but he does make a brief appearance in some Regency letters and memoirs. He was liked on the whole, but thought to be quite mad, sometimes because he did make extremely dogmatic strange statements, but more often because he was at cross purposes with his hearers in his very personal use of terms. So, for example, where most people would say they *imagined* something, Blake would declare he directly *saw* it. Southey was one of those who thought him quite mad, whereas most of us now, comparing the two men's life and work, would be inclined to say that it was Southey who was mad where Blake was serenely sane.

Turner, who had worked side by side with Girtin when they were boys, said of him afterwards, with that gruff generosity of feeling Turner displayed so often, 'If he'd have lived, I'd have starved.' This is not true, because even if they were equal in native genius, Turner had a far more powerful and tenacious character, which played a very important part – as it always does – in the development of his art. Certainly in his later work, especially after he went north, Girtin made what we should call now 'the big breakthrough' in watercolour, transforming it into a splendidly independent art form. And where he led, others, even if less gifted, might follow. But it was not his use of the new cartridge paper, his warm tones but deliberately restricted colour, his sheer skill with the brush, it was above all his direct emotional response to the scene, his deep involvement in it, that were responsible for masterpieces of watercolour like his *Wharfedale* and the *White House at Chelsea*.

Because of its particular limitations as a medium, watercolour tends to be a hit-or-miss form. As we all know if we have tried it (I have, and soon took refuge in gouaches), nothing is easier to do than a bad watercolour. Unfortunately, on the next level, where

PLATE XXXVII. The Peterloo Massacre, 1819, coloured engraving by George Cruikshank
The City Art Gallery, Manchester

PLATE XXXVIII. (overleaf) Representation of the Election of Members in Covent Garden, 1818, aquatint by Robert Havell after George Scharf
The Royal Collection, Windsor Castle

there has been training and there is some facility, nothing is easier than a so-so watercolour, pleasing but empty. It is the next step, towards the watercolour as a masterwork, that is so appallingly difficult, and even when this small high level has been reached, there will still be far more misses than hits. But here, personal taste enters.

To my mind, when Hazlitt called Turner's work 'tinted steam', he was without intending to do so coming close to a definition of true excellence in watercolour painting. Somehow, I feel, it should suggest coloured air rather than a world of solid heavy objects. Turner was charged more than once with trying to use oil as if it were watercolour. If we reverse this – and I am still stating my personal prejudices we can see what is wrong with a very large number of watercolours, often by good men: the artists are trying to use watercolours as if they were oils. I find this fault often in good men like David Cox or John Varley, though not in De Wint, even if he is too steadily autumnal: he could only escape from teaching, to take a painting holiday, when it was already late summer. Another art master, John Crome (called 'Old Crome' to distinguish him from his son, also an artist), who had a sharp eye for tone, brought it off in some of his sketches. He was a Norwich man, and Norwich in those days was very much a provincial capital and a cultural centre, so that Crome was able to collect other painters and create the 'Norwich School'. John Sell Cotman was a member of it for a time but by then he had already produced watercolours quite beyond the scope of even 'Old Crome' himself. In his middle 'teens Cotman went to London, knew Girtin when Girtin was at his best, and may have gone on a painting holiday with him. But Cotman is entirely original: his sense of significant design and his control of broad washes are very much his own; and in watercolours like his famous *Greta Bridge* he is a master and a marvel. As a York-shireman I quote with pride Laurence Binyon's observation: 'It is notable that, as with Girtin, and as with Turner, so it was with Cotman: Yorkshire had something inspiring in its scene that awoke the genius in each of them.' Cotman was a highly nervous type, perhaps to some extent manic-depressive. He never knew Blake's neglect and poverty, but after he returned from London to East Anglia (probably a mistaken move) he spent years and years drudging away as a drawing master and his creative genius was under-nourished. But during his late holidays in Normandy he occasionally painted in quite a new manner, going from broad flat washes to make use of rather dry, intense body colour. This is against my theory of watercolour, but as I am not an art critic and do not have to be consistent, I can add that I possess one of these late paintings – a small *Landscape in Blue* – and find it enchanting.

In 1819, Richard Parkes Bonington, a handsome English lad in

PLATE XXXIX. Chinese corridor, detail from the aquatint in John Nash's *Brighton Pavilion,* 1820–25 The Royal Institute of British Architects, London (Drawings Collection)

(above left) Cheyne Walk, Chelsea,
1811, by John Varley
watercolour
13¾ × 19⅜ in. (34.9 × 49.2 cm.)
The Victoria and Albert Museum,
London

(above right) On the Wharfe, before
1802, by Thomas Girtin
watercolour
12¼ × 20¾ in. (31.1 × 52.7 cm.)
Collection Sir Edmund Bacon, Bart.

his later teens, arrived at the Paris studio of Baron Gros. For his
own amusement he liked to paint lively glowing little watercolours,
which fascinated his new French friends, including Delacroix – and
an errand boy called Corot, who saw one of these tiny watercolours
in a shop window. But Bonington developed consumption, like
Girtin, and died in 1828. John Constable never left England, but his
pictures did and though the French critics, like the English critics,
thought little of them, they excited some important young French
painters. Constable occasionally painted in watercolour – his
Stonehenge: Thunderstorm has often been reproduced, but he was
happier in oils, and many of us are ready to pass over his elaborately
finished pictures to enjoy the oil sketches he made on the spot, to
capture the instant effects of light and shade – the passing clouds,
the shadow under the trees, the dew on the grass. He deeply admired
Wordsworth, and might be called a Wordsworthian in paint.
Throughout the Regency he was not only under-rated but also
constantly attacked; he could say with truth, 'My art flatters
nobody by imitation, it courts nobody by smoothness, it tickles
nobody by petiteness, it is without fal-de-lal or fiddle-de-dee; how
can I therefore hope to be popular?'; but, a very sensitive and
dedicated man, affectionate too in his personal relations, Constable
often felt deeply wounded, and was happiest catching every flicker
of light and shade in his beloved Suffolk.

If we want 'fal-de-lal or fiddle-de-dee' we must return to the
Regent, too busy decorating and rewarding Lawrence to take a
long hard look at Constable. And if there is any evidence that he
took any interest in the great watercolourists, I have never found
it. How surprised he would have been to learn that the age called
after him would be celebrated by art historians as 'the Age of
English Watercolour'! Probably his eye found its greatest happiness whenever it stared, inside or outside, at his Pavilion at

Brighton. This extraordinary building – an architectural white elephant partly responsible for the Regent's huge debts – was not finished even in 1819, but, with the building of the new Royal Apartments begun then, it might be said that the white elephant was on its last lap, in a race that had already lasted over thirty years. The Regent's passion for Brighton dated back to 1783, when he was only twenty-one, had swollen glands in his neck, and was told to try sea-bathing. (For those who do not know Brighton, I must add that the air there is unusually bracing. It is a fine place either to restore your health or, when suitably braced, to ruin it again.) The young Prince of Wales decided he must have a house there, acquired a farmhouse, and then began that summoning of architects, decorators, furnishers, which was to take some of his time and a great deal of his money down and down the years. Here I do not propose to describe in words what can be more quickly and pleasantly discovered in our illustrations. I will merely indicate what happened along the route to the grand completed Pavilion.

The first building, known as the Marine Pavilion, designed by Henry Holland and completed in 1787, was a more or less 'elegant and classical structure on the conventional Palladian plan of a central rotunda with flanking wings'. Between 1801 and 1803, additions and alterations were made by Holland's pupil, P. G. Robinson, who had an eye for the picturesque and added two oval-shaped wings, together with green shell-like canopies above all the windows, a feature widely copied during the Regency. At this time the Prince was given some Chinese wallpaper, and this may have decided him to insist upon a Chinese style, inside if not outside. The taste for *chinoiserie,* well established in the early eighteenth century, had been on the way out; His Royal Highness brought it back again – temporarily. All was Chinese within, and along the southern wing was an astonishing Chinese passage of painted glass, decorated with flowers, insects, fruits and birds, and illuminated from outside, so that guests could easily imagine they

(below left) Henry Holland's design for Brighton Pavilion, 30 September 1795
The Royal Pavilion, Brighton

(below right) The Pavilion at Brighton, showing P. G. Robinson's added wings
The Royal Pavilion, Brighton

The Court at Brighton à la Chinese,
1816, by George Cruikshank
The British Museum, London

were passing through an immense Chinese lantern, which may or may not have delighted them. Low disloyal fellows jeered from a distance, like 'Peter Pindar' who wrote:

> . . . A China view,
> Where neither genius, taste, nor fancy dwells:
> Monkeys, mandarins, a motley crew,
> Bridges, pagodas, swings, and tinkling bells.

But the Prince was persuaded by his architects not to attempt a Chinese exterior, the authentic style appearing to be too light for so grand and solid a building.

By 1808 the Royal Stables and the Riding House were completed, being particularly admired for their roof work, both being engineering feats for their time. The Stables had an eighty-foot cupola, sixty-five feet high; they provided accommodation (first class) for forty-four horses in stalls going round the great circle of the interior, with harness rooms and grooms' quarters above the stalls; and in the centre of the floor was a fountain for watering the horses. Though not a keen student of housing in general, the Prince always said his horses were housed in a palace. But now people noticed that the exteriors of these new buildings were in the Moslem Indian style. Was India coming in and China going out? Before I answer this urgent question I must make a point. Too much must not be made of this age's interest in the Far East just because the poets – Coleridge, Southey, Moore, Byron, Shelley – kept writing about it. They were not students of the

PLATE XL. The Royal Pavilion,
Brighton from the east

Orient but romantics, who wrote about it because it was a long way off and anything might happen there.

What happened in Brighton is that in 1808 a new architect, Repton, submitted plans for buildings and gardens in the Indian style. Delighted, the Prince wrote: 'I consider the whole of this work as perfect, and will have my part carried into immediate execution; not a tittle shall be altered – even you yourself shall not admit any improvement.' But he lacked the money to carry out these designs, and by the time he had crept out of his financial difficulties he had lost interest in Repton's 'perfect' work, thought he wanted something less formal and rigid, and now favoured Gothic. For this, James Wyatt was the man. He had just finished Beckford's fantastic Fonthill (the great tower fell down afterwards), and the Prince was eager for something even more extraordinarily Gothic. In 1812, that romantic year, Wyatt produced plans that had an estimated cost of at least £200,000, but this did not deter the Prince, now of course the Regent. However, the following year, Wyatt inconsiderately got himself killed in an accident. The Regent wept, but more, it was said, for the loss of his vision of Gothic magnificence than for Wyatt. It was time to send for the bold and energetic John Nash, who had already worked on the Windsor Royal Lodge, remodelled part of Carlton House, and was now planning the grand design that would include Regent Street and Regent's Park.

It was in 1815 that Nash began his alterations in a more or less Indian style. He had his faults as an architect, but he was at once clever and original in his use of cast iron, which secretly strengthened many new features of the Pavilion that appeared to be quite airy and delicate and straight out of the Orient, like its bamboo staircases. In 1816 the kitchens were built, and in spite of the palm-tree columns (plus cast iron) supporting the roof, there was not much oriental nonsense about *this* important department. These kitchens were entirely steam-heated, a new device then; and the Regent took a great pride in them. His mother, old Queen Charlotte, not very long before her death, paid him a visit and was so delighted with the new appearance of the Pavilion, she gave him and it a grant of £50,000 from her private purse. In this year, 1817, two imposing new State Apartments were added, with domes not quite Indian, perhaps borrowed from Coleridge's 'Kubla Khan'. Poor Repton, who had first brought the triumphant Nash to the Prince's notice, died an embittered man. It was said that Nash owed much to Repton's original designs, but it is more than likely that he owed much more to his own boldness, sweep and ingenuity. The last thing to be done to the Pavilion – it takes us forward to 1822 – was the construction of an underground passage from the house to the Stables; and it was not intended, as some people

PLATE XLI. The ceiling of the Banqueting Room of the Royal Pavilion, Brighton

supposed, to be of use in secret amorous frolics, a notion that both slandered and flattered the fat ageing George IV. He merely wanted to be able to take his guests to pat the horses on a wet day.

Not everybody exclaimed with delight over the Regent's huge extravagant toy. Even the ultra-loyal Scott could say: 'Set fire to the Chinese stables, and if it embrace the whole of the Pavilion, it will rid me of a great eyesore.' A feminine diarist wrote: 'All is gaudy without looking gay; and all is crowded with ornaments without being magnificent.' And Hazlitt, in his *Travel Notes:* 'The Pavilion at Brighton is like a collection of stone pumpkins and pepper-boxes. It seems as if the genius of architecture had at once the dropsy and the *megrims.* Anything more fantastical, with a greater dearth of invention, was never seen. The King's horses (if they were horses of taste) would petition against such irrational a lodging.' Sydney Smith declared; 'One would think that St Paul's Cathedral had come to Brighton and pupped.' However, according to Lady Bessborough, who probably gave some sign that she did not really care for the place, the Prince excused his oriental fantastifications by pointing out that during the time he was first building and then furnishing the Pavilion 'there was such a cry against French things', he had to go out of his way to avoid any suggestion of them. But as usual he was probably fitting his talk to his company; there is plenty of evidence he loved his Pavilion.

His brother William IV and his niece Victoria did not share this love. In the 1840s the Queen gave orders for the Pavilion to be dismantled, and processions of vans distributed most of its contents between Buckingham Palace and Windsor Castle. In 1850 the municipality of Brighton acquired the building. It is now a kind of Regency museum, well worth visiting, especially as a recent curator, Mr Clifford Musgrave, with the enlightened help of the late Queen Mary and of Queen Elizabeth, has been able to restore at least something of its lost magnificence. I have paid it several visits, and have felt neither the delighted admiration of a Croker nor the savage contempt of a Hazlitt. There is about this Pavilion an air both astonishingly silly and faintly melancholy: it is rather like discovering in the morning some midnight reveller, fast asleep and still wearing his masquerade costume.

There was now a chance for the Regency to discover how it looked through American eyes. In 1819 Washington Irving, that pleasing New Yorker, brought out his *Sketch Book,* to be followed a few years later by *Bracebridge Hall.* At the beginning of the Regency a friend had taken to England copies of Irving's 'spoof' history of the old Dutch settlers along the Hudson, *Knickerbocker;* and Coleridge had sat up all night reading it, and among its other admirers were Byron and Scott. Indeed, after Irving himself came to England he stayed with Scott at Abbotsford in 1817 and they became close friends. It was Scott who made sure that the *Sketch Book* was published by Murray and then widely noticed. Some of its pieces give a charming – though rosily idealised – picture of Regency country life:

> Perhaps it might be owing to the pleasing serenity that reigned in my own mind, that I fancied I saw cheerfulness in every countenance throughout the journey. A stage coach, however, carries animation always with it, and puts the world in motion as it whirls along. The horn, sounded at the entrance of a village, produces a general bustle. Some hasten forth to meet friends; some with bundles and bandboxes to secure places, and in the hurry of the moment can hardly take leave of the group that accompanies them. In the meantime the coachman has a world of small commissions to execute. Sometimes he delivers a hare or pheasant; sometimes jerks a small parcel or newspaper to the door of a public-house; and sometimes, with knowing leer and words of sly import, hands to some half-blushing, half-laughing housemaid an odd-shaped *billet doux* from some rustic admirer. As the coach rattles through the village, every one runs to the window, and you have glances on every side of fresh country faces and blooming giggling girls. At the corners are assembled juntos of village idlers and wise men, who take their stations there for the important purpose of seeing company pass; but the sagest knot is generally at the blacksmith's, to whom the passing of the coach is an event fruitful of much speculation.

But if, for dramatic effect, we set this scene at the end of 1819, then somewhere behind this charming rusticity a vast pot of trouble was heating up and would very soon come to the boil.

The North Drawing Room, Brighton Pavilion

1820

Queen's Move

The year 1820 was just over three weeks old when the Duke of Kent died, quite unexpectedly, for it was thought he had nothing more than a cold, and he was only fifty-three. His death brought his infant daughter Victoria one step nearer the Throne. In the evening of 29 January, without suffering and with no return to sanity, George III died, and a country that had almost forgotten his existence was suddenly moved, once again but for the last time, by pity and affection. Two days later, there was no longer a Regent, our Prince of Pleasure being now proclaimed George IV, though he would have to wait until July 1821 to be crowned. (And from here on, rather reluctantly, I must remember to call him *King*. Somehow, *Prince* or *Regent* suits him better.) Lady Sarah Lyttelton was probably expressing the feeling of her whole society when she wrote, on this same day, 31 January: 'The poor old, old, King George the Third who has reigned over us, our fathers and grandfathers, from time immemorial, is dead! George the Fourth, whom Heaven preserve, was proclaimed today all over London.'

The King while he was actually being proclaimed was down with pleurisy and parting with a lot of his blood, his doctors announcing shortly afterwards that he recovered only because they drained 150 ounces of blood out of him. On 5 February, Croker reported that there was one problem that was delaying the King's recovery: 'His anxiety about the Queen agitates him terribly.' The Queen, of course, was his wife Caroline, who had been living abroad for some years and behaving scandalously, and now he was sure this reckless and insensitive woman would return to claim her rights as his Queen. And in his opinion she had no rights, she was not his Queen (he still called her Princess), and it was unthinkable that this half-mad slut should be prayed for in the liturgy. Something drastic must be done by his Cabinet. So now he set in motion gigantic wheels that would grind out nothing but folly and scandal.

Our Prince no doubt made hundreds of small mistakes; he certainly made three very big mistakes. The first was to marry Caroline at all. The second, in 1811, was to put the Tories into power because the Whigs were being difficult. The third, coming now in 1820, was to deal with Caroline as he did, helping to stage in a few months, with the maximum pomp and limelight, a gigantic

The Proclamation of George IV at
Carlton House on 31 January 1820,
engraving by Robert Havell after
Charles Wild
The British Museum, London

nonsense out of which nobody, as we shall see, emerged with any credit.

However, before picking up Caroline's story, and still remaining in this February of 1820, we must consider the Cato Street Conspiracy. It was not an important historical event, but it is fascinating because it begins in absurdity and ends in horror. And behind the familiar painted gauze, displaying these years in terms of dandies, poetic lovers, eloping maidens, it illuminates balefully the real character of the age. One of the leaders of the republican 'Old Radicals' was a man called Thistlewood, who was supposed to have lost a fortune and then to have served as an officer in the French republican army (he was said to be a magnificent swordsman); he was taciturn instead of being loud-mouthed; and he was very brave and resolute but far from shrewd, rather naïve. He had gone to London during the disintegration of the extreme radical movement, in the autumn of 1819, and had met with a disappointing response in Spitalfields and other centres of unrest. But he had convinced himself, and a small group of rather simple-minded working men he gathered round him, that one violently dramatic blow against authority would raise the country. He and his fellow conspirators met in a barn in Cato Street, off the Edgware Road, to decide upon a target. One Edwards had most suggestions to offer, but after most of these had been rejected by Thistlewood because they would involve the death of innocent persons, it was agreed with Edwards that a grand Cabinet dinner offered them the best opportunity.

These simpletons in fact were being duped. Edwards was a

government spy and *agent provocateur*. There was to be no such Cabinet dinner; the announcement of it had been planted in the press to deceive the conspirators. They were arrested, and during the scuffle Thistlewood ran his sword through one of the Bow Street Runners. This sensational affair at the end of February was just what the government needed; there was to be a General Election in March; and one of the men, Ings, a butcher, was only speaking the truth when, during the trial in April, he cried out: 'I am like a bullock drove into Smithfield market to be sold. Lord Sidmouth knew all about this for two months.' Thistlewood, Ings, Brunt, Tidd and Davidson (a coloured man) were sentenced to be publicly hanged (and then have their heads cut off) on 1 May. Another five were transported.

In court, while the Lord Chief Justice was pronouncing his doom, Thistlewood looked round indifferently and used his snuffbox. Brunt, a shoemaker, boldly informed the court that when his weekly earnings went down from £3 or £4 to ten shillings he began to look about him, and what he found were 'men in power,

Arthur Thistlewood, engraving
published by Humphrey, 10 March
1820
The British Museum, London

Interior of the Hay-loft in Cato
Street occupied by the conspirators,
1820, by George Cruikshank
The British Museum, London

The Execution of the Cato Street
Conspirators 1 May 1820 from
*An Authentic History of the Cato
Street Conspiracy,* by George
Wilkinson
The London Museum, London

who met to deliberate how they might starve and plunder the
country' – a not unreasonable comment on Lord Liverpool's
government. On 30 April, the day before he was to be hanged, Ings
wrote a last letter to his wife, beginning: 'My dear, of the anxiety
and regard I have for you and the children, I know not how to
explain myself, but I must die according to law, and leave you in a
land full of corruption . . .' He was an excitable fellow, and on his
way to the gallows began singing *Death or Liberty* at the top of
his voice. Thistlewood said, 'Be quiet, Ings; we can die without all
this noise.' Somebody should write a novel, a play or a film about
this enigmatic Thistlewood.

The execution was entirely successful as a May-day spectacle. Even the poorest seats fetched half-a-crown, and those with a really good view were going at three guineas. People were arriving from 4 a.m. At five o'clock the City Marshals mustered seven hundred of the civil force from every ward. At six o'clock the infantry left the prison, where they had been all night, and were marched across the scaffold area, while two troops of Horse Guards appeared at each end of the Old Bailey and formed in line. By 7 a.m. all the windows and roofs in the vicinity, all the neighbouring alleyways and streets, were jam-packed. Shortly afterwards, the five men were led out, putting a brave face on it. We are told: 'A gentleman admonished them to consider their approaching fate, and to recollect the existence of a Deity, into whose supreme presence a few minutes would usher them. Brunt exclaimed: 'I know there is a God,' and Ings added, 'Yes, to be sure; and I hope He will be more merciful to us than they are here.' The crowd could not get near the scaffold; there were barricades so that any attempt at a rescue would not be possible and no last-minute speeches would be heard. But the people could see, and the severing of the hanged men's heads was too much for them. So the *Morning Chronicle* reported:

> When the crowd perceived the knife applied to the throat of Thistlewood, they raised a shout, in which the exclamations of horror and reproach were mingled. The tumult seemed to disconcert the person in the mask for a moment, but upon the whole he performed the operation with dexterity, and having handed the head to the assistant executioner, who waited to receive it, he immediately retired, pursued by the hootings of the mob . . .

Thomas Raikes and his friend Lord Alvanley, fashionable fellows who never liked to miss anything, attended the ceremony. But Raikes wrote afterwards: 'It was the first execution I ever saw, and shall be the last.' Moreover, as he also noted, this first day of May, 1820, was a fine morning.

Now we must return to the King and Caroline; and, indeed, to understand the situation in 1820 we must go back six years. We left Caroline making a shrewdly-timed entrance at the theatre, during the 1814 festivities, thus inviting and receiving a round of applause all her own. Later, in August, she left the country, first going back home to Brunswick (where her husband hoped to Heaven she would stay) and then moving on from Germany to Switzerland and finally into Italy. Her progress and her behaviour were noted anxiously in London by two very different men. First, of course, by her husband, the Regent; and secondly, in his capacity as a lawyer, by Henry Brougham, who was now her chief adviser and was soon to play a leading part in her story. It is doubtful if

Henry Brougham, 1st Baron
Brougham and Vaux, 1844, engraving
by John Henry Robinson after James
Stewart

Brougham ever felt any personal loyalty to Caroline. He was very ambitious and he wanted a finger in this rich royal pie. Moreover – and this was probably more important – he hated the Regent and the Tory Establishment, and Caroline was a weapon he could use against them. As for Caroline, though outwardly grateful, she never quite trusted Brougham – but then, nobody ever did.

Henry Peter Brougham was one of the most extraordinary figures of this age. (And of the next age too, for he lived, as Baron Brougham and Vaux and a former Lord Chancellor, until 1868.) Though of English descent, he was born (in 1778) and then educated in Edinburgh, where he made a name for himself in his early twenties and was an indefatigable and dazzling contributor to the *Edinburgh Review*. He could write about anything – and did. It was said of him later, when he was the most brilliant advocate in London, that 'If he had known a little law, he would have known everything.' He entered politics at the radical end of the Whigs, but, in spite of his immense reputation and ability, he was never really successful as a politician: party managers in England favour sound dependable men and mistrust brilliance.

Indeed, it might be said of Brougham that the politicians thought him too much the lawyer, while the lawyers thought him too much of a politician. He was a tall, angular, jerky man, looking like a gigantic marionette when he was making a speech, and he was capable of making speeches, ranging from thunder to dramatic whispers, that went on triumphantly hour after hour. 'By Heaven!' cried Creevey, 'he has uttered a speech which, for power of *speaking,* surpassed anything you ever heard. He could not have roared louder if a file of soldiers had come in and pushed the Speaker out of his chair.' His energy was prodigious, terrifying: meeting an acquaintance, he would offer him two fingers to shake and then hurry on. After referring to a certain glare in some men's eyes, Bagehot wrote: 'Lord Brougham's face has this. A mischievous excitability is the most obvious expression of it. If he were a horse, nobody would buy him; with that eye, no one could answer for his temper.' The Regency Tories feared and detested him, but the Whigs and radicals, whose causes he fiercely defended or pleaded, never quite trusted him. Yet he was deeply sincere about some issues, notably slavery and Parliamentary reform; and, above all, he was from first to last a passionate advocate of popular education, for which he did more than any other man of his time. And he has two smaller claims on our regard. A vehicle – it was a light carriage – was called after him, and *broughams* were much used during the second half of the nineteenth century. And because he built a house in Cannes, then a small fishing village, he may be said to have created the French Riviera.

Brougham had warned Caroline that everything she did on her

travels would be reported to Carlton House. And, after all, though she had long been separated from her husband, who was busy begging his fellow princes not to receive her, she was still the Princess of Wales. But aristocratic English travellers, catching glimpses of her during her progress from Germany to Switzerland and then to Italy, were horrified: 'The natives were, as she would have expressed it, *all over shock*. The suite who travel with her declare openly their fear they shall not be able to go on with her; not so much from wrong doings as from ridiculous ones.' She would waltz all night, dressed – or mostly undressed – absurdly for a woman of her age of any rank. She was – as we say now – 'having a ball'.

And this, I think, is nearer the truth than her reply, when told that everything was being reported back to London: 'I know it and, therefore, do I speak and act as you hear and see. The wasp leaves his sting in the wound and so do I. The Regent will hear it, as you say: I hope he will, I love to mortify him.' No doubt she did; but that was not the chief reason why she was staying up all hours, dyeing her hair or wearing a black wig, preferring diaphanous bodices and short skirts that showed her fat little legs. Unconventional at all times, often thought to be rather dotty, now well into her forties, out of London at last, away from England, she was having her fling. The English members of her suite were now leaving her one by one. Lord Liverpool himself wrote, begging her not to go to Naples. (Murat, Napoleon's brother-in-law, was still king there.) So to Naples she would go.

Bartolomeo Bergami, 1820, by H. R. Cook, engraving from *The Trial of Queen Caroline,* 1820, edited by J. Nightingale
The London Library, London

On the way, she stayed in Milan. And here she met Bartolomeo Bergami – changed later to Pergami because it sounded more aristocratic. He may or may not have belonged to a bankrupt aristocratic family – however, I shall call him Pergami – and it is not certain that he was an ex-officer who had fought in several of Napoleon's campaigns. What is certain is that as Caroline's courier (later, chamberlain) he was extremely conscientious, efficient, resourceful, and that he was very handsome, a fine six-foot figure of a man in his thirties, robust but dashing and magnificently be-whiskered, who, given the voice, would have been the perfect leading tenor in one of Rossini's more serious operas. No man could have been better designed to attract and then satisfy a full-blooded woman in her middle forties, high-spirited, indiscreet, perhaps somewhat randy, and bent on having her fling. But perhaps they kept apart until after Naples, where Caroline spent four months revelling in and out of the palace prepared for her by Murat, King Joachim. After all, Murat, with his black hair flowing in curls over his shoulders, his hats gorgeous with plumes, his splendid uniforms, was himself a famous, regal, super-Pergami, and it was rumoured that before, after, or during the processions, bear hunts, masquerades and balls, Caroline contrived to have an affair with him.

The Neapolitan revels might have lasted another four months, but in February 1815 Napoleon broke out of Elba, Murat prepared to march against Austria. So Caroline and her entourage took to the road again, this time making for Leghorn and Genoa. It was unfortunate – unless of course Caroline was now deliberately making mischief – that English tourists frequently stayed in Leghorn and Genoa. Caroline was seen in Genoa in a pink feathered hat, very low pink bodice, short white skirt that hardly reached her knees, riding through the streets in a shell-shaped phaeton, drawn by two piebald horses and driven by a child dressed as an operatic cherub in flesh-coloured tights. In front was a man on horseback dressed to look like Murat: this was Pergami. Attending a ball in May, Lady Bessborough did not at first even recognise the Princess of Wales. She wrote:

I cannot tell you how sorry and asham'd I felt as an Englishwoman. The first thing I saw in the room was a short, very fat, elderly woman, with an extremely red face (owing, I suppose, to the heat) in a girl's white frock looking dress, but with shoulder, back and neck, quite low (disgustingly so), down to the middle of her stomach; very black hair and eyebrows, which gave her a fierce look, and a wreath of light pink roses on her head. She was dancing . . . I was staring at her from the oddity of her appearance, when suddenly she nodded and smil'd at me, and not recollecting her, I was convinc'd she was mad, till William push'd me, saying 'Do you not see the Princess of Wales nodding to you?' It is so long since I have seen her near before, she is so much fatter and redder, that added to her black hair and eyebrows, extra-

The Villa d'Este – her Majesty's residence on Lake Como from *Memoirs of the Public and Private Life of her most Gracious Majesty Caroline, Queen of Great Britain and Consort of King George IV,* 1820, by J. Nightingale
The London Library, London

ordinary deep, I had not the least recollection of her . . . I could not bear the sort of whispering and talking all round about . . .

As reports of this kind found their way to Carlton House, the furious resentment of the Regent must have mounted steadily. Pleasure he could sympathise with, but this monstrous wife of his was making him look a fool all over the place.

By August 1815 Caroline had bought a charming little villa on the shore of Lake Como, was enlarging it and calling it the Villa d'Este. It still exists and is now a luxury hotel. It had its own little theatre, and Caroline took part in harlequinades there. Pergami was now her Chamberlain, waited upon by his former fellow servants. In view of Brougham's impassioned defence of her in 1820, it is worth noting that at this time he was writing to Lord Grey: 'The accounts of the Princess of Wales are worse and worse.' She was very restless and could not settle in the Villa d'Este or anywhere else. She had to be almost continually on the move. In 1816, after making Pergami a Knight of Malta and giving him the title of Baron de la Francine, she insisted upon making a really long journey (as it was in those days), going as far as Palestine. Discussing her marriage, she once said that the Regent should have been the woman, she the man. There was certainly something womanish often in his behaviour, in the faintings (though tight lacing may have played its part here) and sudden storms of tears. But Caroline was feminine enough in her relations with Pergami, in her exhibitionist dressing-up and dancing – an ageing woman enjoying her Indian summer. Yet she proved herself to be an intrepid and genuinely curious traveller on this long journey.

The Queen's entrance into Jerusalem, from *The Royal Exile,* 1820
The London Library, London

265

She went to Tunis and took coffee with the Bey in his seraglio. From there she sailed to Athens, where later she was reported to have 'dress'd almost naked and danc'd with her servants'. Going by way of Constantinople and Acre, she entered Jerusalem on horseback in July, accompanied by a ragtag-and-bobtail suite, mostly Italian, of twenty-five, and about two hundred servants and camp followers. Genuinely interested, she passed some days visiting the Holy Places, and then went on to Jericho. She had now created a new Order of her own, the Order of St Caroline – 'to recompense the faithful knights who have had the honour of accompanying her on her pilgrimage to the Holy Land'. And who was to be Grand Master of this Order? Why – no other than Colonel Bartholomew Pergami, Baron of Francina, Knight of Malta, and of the Holy Sepulchre of Jerusalem, equerry of her Royal Highness! And he had a large number of his relatives now in Caroline's service.

On the way back, there was a long and tedious voyage to Syracuse in a polacca, which was to figure largely in the 1820 trial because it was said that Caroline and Pergami shared a tent on deck. She returned to the Villa d'Este at the end of September 1816 – and bought Pergami a villa near Milan – moved again in the summer of 1817 but never quite settled down. Perhaps the chief reason why she was so restless was that she knew she was being continually spied upon by her husband's agents.

In 1818 the Milan Commission, appointed by the Regent himself and not by the government, though a law officer, Sir John Leach, was at the head of it, was given the task of collecting evidence for a divorce. No fewer than thirty-one Italian witnesses were examined. The Commission finally concluded that the evidence established 'the fact of continued adulterous intercourse'. In March 1819, Henry Brougham, who was still Caroline's adviser, sent his brother James to discover for himself how things were between Caroline and Pergami. James reported that Caroline seemed very happy, that she and Pergami were 'to all appearances man and wife', that the whole thing was apparent to everyone. He also said that all Caroline wanted was to pass the remainder of her life quietly, that she had not 'the spirits she used to have', and that all the 'work the Prince makes' – she meant the spying and examination of witnesses – worried her. In fact, as she told James Brougham, she was ready to remain abroad and give no trouble, so long as she was left to her own devices and provided with a handsome income to take care of them. It was when he learnt this from his brother that Henry Brougham should have concluded a settlement with Caroline that would have kept her out of England. He was short-sighted and dilatory here, just as he was hypocritical afterwards when he proclaimed Caroline's complete innocence.

We are now in 1820, and the Regent has blossomed into George IV and, whatever he may say, Caroline is his Queen. But he is determined that she shall enjoy no queenly rights and privileges and that her name shall be left out of the liturgy: no subjects of his were going to pray every day for Pergami's paramour. She had made him look a fool from Lake Como to Jericho, and she was not going to queen it now in London. He began collecting various damaging documents, which would show his ministers the kind of woman she was, and had them placed in what was to be soon a notorious green bag. But if Caroline had shown some loss of spirit the previous year, she quickly recovered now, at once angry at being so humiliated and delighted to be the central figure of a national drama. It was the Queen's move – and she left Italy for England.

The Landing of Queen Caroline at Dover to claim her rights – dedicated to the feelings of the British Nation, painting on glass by W. B. Walker Collection Mr Brian Hill

She arrived early in June, cheered by crowds everywhere, and stayed at first with an Alderman Wood, a self-made and very self-important chemist and a former Lord Mayor of London. Later she found a house in Hammersmith, so that her most enthusiastic admirers could go by water to cheer her. It was part of the madness of this time – and if there is a more foolish year in English History I do not know it – that the people should show a frenzied loyalty to Queen Caroline, not only in London, where she was constantly making public appearances, but also in the provinces, which sent to her scores of Loyal Addresses. If she had fought and won more battles than Wellington, instead of making an exhibition of herself and living with an Italian courier, there could not have been more enthusiasm.

Well aware of the people's dislike of the King and the Establish-

(above left) A late arrival at Mother
Wood's, 1820, engraving by
G. Humphrey
Collection Mr Thomas Norbury

(above right) Arrival at Brandenburgh
House of the Watermen & with an
address to the Queen on 3 October
1820, aquatint by Dubourg
Collection Miss Doris Leslie

ment, Caroline made a bold bid for popular support, showing
herself constantly and displaying two qualities she undoubtedly
possessed – an easy good nature and courage. No doubt there was
a general resentment, mixed with chivalry, of the way she was
being treated. But even when all allowance has been made, there
remains something odd and rather crazy about this enthusiasm
for Caroline in 1820. All these people in the provinces, with their
Loyal Addresses, meetings, bonfires, illuminations, had never set
eyes on her; she had never done anything for them; and money
that might have been better spent at home had largely gone on
maintaining Pergami and his relatives.

However, if the people were now in danger of losing their wits,
so were the King and his advisers. Shaken by Caroline's triumphant
return, the King had sent his green bag, crammed with unsavoury
evidence, to the Cabinet, together with a message saying he was
depending upon Parliament to take action. But what action? It
had already been agreed that the King could not bring Caroline
into an ordinary court of law or simply take divorce proceedings.
On the other hand, a committee appointed by the Lords, after
sifting through the nasty stuff in the green bag, had reported that
Caroline could certainly be charged with conduct of a 'most
licentious character', so something would have to be done.

Lord Liverpool then groped into the deepest recesses of the law,
and came up with a Bill of Pains and Penalties. This was an old
and dubious process, outside the common legal system, and never
carrying a death penalty, that would if successful result in an Act
of Parliament, which would have the same effect as a decision in
the highest court of law. In this instance, if the Bill of Pains and
Penalties against Caroline succeeded in proving its case, she
would forfeit her rights as Queen and be divorced by the King.
Though, strictly speaking, what followed now was not a trial, we
are reasonably entitled to call it one. Queen Caroline was in effect

to be tried by the whole House of Lords. (Later it would have to take its findings to the Commons, at present uneasy about this strange procedure.) The Lords would decide if she had or had not committed adultery with Pergami, who, not being a British subject, could not be put on trial himself. It was rather as if a slimy divorce case should be hurried into the fantastic atmosphere of *Alice in Wonderland* and *Iolanthe*. It was a huge solemn piece of imbecility.

The Lords, advised by Black Rod and their Deputy Speaker, took the proceedings with immense seriousness. Unless they were ill, recently bereaved, too young or too old, Roman Catholics or out of the country, all the peers had to attend and were heavily fined if they stayed away. All judges not sitting in the provinces had to be there, not to vote but to give legal advice. The House of Lords was too small to accommodate everybody, so Sir John Soane had to build a couple of temporary galleries. Caroline herself could take no part in the trial, but she was allowed to attend it, had her own chair and footstool in a central position, and her own retiring room; and in view of the fact that some of the most intimate details of her private life were about to be brought out and debated upon, these arrangements for her convenience and comfort were reasonable enough.

In 1820 the Queen could still appoint her own attorney-general and solicitor-general, though they were outside the government. Brougham, of course, was her attorney-general, and Thomas Denman, a good-looking eloquent advocate, her solicitor-general; and these two led for the defence. In charge of the prosecution were the King's attorney-general, Sir Robert Gifford, a sound lawyer but no match for the dazzling and unscrupulous Brougham, and his solicitor-general, John Singleton Copley, a barrister of great distinction who later became Lord Chancellor and lived to be ninety-one. The Lord Chancellor in 1820 was Eldon, getting on in years and a deep-dyed Tory but fair-minded throughout these proceedings, which he heard and considered every day from his seat on the Woolsack. But he would not have been able to do this if elaborate arrangements had not been made to keep the excited crowds well away from the hall. As it was, they cheered their heads off as the Queen, in a special carriage with six bays and all the men in her uniform, went to and from Westminster.

The trial began in the third week of August and did not end until the first week of November. It is hard to imagine how the business of governing the country was carried on. Even the House of Commons kept going into a recession. Judges were missing from their courts, bishops from their dioceses. Too hot in August, too cold in November, there were all the peers of Britain, day after day after day, and, as Hobhouse said, 'sent to pry into foul clothes-bags and pore over the contents of chamber utensils'. And all the

John Scott, 1st Earl of Eldon (detail), *c.* 1826, by Sir Thomas Lawrence
oil on canvas
36 × 28 in. (91.5 × 71.2 cm.)
The National Portrait Gallery, London

time the country itself was in a continual uproar. What Paris, Berlin, Vienna and St Petersburg thought about this gigantic London farce, I have not been able to discover; but it is safe to guess that George IV, his Queen, his House of Lords and his jeering and cheering subjects were regarded with no respect and much mockery. After all, it was the greatest farce ever staged in London.

Much of the evidence, given verbatim, may be found in Mr Roger Fulford's excellent *Trial of Queen Caroline*. I have no space for it here. And it must be verbatim or nothing, because a mere précis of it would be tedious. The best I can offer is a fairly brief account of these daft proceedings. And if I am told that the trial of a queen is no light matter, not to be dismissed as 'daft', several replies would be obvious at once. First, the shocked and sorrowing husband, His Majesty King George IV, had been notorious for his dissolute conduct for over thirty-five years. Secondly, it was impossible for any man of sense and experience to believe that Caroline was the innocent victim of perjured slander. Thirdly, among the peers themselves – and they would not only have to vote, they could question the witnesses – were some who had anything but spotless reputations. So to cynical foreign observers the whole thing must have looked like a monument of British cant and humbug. Finally, it ought to have been clear from the start that no *direct* evidence of Caroline's adultery would be brought out – she and Pergami were careless but not *that* careless – and a mass of circumstantial evidence would soon make the proceedings look ridiculous.

The first witnesses, summoned by the prosecution, were Italians who had been in Caroline's service. They had, of course, been brought to London – and were now being boarded and lodged and possibly remunerated – by the government. The Lords spent one August day after another (there were arguments about opening and shutting the windows) listening to evidence that must often have made the over-crowded room seem closer than ever. There was a great deal about the arrangement of the bedrooms in the Villa d'Este, about the Princess being seen coming out of Pergami's room or Pergami going into the Princess's room and how they were dressed – that kind of thing. There was much, far too much, about that tent on the deck of the polacca, which these witnesses swore the Princess shared with Pergami. But this soporific level could suddenly turn itself into a minefield, when one intimate and rather nasty detail after another exploded. Stains were found on bedclothes. Chamber pots and their contents were mentioned.

There was an odd interlude on behalf of Mahomet the entertainer, who helped to pass the Princess's evenings in the Holy Land. One of his acts was to put his large linen pantaloons to obscene use, contriving a roll out of them with one hand and then making

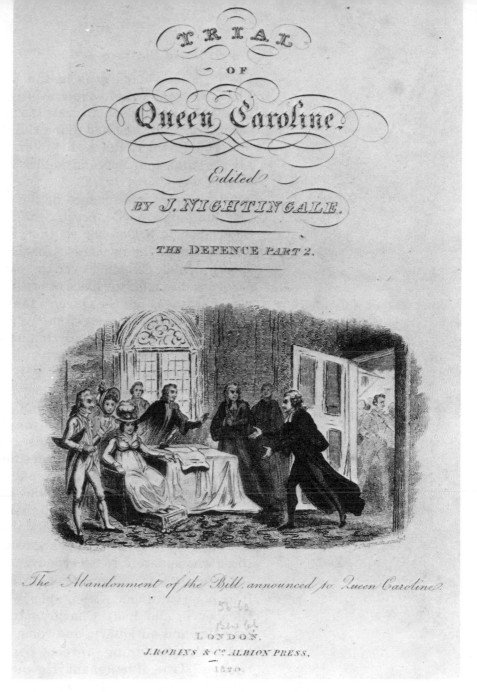

TRIAL
OF
Queen Caroline.

Edited

BY J. NIGHTINGALE.

THE DEFENCE PART 2.

The Abandonment of the Bill, announced to Queen Caroline.

LONDON.
J. ROBINS & C? ALBION PRESS,
1820.

The Abandonment of the Bill
announced to Queen Caroline, from
The Trial of Queen Caroline, 1820,
edited by J. Nightingale
The London Library, London

himself and the rest of his voluminous pantaloons move forwards
and backwards: a tasteless performance for a royal visitor, but of
course no proof of adultery. But Caroline and Pergami shared a
closed carriage on some of their travels, and what went on there
came as close to proof as anything their lordships would hear.
One of the things a witness had to put into the carriage was a
curious bottle with a mouth about three or four inches in diameter.
And the purpose of it? For Pergami to make water in. The last two
Italian witnesses, who could not be shaken, went much further.
One of them, going to the carriage to ask for instructions, saw that

271

the Princess's hand 'was in the small clothes of Mr Pergami'. The other, when they were travelling by night through an Italian July, had gone at dawn to draw the curtains of the carriage, and on several occasions he had found the Princess and Pergami asleep – and 'Her Royal Highness held her hand upon the private part of Mr Pergami, and Pergami held his own upon that of her Royal Highness'.

After Copley had summed up the prosecution's case in a reasonable unimpassioned speech, the trial was adjourned from 9 September to 3 October so that Brougham and his colleagues could mobilise their witnesses for the defence. Brougham's opening speech, which extended over the better part of two sessions, was recognised as a masterpiece of brilliant advocacy. His general line was that it was not the Queen's fault she had had to go travelling alone, that the witnesses, shady characters anyhow, had been bribed to perjure themselves, that most of their evidence was vague and contradictory and that when it arrived at details, then these were so disgusting and offensive they were hardly worth considering and quite impossible to believe; and in a remarkable peroration he begged the assembled peers not only to save the honour of the Queen of England but to save the country and save themselves, save the very altar itself – 'You see that when the church and the throne would allow of no church solemnity in behalf of the Queen, the heart-felt prayers of the people rose to Heaven for her protection. I pray Heaven for her' – and so forth. It was an astonishing performance, all the more astonishing when we remember that only the year before, his brother James had reported that Caroline and Pergami were 'to all appearances man and wife', that the whole thing was apparent to everybody.

The witnesses called on behalf of the defence were no dubious Italian servants but respectable Britons like Lords Guilford and Glenbervie and Lady Charlotte Lindsay, Sir William Gell, the traveller and antiquary, and some naval men. And none of them had noticed anything – except perhaps a few pardonable eccentricities. True, Lieutenant Hownam, who had gone as far as Jerusalem, had been created one of the Knights of the Order of St Caroline – but why not? This question was asked and answered by Denman, who made the final speech for the defence and took ten hours over it. He denounced the prosecution's witnesses and 'those agents who had collected together a set of her Majesty's discarded servants, who had ransacked filthy clothes-bags, who had raked into every sewer, pried into every water-closet, who attempted to destroy all the secrecies of private life . . .' He made it clear he had a very poor opinion of Italian life and character and later even brought in Nero. But after speaking for ten hours, Denman rashly attempted an impromptu emotional peroration,

PLATE XLII. Willy Lott's Cottage, near Flatford Mill, 1810–15?, by John Constable
oil on paper
9½ × 7 in. (24.1 × 17.8 cm.)
The Victoria and Albert Museum, London

PLATE XLIII. (overleaf) The Trial of Queen Caroline (detail), 1820, by Sir George Hayter
oil on canvas
91¾ × 140¼ in. (233 × 356 cm.)
The National Portrait Gallery, London

which ended by his quoting, 'If no accuser can come forward to condemn thee, neither do I condemn thee: go, and sin no more.' And as he had been arguing for two days that no sin had been committed, this was anything but apt, and produced many squibs from the other side:

> Most gracious queen, we thee implore
> To go away and sin no more;
> Or if that effort be too great,
> To go away at any rate.

Copley made the concluding speech for the Crown, and made hay of the idea that Pergami owed his rapid promotion – and the employment of twelve members of his family – to innocent but mysteriously 'extraordinary' services. At the end of his speech he ridiculed Brougham's argument that nothing could have happened in that tent on the polacca because the Princess and Pergami were dressed. But dressed in what? She had been seen wearing a morning gown and Pergami a loose Tunisian robe. 'If such obstructions as these are effectual,' cried Copley, 'what is to become of population?' Then from the last days of October into the first week of November, there was a summing up and much confused debate from peers and prelates, and a tangle of legal and Parliamentary arguments and votes through which I shall slash my way to the final day, Friday, 10 November, when the majority in favour of the bill (which would still have to go to the Commons) had shrunk to nine. The Prime Minister, Liverpool, now moved 'that the bill do pass this day six months', a parliamentary term for abandoning a bill. The motion was carried enthusiastically. The Bill of Pains and Penalties – *A Bill to deprive her Majesty Caroline Amelia Elizabeth of the Title, Prerogatives, Rights, Privileges, and Pretensions of Queen Consort of this Realm, and to dissolve the Marriage between his Majesty and the said Queen* – after all those weeks and weeks of fuss and palaver – was thrown out. The idiotic trial might just as well have never taken place. Even so, it must be understood that the contest was not between those who thought Caroline guilty and those who believed her to be innocent. The real division was between the men who for various reasons were strongly in favour of the Bill and the men who disliked it as a political measure.

Caroline herself knew this: 'Nobody cares for *me* in this business,' she declared. 'This business has been more cared for as a political business than as the cause of a poor forlorn woman.' But I think we must agree that this poor forlorn woman had had her fling. Which kind of fling, though? Are we to believe the English witnesses, who saw almost nothing, or the Italian, who saw almost everything? I doubt if the English witnesses were deliberately

PLATE XLIV. The Royal Banquet 19 July 1821 (detail), aquatint by Robert Havell after Charles Wild 12¾ × 15¾ in. (32.3 × 40 cm.) The National Portrait Gallery, London

telling lies. They had deceived themselves, probably with the help of Brougham, who would be ready to tell them that certain thoughts they had had were unthinkable. It seems to me, however, that this *unthinkable* approach really favours the Italians. No doubt they were capable of adding a few fancy touches to their stories, but it is to my mind unthinkable that these servants could combine to invent a legend of her infatuated and licentious relationship with one of their own sort. And, of course, as James Brougham discovered and his brother Henry well knew, it was commonly accepted that Caroline and Pergami were living together. Her semi-public protestations of complete innocence were nonsense, but then the proceedings against her were equally ridiculous. And they went on too long: Greville could write, 'How great an evil it was when a single subject of interest takes possession of society; conversation loses all its lightness and variety.'

The Queen returning from the House of Lords, 1821, engraving by Dubourg
The Royal Pavilion, Brighton

Caroline took the dropping of the Bill against her as a great personal triumph, to be shared with her innumerable supporters. On 29 November she went in state to St Paul's, cheered by an enormous mob, to offer thanks to God for her deliverance, even though she had to do it without any assistance from the higher ranks of the clergy. This was the last of her spectacular appearances, although, after being given a royal residence and an annuity of £50,000, she did keep visiting theatres, where she was always – as the actors say – 'good for a round'. Meanwhile, the King, who had preferred to stay out of sight in Brighton during the trial, now returned to public life. The reigning favourite was Lady Conyngham, who was to keep the King by her side for the rest of his life. In 1820 she was a plump handsome woman of about fifty-four, who was married to Conyngham, an Irish peer, as early as 1794. The King was in love with her in his rather limited fashion,

(above) A brougham, 1838
The Science Museum, London

(right) A britzka, 1820
The Science Museum, London

279

but it was misusing language to call her, as most people did, his 'mistress'. They probably never went beyond a little elderly dalliance. As one rude popular versifier put it:

> 'Tis pleasant at seasons to see how they sit,
> First cracking their nuts, and then cracking their wit:
> Then quaffing their claret – then mingling their lips,
> Or tickling the *fat* about each other's hips.

Society women thought her rather vulgar and not very intelligent, unlike the King, who in a kind of boyish infatuation, considered her 'wittier than any male or female of his acquaintance'. She was apparently religious, had no political ideas or opinions (a good thing), but, creating a fashion followed by the blondes of our era, had 'a strong leaning to diamonds and money'. It was said later that during George IV's last illness, she carted away sufficient jewelry, plate, etc., to fill two wagons. She was careful to preserve appearances and never stayed under the same roof as the King without being accompanied by her husband, who, incidentally, did very well out of his wife's influence, being advanced to several well-paid offices and posts.

That she had not always been so respectable is proved by a passage in the autobiography of de Quincey. When, years before this, he and a fellow schoolboy were going over to Ireland they had found, sitting in her travelling coach on deck, a beautiful lady of rank and fashion, who was amused by their admiring glances and invited them into her coach for some talk. That night, trying to sleep on deck, not far away, they discovered that a certain colonel, who had been hiding below during the day, crept into her coach late at night – an arrangement 'not entirely a secret even amongst the lady's servants'. And this, of course, was Lady Conyngham. The secret of her long hold over the King was probably – as we find in the Grantley-Berkeley Reminiscences – that 'invariably the lady kept him in good humour with the world', making it clear that 'in her conviction he was a compound of Sardanapalus and Louis XIV, Alexander the Great and Augustus Caesar, Alcibiades and the Admirable Crichton'. Stronger-minded men than George IV have found it hard to resist such flattery; and Lady Conyngham was not only a very handsome woman but also possessed, we are told, 'a sweetly musical voice, low and tender'.

Even that voice, daily delivering butter and honey, could not have induced the King, as 1820 went shuffling out, to forget all his troubles. The Bill had failed; that dreadful woman Caroline, as popular as he was unpopular, was still around; and no matter how great a nuisance the Queen and her cheering mobs might be, 1821 would have to be the year – the truly magnificent year too – of his Coronation.

1821

King of Pleasure

There have been four coronations in my lifetime: those of Edward VII, George V, George VI, Elizabeth II; and I was never near any of them. If I could work a time-trick and hop into the past, the only coronation I would choose to attend would be this one in 1821. George IV might have been vague and dilatory about state affairs, but he made sure that when at last the day had come he would have a slap-up coronation. We might be said to be on our way there now, but we can risk a few brief halts along the road.

At the end of January, in his speech at the Opening of Parliament the King announced that 'notwithstanding the agitation produced by temporary circumstances, and amidst the distress which still presses upon a large portion of my subjects, the firmest reliance may be placed on that affection and loyal attachment to my person . . . and which, while it is most grateful to the strongest feelings of my heart, I shall ever consider as the best and surest safeguard of my throne . . .' All of which, when we remember the various measures to suppress popular feeling, seems nothing short of sheer impudence. Yet oddly enough, though Queen Caroline was still bouncing around to act as a living reproach to him, though Lady Conyngham was very much in evidence as the triumphant favourite, there were signs now that popular disfavour was being left behind.

On 7 February the King went in state to Drury Lane and was warmly applauded for two or three minutes. He went the next night to Covent Garden and was enthusiastically greeted, even though a voice from the gallery cried, 'Where's your wife, Georgie?' The crowds outside both theatres did more cheering than hooting. Chaucer's 'stormy peple unsad and ever untrewe' were now veering towards him, which meant that at last the King and his advisers could begin planning the Coronation.

In this same month, February, John Keats, who was with his friend Severn in Rome, was slowly dying, being bitterly disappointed, morning after morning, to find himself still alive, in a world to which he had already said goodbye. In the evening of 23 February he died. He had asked that on his gravestone there should be nothing but *Here lies one whose name was writ in water*. It has been suggested that what put this into his mind was the sound, to which he had listened through so many feverish hours, of the fountain playing in the square below. But we might remember that among the enduring symbols that appear in our dreams is *water*, symbol of that huge timeless life in the unconscious from which poets take their images. Keats was the first to go; next year, Shelley was drowned; and two years after that, Byron died in Greece. As Wordsworth, years later when another poet died, was to cry:

> How fast has brother followed brother,
> From sunshine to the sunless land!

A rather obtrusive piety had now set in at Carlton House. Perhaps because he had already in mind the more solemn moments of his crowning, the King was becoming more and more devout, banishing all thoughts of a life of idle pleasure-seeking. Here he was much influenced by Lady Conyngham, who could now be discovered among large theological tomes, no doubt with one eye on dogmatism and the other still on diamonds. Another influence – and a much better one – was that exercised by Sir William Knighton, the King's favourite physician and soon to become his chief man of affairs. It may have been piety or it may have been Knighton, but the King appeared to be in better shape than he had been. 'For a man of near sixty.' one observer notes, 'he contrives to look young by the help of a wig without powder; and his air and manner were as graceful as they used to be.' And to be devout gracefully is not given to all men.

There was an odd instance of a simpler and more sincere piety during this summer. After Michael Faraday, thirty, had married Sarah Barnard, twenty-one, he went to make his confession of sin and profession of faith before the Sandemanian Church. This was, as he said himself, 'a very small and despised sect of Christians', but he never wavered in his attachment to it or in his belief in a direct communion between God and the human soul. A great scientist, to whom our whole modern world is deeply in debt, he seemed to have no difficulty all his life in keeping, on a qualitative basis, a complete separation between science and religion. And as he has always seemed to me one of the noblest human beings of his century, I think it is a pity there were so few Sandemanians.

One man who thought nothing of the new piety in Carlton House was Henry Brougham – still not quite to be trusted. In his autobiography he goes to the length of declaring that Carlton House, in its vendetta against Queen Caroline, was now filling the press with libels to deter fashionable ladies from visiting her, and even bringing out new papers just to attack any women of rank who accepted invitations from the Queen. If we are to believe

William Wordsworth, 1818, by
Benjamin Robert Haydon
chalk
21½ × 16½ in. (54.5 × 41.9 cm.)
The National Portrait Gallery,
London

Brougham, it was not psalms and theological treatises that were being studied at Carlton House but guest lists, to make sure that those who visited the Queen were crossed off the King's list, while those who ignored her were to be welcomed with open arms. (Wives of members of both Houses were to be made especially welcome.) The Queen herself took all this far less seriously than Brougham did. 'The Queen bore it all with great patience and even good humour. She used to say, "Oh it is all in the common course. People go to different inns: one goes to the King's Head, another to the Angel".' An excellent remark, but it sounds more like Henry Brougham than Queen Caroline.

On 4 July we are almost back at that trial again. The Queen had claimed that she had a right to be crowned. Her claim had to be examined by the Privy Council, which met in force, with Lord Harrowby in the chair. Once again – but now for the last time – Brougham and Denman put the case for the Queen. Once again, Gifford and Copley argued against them. On this occasion, however, a decision was reached. It was decided that as the Queen was living separately from the King, her claim to be crowned could not be allowed. And here I feel I must continue Caroline's story, leaving the King to wait for his crown. Early on Coronation Day, 19 July, and against the advice of all her friends, the Queen went to each of the Westminster Abbey doors demanding to be admitted. She was turned away, though it was said later that if she had had a ticket she would have been admitted as a spectator. Accounts of her reception by the crowd that morning vary considerably. Sympathisers like Brougham and Creevey declared she was loudly applauded. Fanny Burney wrote: 'The Queen and Wood were hooted by the spectators... The attempt to get admission was therefore only a pretence for a parade through the streets, and that I firmly believe was calculated to try her strength, and it only proved her weakness.'

This fiasco has been called 'her death-blow'. Many of the people believed that she died of a broken heart. In fact she was taken ill at Drury Lane Theatre on 30 July, suffering from an abdominal obstruction and then from too much 1821 medication. She died on 7 August. However, she did tell Brougham she would not recover – and 'I am much better dead for I be tired of this life.' She may have been doomed anyhow, but it is possible to think that her love of high drama and the limelight and storms of cheering might have weakened her resistance. I feel myself that the Queen's move back to England was a mistake, and that if she had been a wiser woman she would have stayed on quietly with Pergami and his twelve relatives, disreputable but cosy. Following the instruction in her will, she was buried at Brunswick – where no tumultuous mobs had ever greeted her, where her family had always thought her a bit

The Coronation Procession of His Majesty King George IV 19 July 1821, coloured engraving by G. Schard Weinreb and Douwma Limited, London

cracked. Brunswick was too narrow and poor, England too cold and suspicious, really to please her, but at least in middle age she had had one huge frolic in the sun, from Jericho to Como.

Now we return to 19 July, Coronation Day. George IV had his faults but nobody could accuse him of being a bad showman – and this was his day. Nothing was spared, including the ears of his subjects, for, beginning at midnight, bells pealed and guns roared every half hour. The King spent the night of the 18th at the Speaker's house in Westminster – a star performer waiting in the wings, we might say, to make his first entrance. The Abbey itself was crammed with boxes, galleries, benches, and might almost have been a giant playhouse, mostly decorated with crimson cloth. Over at Westminster Hall, where there was to be a banquet after the coronation ceremony, the preparations were even more elaborate. A wooden floor had been laid, about fourteen inches above the stone floor; the walls had been draped; there were tiers of wooden galleries for spectators; a dining table for peers and bishops ran the length of the hall; at the south end, a platform, draped in scarlet and gold, had been erected for the King and the Royal Dukes; and at the north end there was a triumphal Gothic arch, about thirty feet high and thirty-six feet wide, and above this arch was a gallery for the band. The coronation procession would move first from the Hall to the Abbey, and it would go along a covered walk, twenty-five feet wide, its blue-carpeted floor raised three feet above the ground for better visibility. This was only fair because spectators in the gaily-decorated galleries lining the route had paid anything from two to twenty guineas for a seat.

At 10.25, preceded by his chief officers of state, the King entered

Westminster Hall. He was twenty-five minutes late because his Lord Great Chamberlain, Lord Gwydyr, had torn his clothes while trying to get into them. The King, a proud and happy man, for once able to wear anything he had ever fancied, made a fine entrance. His train, of crimson velvet emblazoned with gold stars, was twenty-seven feet long; he wore a black Spanish hat that had great plumes of white ostrich feathers; and the curls of his wig fell gracefully over his forehead. 'The way in which the King bowed,' Haydon tells us, 'was really royal. As he looked towards the peeresses and foreign ambassadors, he showed like some gorgeous bird of the East.'

The procession formed up and slowly moved out. It was headed – for the last time in our history – by the King's Herb-woman and six maids scattering herbs along the way. They were followed by the chief officers of state bearing the crown, the orb, the sceptre, the sword of state; and with them were three bishops carrying the paten, chalice and Bible. The peers, in the order of their rank,

The Ceremony of the Challenge. The moment depicted is that previous to His Majesty drinking the health of the King's Champion, who is at the foot of the steps attended by the Lord High Constable on his right and by the Deputy Earl Marshal on his left. On the right of the throne are the dukes of York, Sussex and Gloucester – on the left Clarence, Cambridge and Prince Leopold. In the lower galleries are appropriate peeresses and the Lord High Steward holding his staff of office is on the second flight of the steps in the foreground. Not far from the latter are two of the herbs women who strewed flowers in the path of his Majesty, 1821 The Royal Collection, Windsor Castle

moved majestically in their state robes. Privy Councillors who were not peers all wore Elizabethan costume of white and blue satin with trunk hose. The King walked under a canopy of cloth-of-gold borne by Barons of the Cinque Ports. Processional music was supplied by the Household Band, but what its bandsmen wore I do not know. What I do know is that George IV's coronation cost three-and-a-half times as much as Victoria's. But what a show! And the banquet was still to come.

As the King entered the Abbey he was greeted by the Hallelujah Chorus, fighting to make itself heard above the shouts of welcome. In the Coronation Sermon the King was reminded, perhaps rather pointedly, that 'It is the most essential service that a Sovereign can render to a State, to encourage morality and religion.' Perhaps all that piety in Carlton House, together with Lady Conyngham's theology, had been a kind of preparation to meet this challenging moment. The ceremony itself was very long-drawn-out, and there were signs, noted by Lady Cowper, that the King was beginning to feel exhausted. However, about 4 o'clock he was able to walk, under the weight of his robes and regalia, in the procession back to Westminster Hall. It was now ready for the banquet, the last of its kind and all very medieval, even the backs of the chairs being shaped like Gothic arches. Three hundred and twelve persons (all male) sat down to dinner, in addition to the royal family. And all the diversions between courses had a mediaeval air, picturesque but rather absurd.

After a procession coming through the big Gothic arch had served the first course, there arrived, in their robes but on *horseback*, the Lord High Constable (Duke of Wellington), the Lord High Steward (Marquis of Anglesey) and the Deputy Earl Marshal (Lord Howard of Effingham), which was all very fine but must have made some guests feel they were taking soup in a circus. Moreover, after the Gentleman Pensioners had filed in with great steaming dishes of meat, Lord Howard's horse began to behave badly and his curses rang through the hall. Now came the Ceremony of the Challenge, taking the whole banquet into *Ivanhoe*. An astonishing figure in full armour, with a plumed helmet and carrying a gauntlet, rode a white charger through the Gothic arch. He was in fact the twenty-year-old son of the Reverend John Dymoke, a rector in Lincolnshire, whose family had long held the hereditary office of King's Champion. The white charger had been borrowed from Astley's circus. The gauntlet was flung down three times, but as nobody offered to accept the challenge – the wrong people were there – the King drank to his Champion out of a gold cup, and then he drank to the peers and the peers drank to him and gave him altogether nine rounds of cheering, and they were all jolly good fellows saluting a super-jolly-good-fellow.

The King, who had had a very long day, left about half-past seven for Carlton House, probably to get into a dressing gown and slippers. The peers, free at last of Majesty, horses, gauntlets and challenges, really settled down to dine. They had been well provided for, with about enough to feed a small mining town for a month:

160 tureens of soup, 160 dishes of fish;
160 hot joints, 160 dishes of vegetables;
480 sauce boats (lobster, butter, mint);
80 dishes of braised ham, 80 savoury pies;
80 dishes of goose, 80 of savoury cakes;
80 of braised beef, 80 of braised capons;
1,190 side dishes.
320 dishes of mounted pastry, 320 of small pastry;
400 dishes of jellies and creams;
160 dishes of shellfish (lobster and crayfish);
160 dishes of cold roast fowl, 80 of cold lamb.

The peeresses in the gallery, now feeling very hungry, could only glare down at these wretches of men making beasts of themselves. But round the loaded tables, not all feelings of chivalry or family responsibility were dead. One nobleman at least was seen to tie up some cold chicken in a handkerchief and throw it up to his son, who, I hope, shared the catch with his mother. The great day ended with fireworks and balloons in Hyde Park, which could be enjoyed by everybody – except perhaps the stupefied peerage. And Walter Scott announced: 'Never monarch received a more general welcome from his subjects', even though Parliament had voted £243,000 out of their pockets to pay for this grand occasion.

We left the King riding in his closed carriage to Carlton House, but now we must follow him briefly not in space but in time. He reigned for nearly nine more years. During the first two of them, when he was still able to travel and display himself, which is what he loved to do, he set a fashion still followed, very sensibly, by the British monarchy. He went on tour. He went to Dublin; he visited Hanover; and finally, his greatest triumph, arrived in Edinburgh wearing a full Highland costume.

But he aged fast; his health broke down; he took far more cherry brandy and laudanum than he did exercise; and in his last years, though very stubborn with his ministers about Catholic Emancipation, his mind often wandered and he had various delusions, among them the idea that he himself had won the Battle of Salamanca. But, though no hero, he faced death bravely enough. When his possessions were examined afterwards, it was discovered that he had been a fantastic hoarder. 'All the coats, boots and pantaloons of fifty years were in his wardrobe'; he had had five hundred pocket-books and £10,000 was collected from them, money he had

George IV in Highland costume, 1829, by Sir David Wilkie
oil on canvas
The Royal Collection, Holyrood

His Majesty's Public Entry into the City of Dublin 17 August 1821, engraving by Robert Havell & Son after J. Haverly who painted after sketches made on the spot by John Lushington Reilly
The Royal Pavilion, Brighton

forgotten; and 'there were countless bundles of women's love letters, of women's gloves, of locks of women's hair', which had to be destroyed. All this hoarding suggests a continuing infantile element in his complex character.

Our Prince of Pleasure has been severely dealt with by his critics. Greville, a contemporary well acquainted with him, declared that 'a more contemptible, cowardly, unfeeling, selfish dog does not exist than this king'. Coming later, Thackeray's extremely biased lecture on him in his *Four Georges* was even more damaging than any contemporary opinion. But Thackeray too readily – here and elsewhere – adopted the tone and standards of mid-Victorian middle-class morality. (Notice how he turns the Regent and Caroline into the villain and heroine of a Victorian melodrama.) Certainly the Regent, as I prefer to call him now, was sadly lacking in many bourgeois virtues. He was vain, extravagant, self-indulgent, undependable, and was devoted not to duty but to the pleasure principle, as I have tried to show throughout these chapters. What I might have added – and will do it now – is that at ease among his friends he was extremely good company: not a Sheridan, not a Sydney Smith, but on a monarchical level decidedly a wit; an amusing mimic; fond, perhaps too fond, of a long gossip, but not ill-natured with it; and his talk, like his interests, had a wide range. If the country had been immensely prosperous – or even if Charles James Fox had lived another six years to form a Whig government for him – he would have been seen in a rosier light.

It was his misfortune to occupy the centre of the stage, bowing and beaming, when the scene behind him was darkened by a harshly repressive government and a country wretched in its distress. And it was not simply an idle-minded love of pleasure that made him ignore the scene behind him. He was not himself a cold-hearted man, as many of his ministers were. There were in his nature certain womanish and infantile elements, encouraging him to burst into tears or hide himself, that made it difficult for him to to assert any strong opposition. He liked to please the people around him, and too often they were the wrong people. And while he was very vain, like many other kings and princes, his vanity had no iron in it. So it was wounded continually by the ferociously scurrilous attacks both on him and the various mother-mistresses he doted upon, savagely personal thrusts quite beyond anything the monarchy has known since his time. Finally, it will not do to dismiss him contemptuously, as Thackeray does, as if he were applying for a position as a company solicitor or bank manager: even before his ten years' reign, even as Prince Regent, he was in effect a constitutional monarch.

A constitutional monarch is not expected to rival an imperial Charles V, a Cromwell, a Louis XIV, a Napoleon. He governs his kingdom only in name. But he is not simply a figurehead or life-sized puppet. In the show his country makes, he is the leading performer, with gigantic star billing touched with magic. And he must try to personify, as far as he can, his countrymen's most civilising influences. His official appearances, which have to be sharply distinguished from his private life, must give warmth, colour, vitality, to the idea of his kingdom at its best. And if we accept this, then I think that instead of dismissing the Regent we must applaud him.

Notwithstanding his weaknesses and bad habits, he seems to me to offer us a fine example of constitutional monarchy. Within these limits, I prefer him to his father George III, with his mean court and disastrous meddling in politics, and to Victoria in her middle years, when she mourned and sulked so long at Windsor that even some politicians began demanding a republic. Whenever he was on show the Regent had tact, charm, and a genuine desire to please. He had a real interest in literature, the arts and crafts; his own taste in general was excellent, and where he felt uncertain he had the sense to seek good advice; and, as the result of what was denounced in his own time as mad extravagance, he left his successors and the country itself magnificent collections of pictures, furniture, china.

(below) The Quadrant, Regent's Street (now destroyed, although the Fire Office remains) by John Nash, engraving from Thomas Dale after Thomas H. Shepherd from James Elmes *Metropolitan Improvements or London in the Nineteenth Century,* 1827
The Royal Institute of British Architects, London (Drawings Collection)

(opposite above) John Nash (detail), 1827, by Sir Thomas Lawrence
oil on canvas
18½ × 26¼ in. (47 × 67.3 cm.)
Jesus College, Oxford

(opposite below) The East Side of Park Crescent by John Nash, engraving by J. Redaway after Thomas H. Shepherd from James Elmes *Metropolitan Improvements or London in the Nineteenth Century,* 1827
The Royal Institute of British Architects, London (Drawings Collection)

In many different ways London owes him more than it does to any other monarch since Charles II. Over and above his collections and rebuilding of royal houses, there was his grand plan, designed and carried out by John Nash, of demolishing a clutter of little streets and miserable buildings to drive a broad way, as straight as possible, between Carlton House and the newly created Regent's Park, itself one of the most charming city parks in the world. Some of Nash's work has gone, notably Regent Street as he left it, but the broad thoroughfares and his delightful terraces are still with us. Overseas visitors should explore this whole region, from Carlton House Terrace as far as Regent's Park, and then forget for the time being the follies of the Regent and remember the splendid heritage he left us.

As for the Regency itself – and, after all, the age is more important than the man – while I have done my best to leave some impression of it in the reader's mind, ten volumes of this size could not do full justice to it. The Regency was comparatively brief but had a character, a tone, a tang, all its own. No wonder that writers, from serious historians to popular romancers, have turned to it over and over again. It is like a strange col between the two high plateaux of eighteenth-century and Victorian England, like a

superb bridge passage, modulating various keys, in an ambitious piece of music. Nothing has been settled in it yet; what is old has not been swept out; what is new has not yet taken over society. Down one side of the street may be seen the evangelicals, the prigs and the prudes, and down the other go the gamesters, the extravagant dandies, the drunken womanisers, all having, like Caroline in Italy, a last wild fling.

The age swings between extremes of elegance and refinement and depths of sodden brutality and misery. It has no common belief, no accepted code, no general standard of conformity. It seems horrible one moment, enchanting the next. Anything and everything can be happening. In the North, some men are inventing and setting up new machines while other men are going by night with huge hammers to break them. Wellington is having fifty men flogged while Wordsworth is gazing at a celandine. Jane Austen is sending *Mansfield Park* to her publishers; Lady Caroline Lamb is sending Lord Byron clippings of pubic hair. Wilberforce is denouncing the slave trade when Beau Brummell is denouncing with equal gravity an imperfectly-tied cravat. Under one roof Jeremy Bentham is over-rationalising everything while under another roof William Blake is being visited by archangels. Hannah

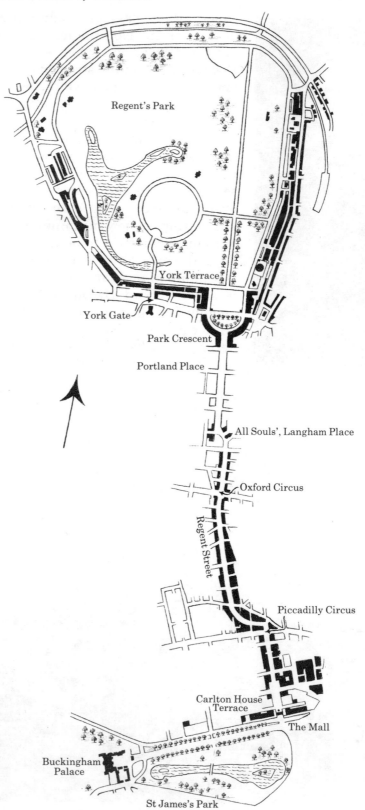

Regent's Park

York Terrace

York Gate

Park Crescent

Portland Place

All Souls', Langham Place

Oxford Circus

Regent Street

Piccadilly Circus

Carlton House Terrace

The Mall

Buckingham Palace

St James's Park

Map of John Nash's executed plan for the redevelopment of Regent's Park to Carlton House

Robert Stewart, 2nd Marquess of
Londonderry, Lord Castlereagh,
c. 1810, by Sir Thomas Lawrence
oil on canvas
29¼ × 24¼ in. (74.9 × 61.6 cm.)
The National Portrait Gallery,
London

(below) An engraving of one of
several cottages built for J. S.
Hartford of Blaise Castle by John
Nash
The Royal Institute of British
Architects, London (Drawings
Collection)

More is instructing the 'good poor' and Harriette Wilson is instructing the bad rich. The sun struggles through the smoke of London to shine both on Lord Castlereagh and on Percy Bysshe Shelley. Davy and Faraday are rapidly advancing science while being treated by doctors who might have come out of the middle ages.

In a city where many people think it is wicked to row a boat on Sunday, young noblemen lose £25,000 in a night at Watier's, tiny boys of six are forced up chimneys, prostitutes of fourteen roam the streets. Down at Brighton, in his fantastic Pavilion, the Regent is believed to be staging wild orgies, perhaps with kidnapped virgins, when in fact, with his stays loosened over the curacao, he is giving imitations of cabinet ministers to amuse the grandmothers who are his favourites. All appearances tend to be deceptive; too many public personages are either drunk or a trifle cracked; sedate grand ladies smile at sons and daughters who wonder who their fathers are; the Tory rulers adopt measures to suppress all opposition, but at the same time the crowds round the printshops roar with laughter at ferocious caricatures of them; lads brought up on sour bread and rotten potatoes go away to command the seas and help to drive Napoleon's marshals out of Spain. And between these extremes, a vitalising electric current seemed to pass from pole to pole; and out of all this rich variety of life that refused as yet to form an overall pattern, there shot up like a fountain the greatest English writing since Shakespeare's time.

Bibliography

Following what I said in my Preface, here is a list of books published in our own time that have been consulted, even though in some instances I have made no use of them in my text. Where I have been particularly indebted, I have named the books and their authors in the appropriate chapters, and I take this opportunity to thank the writers and publishers concerned.

J.B.P.

AIRLIE, Mabel, Countess of, *In Whig Society 1775–1818,* 1955
ALTHAM, H. S., *A History of Cricket,* 1962
ASHTON, T. S., *Iron and Steel in the Industrial Revolution,* 1924,
   The Industrial Revolution 1760–1830, 1954 (first pub. 1948),
   An Economic History of England in the Eighteenth Century, 1955
ASPINALL, A., ed., *The Letters of King George IV 1812–30,* 1938,
   The Letters of Princess Charlotte 1811–17, 1949
BERNAL, J. D., *Science and Industry in the Nineteenth Century,* 1953
BLUNDEN, E., 'On Regency Fiction, A Fragment' in *Essays and Studies,*
   New series, Vol XIV, 1961
BONSOR, N. R. P., *North Atlantic Seaway,* 1955
BOULTON, W. B., *The Amusements of Old London,* 1901
BOVIL, E. W., *English Country Life,* 1962
BRITISH MEDICAL JOURNAL, *Porphyria – A Royal Malady,* 1968
BROWN, F. K., *Father of the Victorians,* 1961
BROWN, I., *Jane Austen and her World,* 1966
BRUTON, F., *Three Accounts of Peterloo,* 1921
Cambridge History of English Literature, Vol. XII,
   The Nineteenth Century I, 1915
CAMPBELL, Kathleen, *Beau Brummell,* 1948
CARROTHERS, W. A., *Emigration from the British Isles,* 1929
CECIL, Lord David, *The Young Melbourne,* 1939
CHANCELLOR, E. Beresford, *Memorials of St James's Street,* 1922,
   The Pleasure Haunts of London, 1925
CHAPMAN, R. W., ed., *Jane Austen's letters to her sister Cassandra and others,*
   1952
CHURCH, R., *The Growth of the English Novel,* 1951
COLE, G. D. H. and POSTGATE, R., *The Common People 1746–1946,* 1946 (first
   edition 1938)
COPE, Sir Zachary, ed., *Sidelights on the History of Medicine,* 1957
COWAN, Helen I., *British Emigration to British North America,* 1961
CRUSE, Amy, *The Englishman and his Books in the Early Nineteenth Century,*
   1930
DRUMMOND, J. C. and WILBRAHAM, Anne, *The Englishman's Food,* 1939
DUDEK, Louis, *Literature and the Press,* 1960
EDGCUMBE, R. *The Diary of Frances, Lady Shelley, 1818–1873,* 1913
EDWARDS, R. and RAMSEY, L. G. G., ed., *The Regency Period, Connoisseur
   Period Guides,* 1958

ELKIN, R., *Royal Philharmonic,* 1947

ELLIS, C. Hamilton, *Railway History,* 1966

ELWIN, Malcolm, *Lord Byron's Wife,* 1962

FALK, Bernard, *Turner the Painter,* 1938

FINBERG, A. J., *The Life of J. M. W. Turner, R.A.,* 1939

FISHER, John, *1815,* 1963

FULFORD, Roger, *George IV,* 1935 and 1949

FULLER, Jean Overton, *Shelley: A Biography,* 1968

GARLICK, K., *Sir Thomas Lawrence,* 1954

GITTINGS, R., *John Keats,* 1968

GOLDRING, D., *Regency Portrait Painting. The Life of Sir Thomas Lawrence,*
    P.R.A.

GORDON, Strathearn, and COCKS, T. G. B., *A People's Conscience,* 1952

GRANVILLE, Castilia, Countess, ed., *Lord Granville Leveson Gower (First Earl*
    Granville) Private Correspondence, 1781–1821, 1916

GRIEG, James, ed., *The Farington Diary,* 1922–6

GRIERSON, H. J. C., ed., *The Letters of Sir Walter Scott,* 1932–7

GRYLLIS, R. Glynn, *Mary Shelley,* 1938

GUTTMACHER, M. S., *America's Last King,* 1941

HAMILTON, H., *History of the Homeland,* 1947

HAMMOND, J. L. and Barbara, *The Skilled Labourer 1760–1832,* 1919

HARPER, C. G., *Stage Coach and Mail in Days of Yore,* 1903

HARTLEY, Brig. Gen. Sir Harold B., *Humphrey Davy,* 1966

HENNING, F., *Fights for the Championship,* 1903

HOBSBAWM, E. J., *The British Standard of Living 1790–1850,* 1958

HOME, J. A., ed., *Lady Louisa Stuart, Selections from her manuscripts,* 1899
    Letters of Lady Louisa Stuart to Miss Louisa Clinton, 1901
    Letters of Lady Louis Stuart to Miss Louisa Clinton, 1903

JACKSON, G. Gibbard, *The Ship under Steam,* 1927

JAEGER, M., *Before Victoria,* 1967

JOHNSON, C., *English Painting from the Seventh Century to the Present Day,* 1932

JOHNSON, R. B., *The Letters of Lady Louisa Stuart,* 1926

KLEMM, Freidrich, tr. D. Waley Singer, *A History of Western Technology,* 1954,
    1959

LAMB, Charles, *Letters,* 1945

LEE, Sydney, *Queen Victoria. A Biography,* 1902

LESLIE, Doris, *The Great Corinthian,* 1952

LEVER, Tresham, ed., *The Letters of Lady Palmerston,* 1957

LONG, J. C., *George III,* 1962

LONGFORD, Lady Elizabeth, *Victoria R.I.,* 1964

LOWKE, W. J. Bassett-Lowke and HOLLAND, G., *Ships and Men,* 1940

MACCARTHY, B., *Later Women Novelists 1744–1818,* 1947

MACDONELL, A. G., *Napoleon and His Marshals,* 1934

MALLET, C. E., *A History of the University of Oxford, Vol. III Modern Oxford,* 1927

MAXWELL, Sir H., ed., *The Creevy Papers,* 1903

MELVILLE, Lewis, *The Beaux of the Regency,* 1908
    Beau Brummell: His Life and Letters, 1924
    Brighton: Its History, Its Follies, and Its Fashions, 1909
    Regency Ladies, 1926

MILES, H. D., *Pugilistica: History of British Boxing,* 1906

MURPHY, C. C. R., *A Mixed Bag, Williams Clowes,* 1936

MUSGRAVE, Clifford, *Royal Pavilion,* 1951
    Regency Furniture 1800–1830, 1961

NEWMAN, Charles, *The Evolution of Medical Education in the Nineteenth*
    Century, 1957

PARTINGTON, Wilfred, ed., *The Private Letter-Books of Sir Walter Scott,* 1930

PASTON, George and QUENNELL, P., *"To Lord Byron",* 1939

PIKE, C. Royston, *Human Documents of the Industrial Revolution in Britain,* 1966

PLUMB, J. H., *The First Four Georges,* 1967

POPE, Willard Bissell, ed., *The Diary of Benjamin Robert Haydon*, 1960

POWELL, G. E., ed., *Reminiscences and Table-Talk of Samuel Rogers*, 1903

QUENNELL, P., ed., *Letters of Princess Lieven to Prince Metternich, 1820–6*, 1937
Byron, The Years of Fame, 1950

REES, J. F., *A Social and Industrial History of England 1815–1918*, 1932

RICHARDSON, A. E., *Georgian England*, 1931

RICHARDSON, Joanna, *George IV A Portrait*, 1966

ROBERTS, H. D., *A History of the Royal Pavilion, Brighton*, 1939

ROBINSON, L. G., ed., *Letters of Dorothea, Princess Lieven, during her residence in London 1812–34*, 1902

ROGERS, Col. H. C. B., *Turnpike to Old Road*, 1961

ROLT, L. T. C., *George and Robert Stephenson*, 1962

ROWLAND, J., *George Stephenson Creator of Britain's Railways,*

SADLEIR, M., *Blessington D'Orday A Masquerade*, 1933

SELWAY, N. C., *The Regency Road*, 1957

SERGEANT, P. W., *George, Prince and Regent*, 1935

SHELDON, Gilbert, *From Trackway to Turnpike*, 1928

SHEPPERSON, W. S., *British Emigration to Northern America*, 1957

SINGER, C. and ASHWORTH UNDERWOOD, E., *A Short History of Medicine*, 1928

SINGER, C., HOLMYARD, E. J., HALL, A. R., WILLIAMS, T. I., ed., *A History of Technology Vol. IV*, 1958

SOMERVELL, D. C., *English Thought in the Nineteenth Century*, 1929

SOMMERFIELD, V., *English Railways*, 1937

STANHOPE, J., *Cato Street Conspiracy*, 1962

STEELE, A. G. and LYTTLETON, The Hon. R. H., *Cricket*, 1904

STIRLING, A. M. W., ed., *The Letter-Bag of Lady Louisa Spencer-Stanhope*, 1913

STUART, D. M., *Regency Roundabout*, 1943
Portrait of the Prince Regent, 1953
Dearest Bess, 1955

TAYLOR, G. Rattray, *The Angel-Makers*, 1958
Sex in History, 1953

TEMPERLEY, H., ed., *The Unpublished Diary and Political Sketches of Princess Lieven*, 1925

THOMPSON, E. P., *The Making of the English Working Class*, 1963

THOMPSON, F. M. L., *English Landed Society in the Nineteenth Century*, 1963
The History of The Times 1788–1841, 1935

TOMKINS, J. M. S., *The Popular Novel in England 1770–1800*, 1932

TREVELYAN, G. M., *English Social History*, 1942

TUTE, Warren, *Atlantic Conquest, 1816–1961*, 1962

UDEN, Grant, *They Looked Like This*, 1965

USHER, A. P., *A History of Mechanical Inventions*, 1929

WARD, S. G. P., *Wellington*, 1963

WATSON, J. Steven, *The Reign of George III 1760–1815*, 1960

WELLESLEY, Muriel, *Wellington in Civil Life*, 1939

WHITE, R. J., *Life in Regency England*, 1963

WILLETT, CUNNINGTON, C. and P., *Handbook of English Costume in the Nineteenth Century*, 1959

WILLIAMS, Neville, *Chronology of the Modern World, 1763 to the Present Time*, 1966

WILSON, Mona, *The Life of William Blake*, 1948

WOODWARD, Sir Llewellyn, *The Age of Reform 1815–1870*, 1962

WYNDHAM, the Hon. Mrs H., *Correspondence of Sarah Spencer, Lady Lyttelton 1787–1870*, 1912

Index

References in *italic type* indicate illustrations.